Herschel H. Hobbs

My Faith and Message

an autobiography

Herschel H. Hobbs

My Faith and Message

an autobiography

Nashville, Tennessee

4253-64
ISBN: 0-8054-5364-4

Dewey Decimal Classification: B
Subject Heading: HOBBS, HERSCHEL H., 1907-
SOUTHERN BAPTIST CONVENTION—HISTORY
Library of Congress Card Catalog Number: 93-34131
Printed in the United States of America

Unless otherwise noted, Scriptures are from the Holy Bible, *King James Version.* Scripture quotations marked (NKJV) are from the Holy Bible, *New King James Version,* copyright © 1979, 1980, 1982, Thomas Nelson, Inc., Publishers.

Library of Congress Cataloging-in-Publication Data

Hobbs, Herschel H.

Herschel H. Hobbs: my faith and message, an autobiography / by Herschel H. Hobbs.

p. cm.

ISBN 0-8054-5364-4

1. Hobbs, Herschel H. 2. Southern Baptist Convention—Clergy—Biography. 3. Baptists—Clergy—Biography. I. Title.

BX6495.H53A3 1993

286'.1'092—dc20 93-34131

[B] CIP

Dedicated to

Emma Octavia Hobbs
My Mother

&

Althea Smitherman Jackson
My Mother-in-Love

both of whom so greatly influenced my life

Table of Contents

Foreword

One of a Kind: Herschel Harold Hobbs

This book will inspire, strengthen, and challenge you on your journey through life. Read it carefully and reflectively. It is the record of what God has done and is doing through the life of one man, Herschel H. Hobbs.

As you read, there will be times when you will be amazed at what God was able to accomplish through Dr. Hobbs; at times your eyes will become misty as you feel the heartbeat of one of God's great servants; other pages will cause you to smile or even laugh out loud as Herschel relates his story.

Without question, Dr. Hobbs will opine that he wishes he could have learned how to serve his Lord better and walk at His side more consistently. Here is a man who experienced a divine call from God, prepared himself to serve wherever called, and simply responded with his whole life.

It is quite a story.

The last year I served Southern Baptists as president and treasurer of the Executive Committee and treasurer of the Southern Baptist Convention was 1992. The annual meeting of the Southern Baptist Convention convened in Indianapolis, Indiana, in June 1992.

As always, one of the highlights of the Convention meeting was the parade of former presidents of the Southern Baptist Convention who were invited to bring greetings and make brief comments. Often their words contain great wisdom and insight; at times, humor. In Indianapolis, the first past president was the familiar voice of one of Southern Baptists' most distinguished leaders, Herschel H. Hobbs. With a twinkle in his eyes and a warm smile, he began with a brief comment about Frances, his beloved wife who inspired and strengthened him:

> I am Herschel Hobbs and my spouse of fifty-seven and a half years is with the Lord and all the hosts of heaven are looking down at what we do here and hereafter. It has been noted that I am the oldest living former president of the Convention. I inherited that title when Louie Newton went to be with the Lord. And I'm saying to the rest of these fellows [former Convention presidents] that I'm going to hold on to that title as long as I can!

In his characteristic way, Dr. Hobbs had words of encouragement and commendation. He continued,

> I can think of a lot of things that are blessings about having lived a long time. One is that you have lived through and remember some history. Fifty years ago if Drs. George W. Truett, M. E. Dodd, L. R. Scarborough, John R. Sampey, and others like them had even dreamed about what has happened in the Southern Baptist Convention since then in growth and world missions, they would have been called crazy. But Southern Baptists have exceeded even the highest aspirations.
>
> I remember being chairman of the committee to allocate funds to the agencies some years ago. They had told us to figure on $19 million for the Cooperative Program, and after we had worked until two o'clock in the morning to get it done, I said, "Brethren, if we ever get the Cooperative Program up to $20 million we will have it made, won't we?" Now it's in the 140 millions.

It is no surprise that he ended his brief comments on the upbeat because that is his habit. Hobbs concluded,

> I am a Southern Baptist—an old-time Southern Baptist. I have been a Southern Baptist since the day I was immersed in Montevallo Creek just outside Montevallo, Alabama, into the fellowship of the Enon Baptist Church. I will be a

> Southern Baptist until the day I die, and I will always be proud to be a Southern Baptist.
>
> Having known a little bit of the history of the past, and looking forward to the future—things we have heard at this Convention—I think that Southern Baptists' greatest era is just ahead.
>
> God bless you, and may God use all of us to His glory.[1]

Dr. Hobbs, now four score and six years old, has not changed his attitude since his youth.

All his life, Herschel Hobbs has been a hard worker, an extraordinary student, a faithful and loving family man, an outstanding preacher and denominational loyalist with a spark of humor, a prolific writer, and a minister of the gospel with a heart for the lost and for missions.

Hobbs was not always a preacher. At the age of twenty he was manager of the Buick parts department of a large automobile firm. But God touched the life of the young businessman, calling him into the ministry.

Herschel became pastor of the Berney Points Baptist Church in Birmingham with a monthly salary of seventy-five dollars! Even this salary became uncertain because of the severe depression in 1930.

He and Frances, an office manager in an insurance office, resigned their jobs in February 1930 to continue their educations. They entered Howard College in Birmingham (now Samford University) on faith.

The young couple received special permission from the dean of the school to take extra courses both winter and summer so long as they maintained a B average.

Herschel and Frances graduated from Howard College in 1932 with A averages. During these years of strenuous academic challenge, he was full-time pastor of a church in Birmingham.

Still pursuing thorough preparation, Hobbs entered the Southern Baptist Theological Seminary in Louisville, Kentucky, in September 1932. While in the seminary, Hobbs was part-time pastor of two churches in Indiana. He received the Th.M. degree in May 1935. He was valedictorian of the class with a grade average of 96. The next September he began his doctoral work at Southern Seminary in New Testament interpretation. While studying toward his doctorate, he was also a fellow in homiletics and taught a class in basic English grammar for first-year students who needed help. Dr. Hobbs received his Ph.D. degree in May 1938.

This man has never known what it is not to work. From age nine until he was twelve, he plowed a forty-acre farm in Chilton County, Alabama. He was the only "man" on the place. In 1920, his family moved to Birmingham. There, rather than loafing around all summer, he got a job with a neighboring farmer until "laying by" time, the last of July. In the six weeks before school started, he had a temporary job in a small restaurant.

In high school, the ambitious Hobbs ushered at the Strand Theater. When the manager learned that Herschel was a captain in R.O.T.C., he made him head usher. For one year during high school, he was floor manager of Loew's Temple Theater where they had afternoon and evening movies and vaudeville six days a week. At that time, there were no Sunday movies. At eighteen, the Loew's chain wanted him to become manager of a small theater. He declined in order to finish high school.

It was from the Dauphin Way Baptist Church, Alabama's largest Baptist church, that the Hobbs family moved to Oklahoma City's First Baptist Church.

At first, Dr. Hobbs did not want to move to Oklahoma. He and his family were happy. The church in Mobile was thriving and the future looked bright. The pulpit committee from Oklahoma City contacted Dr. Hobbs four times before he began to consider moving. God, however, began to move and, under His leadership, Dr. Hobbs accepted the call from the First Baptist Church.

His service as pastor of that church for almost a quarter of a century (1949-72) was marked by growth and stability.[2] While the pastor of this great church, Dr. Hobbs was elected president of the Southern Baptist Convention.

The Convention was meeting in St. Louis, Missouri, in 1961. Carl E. Bates, pastor of First Baptist Church, Charlotte, North Carolina, nominated Herschel H. Hobbs for president. Two others were nominated, but one withdrew his name. After the ballot vote, Joe W. Burton, convention registration secretary, "informed the Convention that the tellers reported the ballot for SBC president resulted in the election of Herschel Hobbs of Oklahoma as president of the Convention."[3]

President-elect and Mrs. Hobbs were presented to the Convention by SBC President Ramsey Pollard of Tennessee. The messenger registration that year was 11,140.

The first year of his presidency reached its climax during the annual meeting of the Southern Baptist Convention in San Francisco in 1962. Dr. Hobbs was tapped for a highly significant task. He was to serve as chairman of a special committee to present "some similar statement" to that of the 1925 "Baptist Faith and Message" for the Convention to consider in 1963.

J. Ralph Grant of Texas presented the following recommendation from the Executive Committee which was adopted:

> 44. J. Ralph Grant (Texas) presented Recommendation No. 14 and moved its adoption. After discussion and amendment by common consent that a report be submitted to the Convention secretary by March 1 for inclusion in the 1963 BOOK OF REPORTS, and a copy be provided the denominational press for discussion prior to the Convention, the motion carried.
>
> Recommendation No. 14
>
> Since the report of the Committee on Statement of Baptist Faith and Message was adopted in 1925, there have been various statements from time to time which have been made, but no over-all statement which might be helpful at this time as suggested in Section 2 of that report, or introductory statement which might be used as an interpretation of the 1925 statement.
>
> We recommend, therefore, that the president of this Convention be requested to call a meeting of the men now serving as presidents of the various state conventions that would qualify as a member of the Southern Baptist Convention committee under Bylaw 18 to present to the Convention in Kansas City some similar statement which shall serve as information to the churches, and which may serve as guidelines to the various agencies of the Southern Baptist Convention. It is understood that any group or individuals may approach this committee to be of service. The expenses

> of this committee shall be borne by the Convention Operating Budget.[4]

In the presidential address that year, Dr. Hobbs preached a sermon entitled "Crisis and Conquest." His message began with the words Soviet Premier Nikita Khrushchev had said, "Our rocket has passed the moon. It is nearing the sun, and we have not discovered God. We have turned lights out in heaven that no man will be able to put on again. We are breaking the yoke of the Gospel, the opiate of the masses. Let us go forth and Christ shall be relegated to mythology."[5]

Hobbs clearly proclaimed the gospel. He spoke of lifting up Christ who will draw all men to Himself (John 12:31-32). He challenged Southern Baptists to give no uncertain sound (1 Cor. 14:8). He asked where Southern Baptists stood in relationship to the theological conflict:

> Where do Southern Baptists stand in relation to the theological conflict that has characterized the modern era? They were scarcely touched in the Modernist-Fundamentalist Controversy. This is explained by the fact that in its midst Southern Baptists firmly positioned themselves in the conservative role which has always characterized their theology. In 1924 when the battle raged the fiercest, Southern Baptists appointed a committee to study the matter. This committee was composed of some of their ablest theologians whose chairman was E. Y. Mullins. In 1925 the committee made its report. In its preamble were the following words. "The present occasion for the reaffirmation of Christian fundamentals is the prevalence of naturalism in the modern theology and preaching of religion. Christianity is supernatural in its origin and history. We repudiate every theology of religion which denies the supernatural elements of our faith." The committee's report was adopted as "a statement" of "The Baptist Faith and Message." And for the time being the issue was settled.[6]

Hobbs concluded his presidential address with the words:

> Yes, this is an age of crisis. But Southern Baptists are not afraid of crises. They were born in a crisis. Their history reveals that they have passed through seven major crises.

> And Southern Baptists emerged from each stronger and more resolute than ever before. They have always turned a crisis into a conquest. God grant that they shall do so now![7]

At the appropriate time in the order of business in 1962, First Vice-President Roland Q. Leavell called for nominations for president of the Convention. Wayne Dehoney of Tennessee nominated Herschel H. Hobbs of Oklahoma. "A motion to close the nominations and instruct Secretary James W. Merritt to cast the unanimous ballot for the Convention for Dr. Hobbs prevailed and this was done. Dr. Hobbs, in acknowledging the election, presented members of his family who were on the platform."[8]

I have already stated that Herschel Hobbs is an outstanding preacher and denominational loyalist. The last time I heard him preach was only a few years ago in San Antonio, Texas. His message was warm, challenging, evangelistic, without ramblings, and Christ-honoring. He inspired me. I stood amazed at the way God blessed him in communicating the gospel.

From the early 1940s until now, Herschel H. Hobbs has served in a variety of denominational positions. He has been a trustee of the Foreign Mission Board (1942-45), the New Orleans Baptist Theological Seminary (1945-49), the SBC Executive Committee (1951-63), and the Southern Baptist Theological Seminary (1965-75).

In 1957, he preached the annual sermon at the Southern Baptist Convention in Chicago, Illinois. He was president of the Southern Baptist Convention (1961-63) and vice-president of the Baptist World Alliance (1965-70).

For eighteen years, Dr. Hobbs was preacher on the "Baptist Hour" sponsored by the SBC Radio and Television Commission (1958-76). When he retired from serving as "Baptist Hour" pastor, his messages had been carried over more than six hundred radio stations around the world, reaching more than fifty million persons each week.

He served as a member of the committee of the "Crusade of the Americas" and was the chairman of the committee to draft the 1963 statement of "The Baptist Faith and Message."

At the Southern Baptist Theological Seminary, Hobbs was national chairman of a campaign to fund the "Billy Graham

Chair of Evangelism" with a goal of $500,000; he raised $750,000. Later he was chairman of the campaign to raise $10 million for the seminary and raised $12 million. At present he is chairman of a committee to raise $750,000 for the seminary.

From 1985 to 1988, Herschel Hobbs was an active, vocal, and faithful member of the SBC Peace Committee.

In his state of Oklahoma, he has served as a trustee of Oklahoma Baptist University and has been chairman on two different occasions. Since his retirement on January 1, 1973, when he was designated pastor emeritus of First Baptist Church, Oklahoma City, Hobbs has maintained almost a full schedule nationwide in preaching, teaching doctrine, and conducting Bible conferences.

Herschel H. Hobbs is a prolific writer. As of April 1993, he had published 147 books, more than any other Southern Baptist. This writing ministry includes *Studying Adult Life and Work Lessons* since 1968. The circulation of this series is about 100,000 copies per quarter. He is the author of *1 and 2 Thessalonians* in the *Broadman Bible Commentary*, has written many articles, and provided contributions to numerous books. A number of his books have been published in foreign languages, including Spanish, Portuguese, Chinese, Korean, and one book published in Braille.

Herschel H. Hobbs has been granted six honorary doctorate degrees, is a member of the Oklahoma Hall of Fame, and was the second recipient of the E. Y. Mullins denominational award (1964), which is Southern Seminary's highest honor. He is a recipient of the highest award of the Republic of Liberia, the Knight Great Band. From the Radio and Television Commission he received the distinguished communication award and was the recipient of the first distinguished achievement award from Samford University in Birmingham, Alabama.

From my first experience of knowing about Herschel H. Hobbs, I have been inspired and challenged by him. I have sat with him in committee meetings, listened to him preach from the Convention platform, discussed numerous matters of deep concern with him at a breakfast table, and had lengthy conversations with him by telephone.

He is a man of God. He is a minister of the gospel to the whole world, a missionary, a denominational statesman, and a warm-hearted person who rejoices in the salvation of the lost.

Read the chapters which follow and profit from them. In it all, you will reflect that God is amazing in what He can accomplish through one life.

Harold Bennett,
Retired president and treasurer of the Southern Baptist Convention's Executive Committee

Notes

1. "Proceedings," Southern Baptist Convention, June 9-11, 1992, Indianapolis, Indiana (tape transcript).

2. Hobbs, Herschel H. *The People Called Baptists* (Shawnee: Oklahoma Baptist University, 1981), 38.

3. *1961 Southern Baptist Convention Annual* (Nashville: Executive Committee, Southern Baptist Convention, 1961), 76.

4. *1962 Southern Baptist Convention Annual* (Nashville: Executive Committee, Southern Baptist Convention, 1962), 64.

5. Ibid., 81.

6. Ibid., 84.

7. Ibid., 89.

8. Ibid., 64.

Tribute to Frances

How can I put into mere words what I feel for Frances? If I could speak all the languages of men, yes, and of the angels in heaven, they would be inadequate to do so.

Other than the little song we sang when first we met, there was never a proposal and acceptance of marriage. Through our brief years of courtship our hearts and souls became as one, so marriage came as naturally as breathing. Without fanfare, one Sunday morning we were married in her parents' living room. Our honeymoon? We went to Sunday School and church that morning and to Training Union and church that night.

My call to the ministry was her call to minister. Together we prepared educationally. Together we ministered to the flocks God gave us. It was never "I" or "you" but "we." Limitless was her capacity to love our people. In every pastoral change she left with tears. But they were soon turned into smiles as she enlarged her capacity of love extended to others.

No daughter ever loved her mother more. No sister ever loved her sister more. No wife ever loved her husband more. No mother ever loved her son and his family more.

When she knew that her days with me were few, she thought not of herself but of me. "Look after Herschel. Don't ever let him be in need" was her plea. Then she went to sleep in our bedroom and woke up in the Father's house to be greeted by the Savior she loved and served.

One day ere long I, too, will enter the House of Many Mansions. And if He wills, I would ask of Him that Frances may kneel alongside me as I place before the Savior my crown—alongside her many-jeweled crown.

Darling, "Many daughters have done well, but you excel them all." (Prov. 31:29, NKJV)

1

Finally—A Boy!

Someone defined an optimist as a woman in church who starts putting on her shoes when the preacher says, "Finally." "Finally" usually suggests the end. But in the case at hand it was a pause in an ongoing series.

My parents were Elbert Oscar and Emma Octavia Whatley Hobbs. (When they married she did not change her initials, only her last name.) Their wedding took place in my Grandfather Hobbs' home. He was a romantic soul. While the ceremony was being performed in the house, he was in the backyard butchering a hog for the bride and groom to take home. I say "romantic"?

Their first five children were girls: Norma, Ila, Gladys, Annie Webb, and Lou Ella. So when my mother was expecting again, a neighbor asked my father if this one would be a boy. He said, "No. We only have girls at our house." But I fooled him. My father had several sisters, but he was the only boy in his family. So I am the only son of an only son.

I discovered America and the world on October 24, 1907, in Coosa County near Talladega Springs, Alabama. A vein of marble runs across parts of Georgia and Alabama. So the rural community where I was born is called Marble Valley.

I was almost born in Oklahoma City, Oklahoma. In 1900 my father sold his hardware store in Talladega, Alabama, in order to move to Oklahoma City, then only eleven years old. But before the family could move, it was found that he had stomach trouble. Doctors advised him to get on a farm. He bought almost seven hundred acres of river bottom land along the Coosa River, farming some and renting out the rest. I was born on that farm seven years later. My youngest sister, Mary Elbert, was born two months after he died in May of 1910.

As was usually the case then, especially with rural people, I was born at home. Knowing that I would probably arrive that night, my sisters spent the night in a neighbor's home. It was during the cotton-picking season. The next morning when they were told that they had a baby brother, they ran all the way home through a cotton patch. Later they told me that you could see the route they took by the cotton on the ground, knocked from the bolls as they ran through the patch.

At that time no way was known to control mosquitoes and malaria, both of which abounded along the river. Chills and fever were a constant problem. My mother told me that I averaged a chill a day until I was five years old.

My father's death was due to complications caused by malaria and typhoid fever. In October that same year, my eleven-year-old sister Gladys died of the same thing. Anxious to get her family away from there before others died, Mother sold her land "dirt cheap" to a banker named Mitchell in Talladega Springs.

A few years later, the Alabama Power Company built Lock 12, a hydroelectric dam, on the Coosa River. It backed water over most of that land. I imagine the banker received a handsome price for it.

Since my father and sister died when I was only two and one-half and three years old, respectively, I have no memory of them, only what my mother and older sisters told me about them. But one of my prized possessions is a picture of my mother, my sister Mary Elbert as an infant, and me when I was three years old. Photographers traveled through the countryside taking pictures in homes. There I stand—barefooted, wearing a "Buster Brown" suit and haircut, bangs and all, and wearing a tie that reached down to my knees. I refused to have my picture taken unless they let me wear my daddy's tie.

As for my spiritual background, my mother was a Baptist and my father was a member of the Church of Christ. However, his personal attitude was more that of the Disciples of Christ or Christian Church. For instance, there was no Church of Christ in the Marble Valley community. The Baptist and Methodist churches had services on alternate Sundays, and my father led the singing and taught the Men's Bible Class in both of them.

One day my mother told him she was going to join the Church of Christ. He always called her "Kate," for what reason I do not know. He asked, "Kate, why would you do that?" She said, "Well, the children are at the age when I think we should be in the same church." He said, "No, you don't believe as I do, and I don't believe as you do. So you stay in your church and I'll stay in mine." As it was, we attended the local Baptist church. In time, all the children were saved and were baptized into the fellowship of a Baptist church. Of interest, however, is that the first time I attended Sunday School Ila carried me "piggyback" to the Blue Springs Methodist Church.

In the fall of 1910 our family moved to Ashland, Alabama, the county seat of Clay County, my family's home county. My earliest personal memories date from that time.

It was "cotton picking time in Alabama." One morning my older sisters were dressed in old dresses. I asked why they were wearing them. They told me they had a job picking cotton. I asked why they were doing that. "To make money," they said. My three-year-old mind could not understand how they could make hard money out of soft cotton.

One day it was raining. Lou Ella and I were playing in the house. She was chasing me. I ran around the corner of an iron bedstead. In those days instead of having carpets we had highly polished pine floors which were slick. I slipped and fell, striking my face on the bedstead. It caused a bruise which became a boil. To this day I have a small scar just left of my mouth. It reminds me not to run and play in the house—rain or shine.

On a more serious note, when I was five years old people would ask me what I was going to be when I was grown. I said, "I'm going to be a *Methodist* preacher like Brother Smith." James Allen Smith was pastor of the local Baptist church. But we had to pass the Methodist church on the way to the Baptist church. In my little mind, I had them confused.

Years later Dr. Smith and I were fellow pastors in Birmingham. One night I spoke at a banquet in his church. Introducing me, he told that story. In response I assured the people I could prove that I made as good a *Methodist* preacher as he did. But I have always felt that even at that tender age God had planted in my mind that I was to be a preacher.

When I was seven years old I started my formal schooling. My first grade teacher was Miss Atkinson. Like most kids, I fell in love with my first teacher. As I recall, during that year I went through four *readers*. At least, that is what we called the books. As soon as I got a new one, Lou Ella would read it to me from beginning to end. As soon as she finished it, I could also read it straight through. Apparently my mind memorized it, for if someone pointed to a word, I could not tell what it was. So my mother soon put a stop to that.

It was about this time that I spent my first and last time as a "jailbird." No judge sentenced me. My mother, at that time, was Registrar in Chancery in the county probate judge's office. Going home from school I had to pass through the town square around the courthouse. Instead of going home, I formed the habit of hanging around the square. I did not bother anyone, just hung around. Mother had told me to go straight home, but you know how little boys are sometimes.

Well, the town constable, Alvin Hobbs, was my third cousin. So my mother asked him to send me home if he saw me loitering about. One day I was just sitting on the curb bothering no one—just sitting there. And along came Cousin Alvin. For some reason, he had a shovel in his hand. He slipped up behind me, picked me up, and set me in that shovel and carried me to the calaboose. It had two cells, one for storing tools and the other for prisoners. He put me in the prisoner cell, locked the door, and went away for an hour. Then he returned and let me go. I ran all the way home. End of *criminal* career!

Like most little boys, I was intrigued by motorcycles. The "Sunbeam Band" met at the church on Sunday afternoons. One Sunday on my way to the meeting I passed a home where a motorcycle was parked. That was like tempting a pig with peaches. So I mounted it. In my imagination I was going ninety miles an hour as with the handlebars I turned the front wheel back and forth. So *rambunctious* was I that the motorcycle turned over with me underneath it. You could have heard me yelling blocks away. Somebody came out of the house and pulled that monster (in sheep's clothing) off me. That was as near as I ever came to being a member of a motorcycle gang. I have never been on one since, nor will I ever be.

Ashland's greatest claim to fame is having been the hometown of the late United States Supreme Court Justice Hugo Black. Following his appointment to that position, he was asked where he learned his first law. He replied, "In the courthouse in Ashland, Alabama, listening to Ed Whatley and Martin Lackey argue court cases." Ed Whatley was my mother's youngest brother. One of my earliest memories is my mother lifting me up so I could see him in his casket. It was my first memory of seeing a dead person and made quite an impression on my young mind. Speaking of Martin Lackey, his wife was my second grade school teacher. She kept order by tapping the culprit on the head with a one-foot ruler. I think I still have some bumps on my head. I was like the young man who was asked how he was *raised*. "I was *razed* with a board and razed often."

My first cousin, Barney Whatley, and Hugo Black were law partners in Birmingham. But in 1912, due to ill health, doctors advised Barney to move to Colorado. It worked, for he died there at age 93.

Justice Black's niece, Evelyn, and I attended school together until my family moved from Ashland in 1916. About sixty years later I was preaching in a revival in Columbia, Mississippi. One day my motel phone rang. A lady said, "You will not remember me, but we went to school together in Ashland." As she talked something clicked in my mind when I heard her voice. I said, "Why, Evelyn Black!" I had not heard her voice in all those years. Had I given her a thousand dollars it would not have thrilled her as much as my remembering her voice and name.

Looking back over my life, I realize I have lived through the greatest period of change in the history of the world. In 1889 the head of the United States Patent Bureau resigned. His reason?

He said there was no future in his job; everything had been invented that could be invented. He stood on the threshold of the most inventive period in history—and did not know it!

When I was a child, automobiles were mostly toys for the well-to-do people. For the most part, they were kept in garages during the week and taken out on Sundays for short afternoon *spins*. I recall hearing a man brag one Monday, "Yesterday I drove my car fifteen miles and didn't have a single puncture!"

I recall the first time electricity was turned on in Ashland. Mother had built a new home which was wired for electricity. The light fixtures were simply single light bulbs screwed into sockets hanging from the ceiling by their wires. It was announced that at seven o'clock on a given evening the electricity would be turned on in Ashland. Our entire family was standing in the hall with our eyes glued to that light bulb. Sure enough, right on the dot of seven o'clock the bulb was aglow. We had entered the Electric Age!

One of my most precious memories of Ashland was an old black man. Everyone called him "Uncle Jeff." His white hair spoke of his age since normally black people's hair does not turn gray as young as for white people. Uncle Jeff lived in a log house about a quarter of a mile from our house. It was surrounded by a large fruit orchard. He played an accordion. He loved children. So we would visit him, eat our fill of fruit, and listen to him play his accordion.

Every day at sunrise and sunset he would kneel in his orchard and pray aloud. If the wind was blowing from his house toward ours, we could hear him. As he prayed, he would start calling names of people living in Ashland and would continue until his memory of names was exhausted. It is no wonder that everyone in town, mostly white, loved Uncle Jeff.

On one occasion, Annie Webb and Lou Ella had visited Uncle Jim Treadwell and his family who lived on a farm near Ashland. He liked to tease. Well, my sisters kept talking about Uncle Jeff. In fun, Uncle Jim told them that Uncle Jeff would not go to heaven. That made them mad. So they said, "Uncle Jeff will get to heaven before you do!"

The first morning after they returned home they saw Uncle Jeff coming down the road pulling his little red wagon. He was on his way to town to buy his week's supply of groceries. My sisters ran out to greet him. I can see him now as with a big smile he took off his hat in the presence of what he called *the little white ladies*. They told him what they had said to Uncle Jim.

He laughed heartily as he said, "Now don't you worry about Uncle Jeff. He's gonna be all right. Don't you know what the Good Book says? No matter how white you be, no matter how black you be, when we get to heaven we are all gonna be *as white as crimson*!" He may not have known his colors, but he knew his Lord!

On second thought, he also knew his colors. For regardless of race, color, or clan—all who believe in Jesus as Savior will be cleansed of all sin, washed in the blood of the Lamb!

I had a friend named Leon Jordan. Everybody called him "Pete." He was always doing something he had no business doing, not mean, just mischief. But he blamed me for it and got me in trouble. One fall day he and I were playing in the unused part of the town cemetery. Due to the time of the year, the broom grass was dry. We were smoking *rabbit tobacco*. It was just a weed. But we rolled its dry leaves in paper like a cigarette and pretended that we were smoking.

Well, Pete accidentally set this dry grass on fire. We tried to put it out, but it was getting ahead of us. So he tore out for town while I was still fighting the fire. Seeing him run, a man asked why. He said, "Herschel Hobbs set the graveyard on fire!" I soon had the whole town helping me put out the fire. But I never did tell that Pete was the culprit. Our "Marlboro Country" almost became a disaster.

Pete died some years ago. But the last time I saw him, we had quite a time laughing about our childish escapades. The occasion of this was when I preached in a revival in Ashland. I am sure that that day in the graveyard no one would have predicted that I would be a preacher. But God does the best He can with what He has.

In 1916, we moved from Ashland to a farm in Dry Valley. It was on advice from my mother's doctor that she get out of an office and onto a farm. She bought a sixty-acre farm, forty acres in cultivation and the rest in timber. It was located in Chilton

County, Alabama, a quarter of a mile from the Shelby County line. The community was known as Dry Valley. The water table was so low it was too expensive to drill wells. Each farmer had cisterns in which he collected the runoff of rain water on the roofs of house and barn.

Though we lived in Chilton County, it was more convenient for us to trade in Montevallo and Calera, each about four and one-half miles away. Also, we attended a two-room school in Shelby County. We also attended Enon Baptist Church which was about one hundred yards from the school. My mother and older sisters were members of that church.

It was at that school that I faced my first major physical test. When a new kid moved into the community the boys wanted to know if he could/would fight. Just barely nine years old, I had never been of a fighting nature. Reared in a small town, neither had I been subjected to hard work. These boys had worked on the farm. So they were physically stronger than I was.

Well, they picked on me, trying to provoke me to fight. There was a pond just off the school yard. I had to walk home, a mile and a half, in wet clothes. Trying to put some steel in my backbone, my mother kept telling me to take a stick and hit these boys on their heads.

There was another boy who did not like to fight. His last name was Mitchell. I never knew his given name. We called him "Piggy." These boys would get Piggy and me facing each other. Then a third boy would stick out his hand between us and say, "The best man will spit over my hand first." We would let it fly right into each other's face. And that was followed by fisticuffs. But as unskilled as we were, neither did any damage.

But one day when they tried that, I decided I had had enough. Following my mother's advice, I picked up a fallen limb of a small tree and flew into them. In Bible terms, I "smote them hip and thigh." They scattered and never bothered me again. I had passed the test. And I learned that I had to fight my own battles.

It was on that little farm in Dry Valley that I became a *man*—a nine-year-old man! Dire necessity became the mother of invention. In November 1916, my mother hired a man from

Marble Valley as a farm hand. In order to have someone to make a crop, she paid him through the winter with nothing to do but odd jobs so that she would have him to do the farming in the spring.

About that time, President Woodrow Wilson, anticipating our involvement in World War I, issued a call for volunteers for our armed forces. Most young men in the community responded. Our man said he was going home to volunteer. The fact was that he was homesick. Just before the war ended, he was drafted. But that left us with no one to do the plowing.

So I asked my mother why I should not do it. After all, I was the only *man* on the place. I had never plowed an inch in my life. Mother said, "Aw, son, you can't do it; you are too small." But when I insisted, she let me try. Using an Avery breaking plow, she plowed the first furrow around the field. It is called "laying off a land." Then I took over. I was so short I had to reach up to hold the plow handles. Each time the plow hit a rock or a root, the handles would pop up and hit me under the chin. But from then on it was my job. That went on for several days. We were making progress, slowly but surely. I don't know how long it would have taken for me to break forty acres and get seed in the ground. But then something happened.

One morning at sunrise we looked down the road and saw a long line of wagons coming. We wondered what on earth was taking place! But finally they turned up the lane leading to our house. They brought along every kind of plow except breaking plows—Johnson plow stocks, guano distributors (we had the guano), and cultivators. The ladies brought food and big wash pots in which to cook it. They knew of our predicament and had come to help out—men, women, boys, and girls. They had come to plant our forty-acre farm in one day! What wonderful neighbors they were!!!

How was it done? With a Johnson plow stock, one man would plow the row. Behind him came another with a guano distributor. Then a child followed dropping the seed, such as corn. With our nimble fingers we could drop the seeds as fast as we could walk. Finally came the man with a cultivator covering the seed. They did not plow up the middles between rows. The object was to get the seed into the ground. Later our family dug up the middles—with hoes, no less! Try digging up forty acres with hoes! But we did it. Throughout the growing season I did the plowing, tilling the growing plants. And we made a crop that year. And the years after that with yours truly doing the plowing.

People have always asked me where I got my vocal training. I got it plowing with a stubborn horse in Alabama when the only way I knew how to handle him was to holler at him. Neighbors said they knew that when I stopped hollering I had quit plowing, either sitting in the shade or on the plow handles. When old Rex decided to go to the barn, he went. The only way I could stop him was to throw the foot of the plow about any convenient stump.

One day I was hoeing corn at the farthest spot from the house on our forty acres. Thirsty, I kept yelling for my youngest sister, Mary, to bring me some water. But none was forthcoming. She was playing in the shade of a large oak tree in the backyard. At the time, she was about seven years old. My mother asked why she did not answer me. She said, "I've answered every time he called!" But it was a very quiet "Heyo!"

Of course, Mother told her to take me some water. She filled a little bucket and started on her way. But she stopped at a plum thicket and ate a bait of plums. Almost an hour later, she arrived with trash floating in water so tepid I could hardly drink it. I have never let her forget it. We chuckle over it now, but it was not funny then.

Speaking of sisters, after Gladys died I had five left. While a very closely knit family, we paired off according to ages and interests. Norma and Ila; Annie Webb and Lou Ella; myself and Mary. By that time Annie Webb and Lou Ella were more interested in boys than dolls. So Mary and I played together. One day we would play boy games and the next girl games. As a result of the latter, I had as fine a collection of paper dolls cut from a Sears and Roebuck catalog as any girl in the community.

Of course, having four beautiful sisters eligible for dating, there were plenty of young swains coming to our home. And that is where I enter the picture. In the summer and fall, farmers would cut enough firewood for stove and fireplace to last all winter. But as a small boy, I lived from day to day in my firewood supply. Late each afternoon I cut just enough wood for that night and the next day. As I used the one ax we owned, Mary would hack away with an old ax head I had found and for which I had made a makeshift handle—just to be with me.

More often than not, some boy would phone and arrange to come over and see one of my older sisters. That called for a fire in the fireplace in the parlor. It also meant that I had to go out in the dark and cut more wood. Well, I got fed up with it. One night Cecil Lucas called and came to see Annie Webb. While they sat in the parlor toasting their feet before *my* fire, I was in the adjoining room preparing for bed. I called out, "Cecil, the next time you come to see Annie Webb, come a little early, bring your ax, and help me cut some firewood." Of course, that embarrassed them. And my mother gave me a switching. But a few days later, here came Cecil with a wagon load of firewood. Word of it got around. And a few days after that, here came Orion West, Ila's beau, with another wagon load of firewood. I got a switching, yes. But I thought it was a pretty good bargain—two wagon loads of firewood for one switching!

Ila's longtime sweetheart was John Owens of Ashland. He was a medical student at the Alabama Medical School in Mobile. To go from Ashland to Mobile, he had to go by train to Birmingham, then catch another to Mobile. It went through nearby Calera. One Saturday he got off the train at Calera and came out to our farm by taxi to see Ila. He stayed overnight, and the next day I took him to Calera in the buggy. As he was boarding the train he handed me a dollar bill—the first I ever earned. I wanted to spend it on something that would last a long time, so I bought a dollar's worth of chewing gum.

And it did last a long time. When a stick of gum had lost all its flavor, I did not throw it away. I simply added another stick. Of course, I gave Mary a pack or two. To this day, I have a picture another sister made of us sitting on a scuppernong vine in the backyard. Naturally we were eating scuppernongs (a variety of grape). In my hand I had a wad of gum so big it shows in the picture. You see, from an early age I have always believed in making good investments.

My mother was quite a psychologist in disciplining her children. When we lived in Marble Valley, a lady who dipped snuff came to visit us. Annie Webb and Lou Ella saw her snuff on the mantle and decided to try it. It made them deathly sick. When Mother noticed, she asked as to their trouble. They said they were having a chill. Mother knew better, since she could see the snuff on their mouths. But she took them at their word and treated them accordingly. She wrapped them in quilts and put them on the front porch steps in the hot sun, the very thing they did not need. That was her punishment for them.

In Ashland when I was seven years old I saw men with small sacks of Bull Durham tobacco in their pockets with the tag hanging out on a string. I wanted to be a *man*. Cousin Brady Levie had a store. One day I took a sack of that tobacco from a glass case. It never occurred to me that that was stealing. When my mother saw it in my pocket she asked where I got it, and I told her. Of course, it had not been opened. So she placed it on the mantle in the parlor. It stayed there for a month.

Each time a lady came to see her she would call me in there. Taking the sack from the mantle she would say, "Here is a sack of tobacco my son stole." It seemed that every woman in town visited her that month. Then she made me return it to Cousin Brady and tell him how I got it. I must confess that I waited until he was in the back of the store and then put it back in the case. But it cured me.

In Dry Valley, school sessions were fitted into the farming year. School let out in early spring so the kids could help in the field. "Laying-by time" came about the middle of July when we finished tilling the crops. School began again and lasted until early fall when harvest time arrived. After that, we went to school until spring.

One year we planted some late corn in fertile soil just behind the barn. Thus, we would have late roasting ears (we called them "rossneers") in the fall. It had grown beyond the plowing stage, but the rows were full of grass. One day Mother told Lou Ella and me to hoe out that grass and we would be through *laying-by*. We were thrilled to know we would have no more field work until harvest time. So we simply hit the high spots, but removed very little grass.

Mother came to inspect it when we said we were through. She said, "Why you children haven't finished. Just look at that row of grass!" Lou Ella said, "Herschel did it." Row after row, it was the same. Mother did not accuse her of not telling the truth. But she got a switch and wore her out for sitting around, doing nothing, and letting me do all the work.

Speaking of discipline, I will never forget the last time my mother switched me. In the community was a man who prided himself in having the first ripe watermelons each year. One day his family went somewhere. But he *chained* one of his boys in the barn where he could watch the melon patch. We boys knew about that and it made us mad. So passing by, someone suggested that we get one of the melons. Two boys did so. We "busted" it and ate it. Though I did not steal it, I helped eat it. So I was as guilty as the others.

About that time the man returned home to learn what we had done. He phoned our parents. When we reached the home of the two boys, their father was waiting with a switch. And he gave them the full benefit of it. I knew that when I got home the same thing awaited me.

But when I arrived, my mother said nothing about it. Two weeks went by and I thought I was home free. But one day while plowing, I broke a singletree on the plow. The next morning before breakfast, Mother told me to go to a neighbor's house and borrow one. Then she said, "On the way back, bring me a switch." I knew that judgment day had come.

Had she only switched me, it would simply have made me mad. But she talked to me about what I had done. It was the first time I ever heard the Bible truth about sparing the rod and spoiling the child.

Then she put her arms around me and pulled me to her bosom. She literally wailed as she whipped me across the back. And I cried, not from the whipping, but because her words and wailing broke my heart. She never had to lay a hand on me again.

The highlight of my stay in Dry Valley came in August, 1919. It was the time of our annual revival. Our pastor was a farmer-preacher named Davis. That year he had his son, Ernest, a ministerial student at Howard College, Birmingham, do the preaching. At a week-day morning service, I went forward and made my profession of faith in Jesus Christ as my Savior.

At the close of the revival, along with others, Ernest Davis baptized me in Montevallo Creek just outside Montevallo.

In 1961, I was elected president of the Southern Baptist Convention. Back then, Dr. Porter Routh wrote articles about the presidents for *The Baptist Training Union* magazine. In interviewing me, he asked me to relate my conversion experience. I told him I did not recall what the sermon was about. But I remembered the invitation hymn, "Let Jesus Come into Your Heart." I also told him that Ernest Davis was the preacher. But I had lost track of him and did not know if he was still living.

Shortly after this issue came out, I received a letter from Dr. Ernest Davis. He was retired and living in Birmingham. After graduating from Howard College, he had earned his doctor of medicine degree at the University of Mississippi. Thereafter, while serving as a county health officer, he had been pastor of rural churches in Mississippi. His medical training showed in that he had kept careful records. He sent me a copy of his sermon outline he used when I made my profession of faith. His text was, "What shall I do then with Jesus, who is called the Christ?"

Sometime later, I preached at the Alabama Baptist Evangelistic Conference and he came to hear me. He asked if I knew what I said the day I made my confession of faith. He asked me, "Son, why did you come forward today?" I replied, "Back there [in the pew] I felt bad. I came, and now I feel good." That was an eleven-year-old country boy saying that he was under conviction, making a public profession of faith in Christ, and feeling good because of being saved. Some years later, Dr. Davis went to be with the Lord.

I now have a photostat copy of the page in the church membership book where my name was listed and numbered. My number is "100."

One of the most intriguing stories written in my lifetime is Alex Haley's book, *Roots*. It is his account of his efforts to determine the origin of his family line, a search which ultimately led him back to tribal Africa.

Frances and I had been married over fifty years. Through our years together we had spoken of people and places in our lives prior to moving to Birmingham. But neither had seen the places related to the other's beginning. So one year we spent our vacation visiting these places. For one thing, we learned that as children we had lived almost three years only a few miles apart.

We started at West Blocton in Bibb County, Alabama, where Frances was born and lived as a small child. Then we drove the short distance to Montevallo. We went to the place where I was baptized. I have a picture someone made of me and another boy standing in the creek with Brother Davis. I was waiting my turn as he prepared to baptize the other boy. So I know how wide the creek was. In Oklahoma we would call it a river. Today you can step across it. Several years ago it was flooded, filled with soil, but never cleaned out. Small trees now grow in what was once the creek bed. But I could still see the wagon tracks once made as the creek was forded just below where I was baptized.

From there we drove out to the farm site. The old house still stands, but in a cotton patch instead of in a grove of beautiful trees. Somebody loved cotton money more than beauty. We drove by the site of the little church building and two-room schoolhouse. Both are gone. But a beautiful new church building had been erected across the road from the old one.

The following Sunday we drove to Marble Valley and Ashland. In Marble Valley, the house where I was born had been destroyed in a tornado some years before. But we visited the graves of my father and Gladys. In Ashland we saw the house my mother built, the one where I had first seen electric lights. Small trees my mother had planted in the yard are now mighty oaks.

But back to the little church in Dry Valley. Frances, Norma, and I had visited there in 1937. The previous April I had passed my oral exam and was writing my thesis for my Ph.D. degree. I supposed that I was getting to be *somebody*. But the Lord knows how to humble us.

It was their *preaching* Sunday, but the pastor did not come. So they asked me to preach. Afterward they announced that it was time for the business meeting. In the pastor's absence, they asked me to preside and Norma to be the church clerk. I asked if there was any business to come up. To my consternation, I was told that it was time to consider the annual call of a pastor. A suggestion was made that they not call the present pastor for another year. I was in a tough spot. I did not want it said that I went there and got the pastor fired. So I suggested that they postpone any action until he was present. Happily they followed my suggestion.

Then they called on Aunt Becky Lucas to pronounce the benediction. Now Aunt Becky had known me since I was a boy. She had a heart of gold and a bullhorn voice. So she prayed:

"O Lord, today we have seen Scripture fulfilled before our eyes. Thou hast said that out of the mouths of babes and sucklings you have perfected praise. We have heard it today from thy servant, who just a few years ago was here as a barefoot boy and going in a washing!"

A candidate for a Ph.D.? No, a barefoot boy going in a washing! And you know, I wish I was that again!

2

"*The Magic City*"

Birmingham's slogan is "The Magic City." In less than fifty years after its founding it was the largest city in Alabama and one of the largest in the South. It was a great steel center. Only there in all the world could be found within a few miles of each other the three ingredients necessary for making steel—iron ore, coal, and limestone. With its towering skyscrapers it was quite a sight to this small-town country boy who had never seen a building over three stories high.

In April 1920, our family moved to Birmingham. Norma and Ila were already employed there. However, I remained in Dry Valley for the time being. Our school was already out due to the farm demands. I could not enter Birmingham schools since they too would soon be out. So I suggested that I get a job with a neighboring farmer. I was to receive twenty dollars per month and board. A month later I was one proud youngster of twelve years when I went to Birmingham and put my first month's salary in my mother's hand. On the farm I had contributed to family support by working. Now I had put some cash in the family till.

In August I moved to the city also. Since I was nine years old I had formed a work habit. It was two months before fall school would begin. So I told Mother I was going to get a job. It was in a greasy-spoon restaurant run by two bachelor Irish brothers. The principal customers were workmen at a nearby railroad roundhouse.

In that little restaurant I saw varieties of food I never knew existed. And I was told I could eat any and everything I wanted. Those brothers knew what they were doing. For after three days I was off a day with a sick stomach. Thereafter I lost all temptation for the food which I served to others.

By the time school opened in September, we had moved to Southside in the city. We joined the Southside Baptist Church. Our pastor was Dr. J. E. Dillard. Also, I enrolled in the South Highlands Grammar School. T. C. Young was the principal. I have three vivid memories of that school.

One night I won the silver medal (first place) in a W.C.T.U. speaking contest held in our church. I was so proud of that medal that I wore it to school the next day. That afternoon we were watching a basketball game after school. Just for fun another boy and I were scuffling. Somehow I lost the medal and haven't seen it since.

The pupils put on a pageant to raise money to purchase equipment for the school playground. I had the part of an Egyptian slave—no speaking, just scenery. But every time I drive by Magnolia Park I still see swings and slides bought with the money we raised.

It was in this school that I learned I was not to be a carpenter. Miss Lanehart taught woodwork. Each student was to make a footstool. I worked two and one-half years without finishing mine. In next to the final class I finished all the parts and planned to assemble it in the last class period. I found that someone had taken the parts. End of footstool. I think it was simply to get me out of the class that Miss Lanehart gave me a passing grade—probably a C for *clumsiness*.

In 1926 I graduated from Phillips High School. Nothing world shaking took place during those years. Well, not much anyway. I have never liked math, so I did not study it much. In fact, I flunked one course in math. Miss Chase was the teacher. In the senior yearbook I stated my ambition: "To find Miss Chase's '60' stamp." I had to take the course again. That time the class thought I was a math whiz. They didn't know I had already been through it.

Oh, yes! I also flunked one course in chemistry because it included working equations. The teacher was Peggy Eberhardt. Later her brother, Wallace, married my oldest sister, Norma. In college, Frances and I made A's in chemistry. I have never let Peggy forget that it proved that my flunking her course was the teacher's fault. Her reply? "You simply did not study." And I suspect she is right.

In high school I took R.O.T.C. and rose to the rank of captain. In fact, on a Friday my name was sent to the principal for approval of my promotion to major, the highest rank over the entire battalion. But on Sunday I had an emergency appendectomy. So on Monday my name was erased in favor of Neil Armstrong. Within two weeks I was back drilling my company—everyone called it a miracle. But it was too late. I remained a captain.

But that helped me in another way. During most of high school I had a job ushering in the Strand Theater. It required afternoons, nights, and Saturdays. In those days we did not have Sunday movies. Mr. J. Roscoe Faunce was the manager. He made me the head usher because, being a captain in R.O.T.C., he figured I knew how to handle other boys.

Until moving to Birmingham, I had never seen a football. But in my junior year I decided to try out for the school football team. I decided to try out at left guard, even though I only weighed 127 pounds. The first week of practice I was running drills on the first team, so I thought I had it made. But the second Monday, Fred Sington showed up for the left guard spot. He was sixteen years old and weighed 215 pounds! I knew I would never get to play, but simply be meat for him to pound on in practice. So I turned in my uniform.

Later, Fred made an all-American tackle at the University of Alabama. I still remind him of the sacrifice I made by stepping aside so he could go on and become an all-American.

In Dry Valley when we chose sides for teams to play baseball, I was always the last to be chosen, which gives you a hint as to my prowess in the game. Anyway, I went out for the Phillips baseball team and was chosen to be manager. In school sports the coach runs the team, so my high-sounding title was a synonym for *glorified bat boy*!

On that team we had some great players. At least seven of them went on to play professional ball. The two greatest were Fred Sington and Ben Chapman.

Fred was our star pitcher and pinch hitter. He could knock a ball a country mile, but he excelled as a pitcher. Even at his age he could throw a ball as hard as any man I ever saw. In one game in a summer Industrial League in Birmingham, he struck out all twenty-seven men.

Had he not broken his shoulder in football, he probably would have been another Walter Johnson, the immortal great of the old Washington Senators. As it was, he played outfield for the old Brooklyn Dodgers. Later, while playing in the Southern League, I saw him catch a fly ball with his back against the right field fence. He then threw a *strike* to home plate throwing out a runner trying to score from third base. He could still *pitch*, but not for nine innings.

Right out of high school, Ben Chapman signed a contract with the New York Yankees. Two years later he was playing outfield with the Yankees, along with Babe Ruth. Later he managed one of the Philadelphia teams for several years.

A few years ago I preached in a Bible Conference in the Huffman Baptist Church, Birmingham. When I entered the pulpit the opening Sunday morning, on the second row center, the entire pew was filled with former members of that team—including Fred. Due to illness, Ben was unable to be there.

Why do I recite all this? It is like the story of the boy who entered his mutt dog in all the dog shows. The boy said, "He never wins anything. But he gets to associate with some mighty fine dogs." This *dog* also has had his day!

Frances and I met by accident. My family had moved to Ensley Highlands in Birmingham. She, her sister Louise, and I were active members of the Ensley Baptist Church. It was there that I made my first commitment to the ministry. Louise and I are the same age. So one day I asked her for a date. She turned me down by asking why I did not ask her sister for a date. I asked her age and found that she was younger than my sister Mary. I said, "My baby sister is older than that. I don't want to date a baby!"

The Ensley church planned to build a new church building at a better location. The pastor was Dr. David M. Gardner, later the editor of the Texas *Baptist Standard*. Agnes Durant (Pylant) was the youth director.

Under her leadership the young people planned to put on an operetta to raise money for the building fund. Frances had a part in it. At that time Japanese umbrellas were the *in thing*. One skit in the operetta featured several couples under these umbrellas singing to one another. But Frances' partner became ill and had to drop out. Frances suggested she also drop out, but Agnes disagreed. She said, "I'll have you a new partner tomorrow night." I was asked to be that partner.

Since we were supposed to be sweethearts, I tried to hold Frances' hand. But she would not let me. Learning of that, Agnes said, "Frances, let Herschel hold your hand! You are supposed to be sweethearts!" Well, she did. And then, together with the other couples, we sang our song. I would sing a question and she would reply.

Herschel: *How'd you like to have a little home for two?*
Frances: *I'd love to!*
Herschel: *Now would you? How'd you like to bill and coo?*
Frances: *I'd love to!*
Herschel: *Now would you? How'd you like to have a little home for two, where you and I could live and love our whole lives through? Oh, how'd you like to be my loving wife for life?*

Herschel and Frances together: *I'd love to!*

We always said that the first time we met I proposed to her and she accepted.

(More than fifty years later we received a letter from Agnes. Retired, she was writing a book for young people, including games and other projects for them. She wanted to include that operetta but could not find the words of that little song. Did we have a copy? We did not. We remembered the tune. So one night we kept singing it. As we did, the words gradually returned to our memories. Then we sent her a copy. They had been in our subconscious minds—and hearts—all those years!)

Soon after the presentation of the musical we began dating. By that time my family had moved back to Southside. But every

Sunday we were together at church. I went to her home for lunch, stayed all afternoon, then back to church. At least once during the week I was back at her home. I kept the streetcar line in business. To this day I remember Frances' house and phone numbers: 2113 Avenue G and Ensley 2560 J. I should remember that number; I called it enough. I knew she was the girl for me. And she began to feel the same way toward me.

However, one night I was not so sure about that. It was a time when teenage boys thought it was fashionable to grow a mustache. So I grew one. Mine was just at the scratchy stage. But Frances did not think it was so fashionable. One night I had a date with her when she expressed her opinion of it. Just for meanness, when I was leaving I took her hand and, like a Frenchman, I bent over as if to kiss it. Instead, I rubbed it across my scratchy upper lip. She jerked it loose and slammed the door in my face. As soon as I arrived home, I shaved it off.

Well that put a temporary lull in our courtship. It lasted about two weeks. Then one day I got an idea. It was to use two popular songs. One was "I'm Lonesome and Sorry." The other was "I Wish I Had My Old Girl Back Again." I mailed her the sheet music copy of the former. Two days later I mailed her the other one. That did it! Once again I was at 2113 Avenue G, and Ensley 2560 J was a "hot line" once more.

By 1926 when I graduated from Phillips High School I had turned my mind more toward becoming a lawyer. My cousin Barney Whatley had his own law firm in Denver. He said if I would come to Denver and live in his home he would put me through law school. When I finished my legal training he would take me into the firm. He planned to retire in 1936 and would give me the law firm. Talk about a temptation! It seemed to be the chance of a lifetime!

But it would mean at least six years in law school. So I asked Frances if she would wait for me. I can still remember almost her exact words in her reply. "I can't make that promise now. We would be separated most of that time. At our ages, we would be dating someone else. And either of us might fall in love with another person. All I can say is that if at the end of the six years we feel toward each other as we do now, we will then get married." I turned down Barney's offer. I knew what a prize I had and did not want to lose her. Also, I can see now that God was working to hold me to my commitment to the ministry.

Shortly thereafter, Frances' family moved to Brighton, a town in the Birmingham-Bessemer area. But we continued to attend the Ensley Baptist Church.

About a year later on a Friday night, we agreed to wait two years before we would marry. What happened to change our plans, neither of us ever could recall. We were married at 8:30 the following Sunday morning, April 10, 1927, in a simple wedding in the parlor of her home. For our *honeymoon* we went to Sunday School and church that morning and B.Y.P.U. and church that night. Six weeks later, Frances graduated from high school under her maiden name.

Both of us were leaders of B.Y.P.U.—hers were Juniors called "Go-getters"; mine were Intermediates called "Live Wires." Mine lived up to its name! At closing assembly that night, the youth director, Gladys Rickles, said, "We have some newlyweds with us tonight. You two stand up." The leaders sat with their unions. So Frances and I stood up—she was on one side of the room and I was on the other side. Then Gladys said, "Before we dismiss, let's sing a song. Someone suggest one." A boy said, "Let's sing 'The Fight Is On.'" I hope he did not have us in mind, but it got a laugh.

Ours was as near an ideal marriage as I ever knew. I will not say that we did not have our differences, but we resolved them in love. The Bible says that married couples become one flesh, not one mind.

If a man says he and his wife have been married for fifty years without a cross word between them, I know that he is one of three things: either he is a liar, has a bad memory, or is so hen-pecked that he does not dare open his mouth around the house.

After our marriage, Frances and I, along with her family, joined the Brighton Baptist Church. Since we had been active in a larger church, they offered us about every job in the Brighton church. During our brief stay there, about eighteen months, I was ordained a deacon, served as superintendent of the Sunday School, and as secretary of the B.Y.P.U. Frances and

I sang in the choir (she was also active in various leadership roles). I even led the singing and directed the choir, in spite of the fact that I did not know one note from another. I had never heard of one-two, one-two-three, or one-two-three-four time. The only thing I had that other choir members did not have was more *brass*. I beat time by rolling up a cloth-bound Robert Coleman Hymn Book and banging it in my hand. But the object was to get people to sing. And, brother, how they sang!

In fact, at that time people were divided in opinion as to whether I should preach or sing. After all these years they are still divided, although they have changed sides.

But whatever I was asked to do, I did it. Lucy Gibson, my secretary for twenty-four years, always said that I never learned one word in the dictionary—"*No*." The truth of the matter is that I was trying to satisfy my sense of call to the ministry by doing other things in the church.

One of our most signal experiences was that for the first time we started tithing. I had just been elected a deacon. It was a Sunday night following the church service. A full moon was shining. Our pastor, Leroy Priest, Frances, and I were walking up the street toward our home. Leroy said now that I was a deacon we should become tithers. We told him we would think and pray about it.

We had bought our first furniture, a bedroom suite on which we had to pay three dollars weekly. In fact, every cent of my pay was committed, including one dollar each week for the church.

I suppose we were like the man whose excuse for not tithing was that he owed so many people. His pastor asked, "But do you not owe the Lord, also?" "Yes," said the man, "but He isn't pushing me as much as the others are."

Well, after much figuring and praying, Frances and I agreed that one month from then (January 1) we would start tithing. If anyone had to wait, it would not be the Lord.

The first Saturday in January I received my pay envelope. As I walked away, I looked at the amount written on it. It was more than I had been receiving, so I went back to the paymaster. "Mr. Kelly," I said, "you have made a mistake." I mentioned the amount I was supposed to receive. He said, "No, that is correct.

Mr. Drennan told me to give you that amount as an increase in your pay." Arriving home, Frances and I figured the amount needed for our expenses—plus the tithe. There was enough to meet it all—with fifteen cents left to spend foolishly!

Which has led me to say through the years, you can tithe if you will to do so. I firmly believe that had we said, "Lord, we will tithe if you will give us a raise," it would not have happened. But when we said, "We will tithe—*period*," the Lord provided the way!

Finally our church was in a revival. One night, for some reason, Frances and her mother did not attend. But during the invitation I felt God calling me again. So I went forward and made a new commitment to His call into the ministry. And I have never turned back!

Arriving home after the service, I told Frances and "Mrs. Jack" (Jackson) about it. Mrs. Jack was a diamond in the rough. She told it like it was. She said, "Well, if you are going to preach, you and 'Sis' (Frances) are going to Howard College." I said, "I can't go to college. I have a wife to support!" She replied, "I don't care. You are going to college. We don't want a 'jack-leg' preacher in the family!" Poor thing! She got one anyway. But she did the best she could. Incidentally, I always referred to her as my *mother-in-love*. I told her we were united in love before we were united by law.

Preaching my first sermon came purely by accident. One Sunday morning about eight o'clock the pastor called to tell me he was sick and asked me to find someone to preach. In my usually humble (?) fashion, I asked, "Why don't I do it?" What could he say? I am sure that in spite of his better judgment, he agreed that I should.

Frances' father was a bi-vocational pastor. He earned a living in his hardware store and, by choice, was pastor of rural churches. He had a very limited library. In it I discovered a book of sermon outlines. I found one on John 1:39, "Come and see." Using it, I called it "God's Universal Call to Humanity." By 8:30 a.m. I was ready to preach. (The older I get the longer it takes me to prepare a sermon!) In the words of the late Dr. R. G. Lee, I had a text and topic large enough to support a skyscraper. And I built a chicken coop on top of it.

Once I declared myself for the ministry, it was surprising how many Sundays Frances' father did not feel well enough to go to his churches. He would give me the keys to his Model T Ford and tell me to go in his place. I have never forgotten his advice the first time he gave me the car keys. He always called me "Boy." He said, "Now, boy, drive this car as far as it will go without gas. But don't drive it one foot without it has sufficient oil."

And I will never forget the first person to make a profession of faith in Jesus when I was preaching. It was in the Mud Creek Baptist Church near Bessemer, Alabama.

My first pastorate was the Vinesville Baptist Church in Birmingham. Its call to me came unexpectedly. Two families from the Brighton church moved into the Vinesville community. Dr. M. M. Wood, an elderly preacher, was secretary of the Birmingham Baptist Association. At that time no one had even thought of what we now call a Director of Missions. Neither had the Southern Baptist Annuity Board become the tower of strength for retired pastors, etc., that it is today.

Dr. Wood's work consisted largely of office work in the associational office. He rendered a valuable service. But it also enabled a grand old soldier of the cross to live in the dignity he deserved. In addition, he was pastor of the Vinesville church. Today it is a strong church, but then it was in its beginning stage. Dr. Wood resigned the pastorate, giving all his time to the associational position.

The two families from Brighton church had joined the Vinesville church. Unknown to me, they recommended me to the pulpit committee. Eventually they called me as their pastor. At the time they had only a one-room frame building. Other than Sundays and Wednesday nights, the pastoral demands were minimal. So I continued to work at Drennans. Though I had never heard the term "bi-vocational pastor," I was one. A very practical reason for this was that the church paid only fifty dollars per month. That may sound like *poor pay*. Well, in return they got *poor preaching*.

One of my first pastoral visits to a prospective member I remember well. She was a Baptist who lived just across the street from our church. When I approached her about uniting with our fellowship, she countered, "I do not know how long I will live here. I am not settled." I asked how long she had lived there. She answered, "Sixteen years." I had not learned the finesse of dealing with such *excuses*. So I rose, picked up my hat, and said, "Well, if you are not settled yet, you never will be until they pat you in the face with a spade." You know, she never did join our church while I was there. I wonder why!

When the church called me I had not been ordained. I wanted the Ensley church to do that. On a Sunday in June 1929, at the eleven o'clock church service, Dr. Gardner resigned to go to First Baptist Church, St. Petersburg, Florida. At two o'clock that afternoon, he presided at my ordination to the ministry. Dr. Leroy Priest, my pastor at Brighton, preached the ordination sermon. In preparation for being examined for ordination I asked Dr. M. M. Wood if he had a Baptist *creed* I could study. The kind old man did not lecture me. Instead, he smiled and said, "No. If you find one I would like to see it. I have never seen one." Then he explained that Baptists' only creed is the Bible. Who would have thought that day that the time would come when I would chair the committee that drew up the revision of the 1925 "Baptist Faith and Message?"

In my examination prior to ordination, one pastor asked, "Does the Bible *contain* the word of God or *is* the Bible the word of God?" Frankly, I had never even thought about it. Quick as a flash Dr. Gardner said, "I'm not going to let him answer that question. He isn't ready to answer it." I soon learned and still believe that the Bible *is* the word of God.

My first wedding was a church wedding with all the trimmings. I had never even seen such. But thanks to Frances' know-how we came through it fine.

My first revival was in the Vinesville church. I did the preaching—such as it was. It was a two-week affair. I had no sermon storehouse from which to draw. Each day during my lunch hour I *prepared* the sermon for that night. Talk about living from hand to mouth. I lived from lunch time to service time daily.

But the building was packed each service. On the opening Sunday morning we had one addition by letter. We were on our way! But we went from that morning through two weeks, including three Sundays without another *move*. My preaching was largely by main strength and awkwardness.

I said we did not have a *move*. Well we had two, but the kind we did not want. The song leader was a member of the church. One night after I had preached my heart out, I called for the invitation hymn. The song leader stood up and said, "During the sermon I was thumbing through the song book. I discovered a song I had never seen before. I think this would be a good time to sing it." Talk about a mess! We had it! The people, including the song leader, couldn't sing it. It sounded more like a cat and dog fight. After two stanzas I changed it to "Just As I Am." The song leader got mad and sat down. We sang that hymn, had the benediction, and went home.

The other *move* came in the final service. At the invitation a woman came down the aisle weeping aloud. She made a confession of faith. You hear of people being on "cloud nine." Well, I was on cloud *ninety-nine*. I told the people that this one conversion was worth all the effort put forth in this revival. After the benediction, people came to shake the lady's hand. A deacon came to me and said, "Pastor, I hate to tell you this, but this woman is mentally off. She does this at the closing service of every revival we have." Oh well! It was great while it lasted!

The above has nothing to do with the fact that we were at Vinesville for only six months. Since the gentle (?) nudging by "Mrs. Jack" about going to college, Frances and I had that as our immediate goal. Frances had been employed by an insurance agency, beginning as a clerk and winding up as office manager. Our purpose was to live on my salary and bank hers as a reserve fund while in school. We had even drawn up a potential budget for living needs once we were in school. It amounted to seventy-five dollars per month. Once we resigned our jobs, our total monthly income would be fifty dollars.

One day I received a phone call from Fred Schatz, chairman of the pulpit committee of the Berney Points Baptist Church, Birmingham. He invited me to preach one Sunday with a view to a call as their pastor. He said, "I'll tell you now that the salary is seventy-five dollars per month." I knew then that if they called I would accept, for Frances and I had been praying for such to happen. It was not a case of Frances packing while I prayed. We had already prayed. So it was simply a matter of packing. And at that time in our lives that did not take long. It is a simple task to pack one bedroom suite.

We moved to the Berney Points church in the fall of 1929, just after the stock market crash in October of that year. This ushered in the depression of the 1930s. Trying to describe it to someone who did not live through it is like endeavoring to describe a sunset to a man born blind. Banks failed by the thousands over the nation. Businesses without number went under. The ranks of the unemployed soared into the multiplied millions. Jobs were hardly to be found.

Naturally this made it hard on churches financially. Our congregation was composed of wage earners who lived from payday to payday. The church lived from Sunday-offering to Sunday-offering. With more people losing their employment, the offerings dwindled.

Our building was a shotgun wooden structure. The church had bought the vacant lot next to our building. But due to our inability to meet the payments, we were in danger of losing it. Our church treasurer bought the lot and sold it to the church. In later years I kidded him. The offerings might not be enough to pay the pastor's salary. But there was always enough to meet the payment on the note for that lot.

But despite the hardships, the church carried on. In those days we had our formal worship service on Sunday morning, for the attendance was largely composed of church people. Lost people were sleeping off Saturday night. By Sunday night they were up and about and wanted to be with people. We had no television, Sunday movies, or sports, so the only place people were congregated was at the churches. The lost came, we preached the gospel to them, and many were saved.

When I became pastor of the Berney Points church it had ninety-nine members. The families were confined to a community area. Though I had no automobile, I visited every one of these families monthly—walking all the way. At that time I weighed only 127 pounds. As I now view myself in a mirror I think it might have been well had I never owned a car. But, of course, that would have been impossible.

Frances and I knew nothing about planning visitation. So the first Sunday afternoon at that church we picked one block and visited every family living there. Most of them were of other denominations. And I am sure we were more of a nuisance than a blessing to them. Well, one thing was sure. We soon learned how *not* to visit. Having no formal training for the work, what we did was mostly by main strength and awkwardness. But God blessed it in spite of that.

Looking back, we always regarded Berney Points as a happy pastorate. We had problems. But we had joys and sorrows as Frances and I were learning how to be a pastor and *pastorine*. We were always a team!

With your indulgence, let me share some memorable experiences. There could be many more, but these are typical.

Frances taught in the Primary Department, ages five to eight. In this department were two boys: Blakie Adams and Mike Edwards. The classes sat around tables. But Blakie had the habit of table-hopping and pestering boys at other tables. Nothing the teachers said or did stopped him. One Sunday Blakie was pestering Mike, who was at Frances' table. She was telling a Bible story which Mike wanted to hear, so he kept pushing Blakie away. But he came right back at him. Finally Mike got out of his chair, threw Blakie to the floor, and began pounding his face with his fist. Conveniently, Frances was looking the other way. But when she figured that Blakie had had enough, she looked back, saw it, and stopped it. Mike returned to his chair and Frances continued the story. Blakie returned to his table and never bothered anyone anymore. What the teachers could not do over a period of weeks, an eight-year-old boy did in a few seconds.

Then there was this beautiful redhead about eighteen years old. Since she may still be living, I will not give her name. Though a Presbyterian, she had attended our church for some time. One Sunday she presented herself for baptism saying that she wanted to be baptized in running water.

There was no such water in the area. But I found a large pond nearby. The water seemed to be clear. But it was in an iron ore district. What I did not know was that its bottom was red silt. We had several to be baptized. The men and boys were dressed in dark pants and white shirts. The ladies wore white dresses. But this young lady did not show up.

When I walked into the pond, that red silt boiled up. But we went ahead with a baptizing anyway. When each candidate came up out of the water, to every hair on his/her arms were clinging globs of this red silt. You can imagine what it did to the white clothing!

That night the absentee was at church. I reminded her of her absence, but told her I would baptize her the next Sunday afternoon. She still insisted that she wanted to be baptized in running water. I told her that we went through that ordeal just for her sake, and that we were not going through that mess again. I added, "We are going to the Hunter Street Baptist Church. Just before I immerse you we will have the janitor open the drain." We did just that. And she was baptized in running water—running out of the baptistry into the *sewer.*

His name was Seeb Gant. His aged parents were Christians, as were his wife and widowed daughter, Amelda Merk. Amelda was very active in our church. But Seeb had not been inside a church building for fifty years. To show his contempt for religion, when Amelda had the radio tuned to a religious program he would place the radio on the floor and kick it around.

But his father died. Frances and I went to see Seeb's bereaved mother. When we entered the room where she sat alone, she began to weep. I read the Bible to her, talked and prayed with her. Later I learned that Amelda prevented her five brothers from entering the room to throw me bodily from the house for making their grandmother cry.

The funeral was held on Saturday. After the graveside committal, I shook hands with the family. When I came to Seeb, I said, "I'm praying for you and hope to see you in Sunday School and church service tomorrow." He promised to be there. At the morning worship service he was gloriously saved. That night he was back with his mother. During the service she "shouted," the last time I have heard someone do so.

Seeb became one of our best members, finally being elected as a deacon. One day he said to me, "Pastor, I know I am saved. I have tried to lead my sons to Christ and can't reach them.

They say, 'Dad, you made us what we are! Now leave us alone!' If I died right now I know I would go to heaven, but I am living in a saved man's hell!"

In the Berney Points church was an ideal couple. When I married them I thought she was one of the most beautiful brides I had ever seen. In due time a baby was born. In the hospital mother and baby did fine, but a few days after they went home, the mother had blood poison and died. Grief-stricken family and friends blamed the doctor for neglect. But he asked the husband, "Did you give her the medicine I prescribed when she left the hospital? It was to prevent blood poison." The husband's face turned white as a sheet as he pulled the prescription from his coat pocket. He gasped, "My God! I forgot to get it filled!"

In our little church building I stood by his side as we took our final look at her face. And I do not know which of us was crying the more. But I have often thought through the years of the multiplied people over the earth who have in their hands the "prescription" (Bible) of the Great Physician for salvation—but they never get it filled!

3

Letting Go and Letting God

From the time of Mrs. Jack's "jackleg preacher" speech, Frances and I had set our goal to attend Howard College (now Samford University). Humanly speaking, we picked the worst of all times to do so. The stock market crash of October 1929 ushered in the bleakest economic period in our nation's history. By January 1930, the squeeze was really on. Most of the wage earners in our little church had lost their jobs. At the same time, Frances and I had secure jobs. Both of us were managers of our departments. So long as the companies stayed in business, our jobs were safe.

So when we announced that we planned to enter Howard College at midterm, some men in the church said that we were crazy. They were out of work and could find no job, and we were giving up secure ones. We could not see it then, but looking back it was the best time in our lives to get an education. Yes, we were poor, but we did not know it, for everybody was poor!

When Frances told her employer of our plans, he asked, "What are you going to live on?" She said, "Faith." He replied, "Faith is a good thing, but you can't eat it. Why don't you go to school in the mornings and work in the afternoons?" She said, "I can't. My husband is pastor of a church which will require some of our time. And I will need time to study." So he told her to try it for six months and if we could not make it, her job would be waiting for her.

Well, finally, we went to work one morning making over three hundred dollars per month, a good income then, and returned home that evening making seventy-five dollars. This was my salary from the church. Due to economic conditions it often could not pay all of that. But we were all in it together, and somehow we got by.

Frances and I entered Howard College in February 1930. Dean P. P. Burns gave us permission to take all the extra work we could, provided that we averaged a B. So we went summer and winter, graduating in two and one-half years in August 1932. We averaged A-. We had two purposes for this. One was to make up for lost time between high school and college. The other was that Frances' sister, Louise, and her husband, Henry L. Lyon, Jr., were already attending the Southern Baptist Theological Seminary in Louisville, Kentucky. We wanted to have one year there with them. In the meantime, Frances' mother had come to live with us. She carried her part of the load in cooking and other housekeeping while we went to school, did our church work, and studied. Our church was located in West End and the college was in East Lake. Much of our studying was done on the two-hour street car ride each day. We could not afford to buy lunch at school, so we ate a good breakfast, studied during the hour lunch break, and Mrs. Jackson had us a hot meal waiting when we arrived home at three o'clock.

Monday afternoon was "wash day." We all pitched in, with me doing the heavy work such as using the scrub board. We had no washing machines then. Tuesday afternoon was "ironing day." That was my job. Yes, I can iron a shirt as good as any woman! In the summer, I had a white starched pulpit suit. I washed and ironed it every week. Through the years Frances washed clothes on Monday in a washing machine. Monday nights I ironed while watching Monday night baseball and/or football. Frances said that was the only time she was thankful for these programs. Since her death I have joined the *folding brigade*. But I sure do miss Monday night games!

But back to college. Our first class to attend was in freshman French. It was taught by Mrs. Acton, wife of the head of the romance language department. She was a young and beautiful blond. According to our schedule, the class met in a certain room. New on campus, we had difficulty finding it. So we arrived late. We found a class in advanced French meeting in the room. We knew something was wrong when we heard them speaking rather fluent French. But we sat on the back row.

The teacher was Dr. Martin, a bachelor. He had absolutely no sense of humor and as much personality as a board fence. Finally, he spoke to me in French. I apologized, explaining that we thought this was Mrs. Acton's freshman French class. He asked, "Well, do I look like Mrs. Acton?" I replied, "No sir, you certainly do not!" With that we left and finally found our class. We were in the right room but in the wrong class.

James Dillard and I were former backyard neighbors and good friends. Also, he was our teacher in freshman English. One assignment was to read through the *Winston Collegiate Dictionary*. Many times at 2:00 a.m. Frances and I were still taking turns reading it aloud to the other. It happened years later that I was fellow in homiletics at the seminary. Jim had surrendered to preach and entered Southern Seminary. One of my duties was to teach a class in basic English grammar to first-year students making below 70 on a placement exam. I was so in hopes that Jim would fail the exam. If so, I was going to give him a personal, handmade assignment—read through the dictionary. He crossed me up by making 93. But I now know his purpose—to familiarize us with the origin of words. It has helped me through the years.

In those days, a married woman attending college was almost non-existent. So much so that *The Birmingham News* interviewed Frances and ran a story, her picture and all. On one occasion our Bible teacher, Dr. L. O. Dawson, complimented Frances for going to college along with her husband. He told her to stay in school as long as I did. Wanting a little credit myself, I said, "Doctor, you do not need to worry about that. I will see that she does. You see, I am a model husband." With a sly grin he replied, "Yes, I am sure that you are. The dictionary defines 'model' as 'a fair imitation of the real thing.'" Yipes!

Incidentally, we were in Dr. Dawson's Monday afternoon church history class when he said, "Yesterday afternoon a little group of us gathered to organize a little Baptist church. We call it Edgewood Baptist Church. It is not much now, but it will be a great church someday. Today it is known as Dawson Memorial Baptist Church, one of the great churches of the Southern Baptist Convention.

Professor James H. Chapman taught religious education. One day he asked, "Brother Hobbs, do you like books?" I said, "Yes, sir!" There came back the reply, "Well, Brother Hobbs, on my reserve shelf in the library is a little book of five hundred pages. Will you read it and give us a digest at the next class?" That was two days later. Carrying extra work and serving as pastor of a local full-time church, I didn't have time to read that book. So I went to the library and made some hurried notes: chapter headings, introduction and conclusion, and some publisher's notes on the jacket.

At the next class, Professor Chapman asked for my digest. From my presentation he knew I had not read the book. So he said, "Now, Brother Hobbs, I asked you to give a *digest* of the book. What you have just given sounds more like *indigestion* to me." That gave me a case of the same.

Due to my aversion to math, I asked Dean Burns for permission to substitute an extra year of Greek for college math. Since I was to be a pastor I felt that I already knew enough arithmetic to enable me to figure my salary and that an extra year of Greek would be more beneficial. He agreed with me.

Poor Frances! She had no such alternative, so she had to take math. At the end of the year, I waited in front of old Main Building while she went to ascertain her grade. She made a B. When she left the building, Vice-President Eagles and Dr. Dawson stood there talking. So happy was Frances over her grade that she danced a jig right there in front of them.

As for my Greek, my professor was Dr. Thomas, an eighty-five-year-old man. I thought of him as an old man. But now that I am eighty-six, I know that he was in his prime. In fact, at eighty-five he married "Miss Lottie," the assistant registrar. Shortly before their marriage I studied Latin under him. The class met at 8:00 a.m. She rode a street car to work that arrived at 9:00 a.m. We were always assured a short class, since at 8:45 he hurried to meet her and walk with her to her office.

Dr. Thomas taught us classical Greek grammar. In those days at Southern Seminary, if you passed senior Greek you automatically received credit for junior Greek. After three years of Greek under him he told me to take senior Greek. Instead I started out with *baby* Greek, a non-credit course for students who had had no Greek. That hurt his feelings, since he said it reflected against his teaching.

I said, "No, Dr. Thomas. I went to the seminary with the intention of earning a Ph.D. degree. To be admitted to the doctoral school I had to have a certain grade average. You taught me classical Greek grammar. In the seminary I needed to know Koine Greek grammar. That is why I took baby Greek instead of senior Greek." That seemed to satisfy him.

In any study we learn not only the subject matter, but also from the philosophy of the teacher. This was true of Miss Anne Boyette. She taught English literature but was drafted to teach one semester of history. Just before the fall term the history professor resigned to go to another school. While the school sought a replacement, Miss Boyette filled in.

At the final exam she wrote questions on blackboards all around the room. Then she erased the first section of blackboard and wrote other questions. When the first question was on the board I began writing as rapidly as I could. By the end of the hour I had only answered those on the front board, so I resigned myself to a failing grade on the exam. She gave me an A.

When she returned the papers she explained her philosophy about exams. "Anytime the pupil can complete the exam in the allotted time, it is not a true test of the pupil's knowledge of the subject."

I applied that to preaching, and it has been a guiding principle ever since. Anytime a preacher exhausts his knowledge of a subject in a thirty-minute sermon, he is not properly prepared. So I have always tried to preach out of the *overflow*. I never really finished what I wanted to say in a sermon. I simply quit somewhere near the stopping time.

When Frances was living, they used to tell this story on me in Oklahoma City. At 12:30 on Sunday she was standing in front of the church. Someone asked her, "Is the preacher through yet?" She replied, "He's been through for thirty minutes. He just won't quit."

My college athletic career was short-lived. One day in gym class we were playing basketball. All of us were under one goal fighting for the ball. One was a boy named Davis, varsity center on the college football team. He was big and rough. Suddenly he came charging into the group reaching for the ball. Instead, one of his fingers went into my eye. It felt like he had gouged my eyeball out. They rushed me to first-aid, where they put a large bandage over the eye. After that, I went to chapel where Frances and I sat together. Imagine her surprise when she saw my condition! I haven't touched a basketball since.

Each year in intramural sports we had a football game between the ministerial and pre-medical students. It was billed as a game between the "Saints" and the "Devils." This particular game was played on a muddy Berry Field. We had no football gear such as shoulder pads and helmets. All the pre-med students wore cleated football shoes. Howard Bryant (later he and his wife, Sarah, were missionaries in Chile) was the only "Saint" wearing football shoes. The rest of our team wore rubber-soled gym shoes.

In that mud our team was simply slipping and sliding. We would get set to tackle a ball carrier. But instead our feet would slip from under us, and we fell face down in the mud. Well, the "Saints" got to laughing—all but one. Oley Kidd (we called him "Mule") got mad. I can still hear him shout as he made a successful flying tackle, "You preachers get *mad*!"

On one play a "Devil" wearing football shoes accidentally kicked me on my foot, which had no protection other than wet canvas. It was on a Wednesday afternoon. That night I conducted prayer meeting, half sitting on the altar table in order to protect a sore foot. End of football for me! It was the end of my athletic career—before it even budded.

I was never a hero in sports. But I *thought* I was one on one occasion at Howard College. One day during lunch time (for others) Frances and I were at our usual place—sitting under Sherman Oak (named for the school's first president) in front of the library. I happened to look across at Renfroe Hall, the men's dormitory. The third floor was on fire. Smoke was boiling out of windows through which students were throwing trunks, suitcases, etc. I ran to a phone and called the fire department. They came and put out the fire, thus saving the building. Only Frances and I knew that I had done it.

A few weeks later, Dr. Dawson gave the Howard College report at the Alabama Baptist Convention. He said, "Everything is fine at Howard College. We have a fine student body and a great spirit. Old Renfroe Hall caught fire the other day. It was fully insured. And we would have a new building if some *fool* hadn't turned in the fire alarm." We certainly weren't going to tell about it after that.

In fact, it was our secret for over twenty-five years. After I had been in Oklahoma City for several years I was invited back to speak at the Alabama state convention. And of all things, I was asked to speak following the Samford University (Howard) report. I started off by saying, "Now it can be told." After relating the incident, including Dr. Dawson's remarks, I thought the crowd would never stop laughing so I could speak.

The same thing happened years later when I told it in a Founders' Day message at Samford. Dr. Leslie Wright invited me to deliver this address. I said, "Leslie, I have sat through many such addresses that almost put me to sleep. You have here a new campus where every building and street bears the name of people, many of whom I knew personally. Unless you object, I want to put some meat on those bones." He agreed.

So I told of experiences with them, some serious, some humorous. Students have ways to let you know if they like or are bored with a speech. They sat silently as if they wanted to catch every word. They responded with laughter at humorous events. At the conclusion they gave Frances and me a standing ovation. Dr. Wright told me that was the only time he had seen such a response to a Founders' Day address. Why? Because I was talking about something in which they were interested.

Since writing the above I was asked to be the representative ministerial student at the sesquicentennial of the school (1991). The state convention met on campus, with one night given over for the celebration. The interviewer asked me to relate some of the experiences I had had as a student there. At the telling of my "hero" experience, again the crowd roared with laughter. I guess they agreed with the "fool" title. At the close there was another standing ovation. Yes, humor is a good medicine.

How were we doing financially? It was rough! By 1932 the depression had really settled in. Most of our people were out of work. At times we did not receive all of our salary. The people were faithful, but they could not give what they did not have. Fortunately some dear soul whose name we did not know had established an aid fund at the college. When we had gone as far as we could go, we could always get a few dollars to tide us over.

And I must say that God provided help from an unexpected source. Dr. James Randolph Hobbs was pastor of the First Baptist Church, Birmingham. Couples wanting to get married and wanting a Baptist preacher knew that a "Hobbs" was there. So they looked in the phone book. "H" ("Herschel") comes before "J"("James"). I was listed as "Rev."; he was listed as "Dr." So they thought I was the preacher. I got more wedding fees which I am sure were intended for him. But the Lord takes care of His own and fools, too. And I am sure I come in there somewhere—maybe in both categories. And those errant fees sure came in handy.

One Christmas Eve I did not have Frances a present. And I had no money with which to buy one. She needed a new fountain pen. A druggist had offered to sell me one at cost—five dollars, but I didn't have five cents. Then a call came; a couple wanted to get married. The groom gave me five dollars. I don't know who hit the sidewalk first, the couple leaving or me going to the drug store.

Years later we still had that pen, retired with age. But it still served the Lord. At times when I was worried over a church problem I would get the pen and remember how God had helped me in the past. I was assured He would do so then.

Years later I told that story on the "Baptist Hour." Soon I received a small package from another druggist in Birmingham. He had heard the story on the program. So he sent me a ball-point pen and pencil set with my name engraved on it. The original pen is in my lock box at the bank. Precious memories! Wonderful Lord!

Finally we were nearing graduation. When we went to the seminary Mrs. Jackson planned to live with another daughter.

By that time, between the three of us, we had a house full of furniture. Mrs. Jackson would not need it, and it would not fit the small seminary apartments. So as a last resort we began to sell our furniture and use the money to buy groceries. One Sunday after church services Fred Schatz, the church treasurer, asked, "Mrs. Jack, how are you all getting along?" She replied, "Oh, all right I guess. We've eaten the living and dining room suites. Now we are starting in on a rug."

By that time we needed to order our senior rings if we were going to get them. Two would cost fifty-six dollars, and where it would come from we did not know. But we ordered them, trusting the Lord that we could pay. Unknown to us, the ladies of the church learned about it. So they started quilting a *name* quilt. For ten cents they would sew a person's name into the quilt. By the time the rings arrived C.O.D., they presented us fifty-six dollars with which to pay for them. I still have that quilt as a constant reminder of God's providence through the love of some of His wonderful handmaidens, every one of them a Dorcas (Acts 9:36).

But I am getting ahead of the story. During our college days we lived in four different houses. The first was a duplex which we shared with a young couple. The man managed a store in Bessemer and usually arrived home after dark. He had to change displays on Saturday nights and did not come home until about 2:00 a.m. Sunday. We told his wife if she ever needed help at night to knock on the wall which separated our bedrooms. One Saturday night she knocked on the wall saying she thought there was a prowler in her backyard. I turned on lights in our bedroom, living room, and front porch. When I left the house I slammed the screen door. Then I saw a big dog jump the fence and run away. It had been turning over garbage cans.

When I returned to the house, from Mrs. Jack's bedroom came her voice. "My land, with all those lights and noise, if somebody had been back there he would have been gone when you got there!" I said, "Why do you think I did that? I wanted him gone!" My mama didn't rear any foolish children!

The second house was a private dwelling which enabled us to take in two men as boarders to help pay expenses. We moved to the fourth one simply because it was next door to the church.

It was the third one that carries a unique memory. It was just across Tuscaloosa Avenue from the second house and was a nicer one. This unique memory was Mrs. Jackson's idea to provide us meat to eat at a minimum cost.

We bought eggs in large quantity and had a hatchery to hatch them on a scheduled basis. In the meantime, we put two tables in the kitchen where it was warm. Another we put on the back porch. Then we built chicken-wire fences of varying heights around the edges of the tables. On one we placed upside down a large metal dishpan, in the bottom of which we cut a hole. An electric wire, on the end of which was a bulb, was run through the hole. The lighted bulb gave heat under the pan which rested on wooden blocks. A cloth was fixed around the edge of the pan, with slits cut in the cloth. This enabled the little chicks to go in and out of the heated area. This contraption made an ideal brooder. Small-ground grain was placed in troughs around the fence. The other tables had higher fences to contain larger chicks. The garage we made into a chicken house by building roosts in it.

The first batch of chicks was placed on the brooder table. By the time the second batch arrived, the first one was large enough to put on the second kitchen table. When these had enough feathers to keep them warm, we placed them on the porch table. Finally, they went into the garage. Thus, we soon had an abundance of frying-sized chickens to eat. In fact, early in the process we each had a chicken (quail size) for breakfast.

Also, we had some laying hens in a small chicken house. They kept us supplied with eggs. One was a small French hen; another was a large Bufforphington. Several times daily the French hen came out of the hen house cackling. We thought she was really laying eggs. From the other hen we never heard a sound.

So one Sunday we had roast hen for dinner. You guessed it—the Bufforphington. The tragedy is that when they opened her they found her full of little eggs. We had killed a prized layer. The moral is, "It pays to advertise."

But hear "the rest of the story." The next day a lady came to cull the flock. Having examined the French hen, she said, "This hen hasn't laid an egg in years." A few Sundays later we had another roast hen dinner—French style, that is. Moral: "False advertising will get you into serious trouble if you can't deliver the goods."

The time finally arrived for us to apply for our degrees. Frances and I went to see Dean Burns. After checking our records, he said, "But you have been enrolled only two and one-half years. You are supposed to have been enrolled three years to qualify for a degree." I said, "You did not tell us that when we first talked to you. You said we could take all the work we wished so long as we averaged a B, and we have averaged an A-. I have already enrolled in the seminary, accepted a call to a church in Indiana, and resigned my church here. I suppose we will have to attend summer school at the University of Louisville and graduate there." He thought a moment and then said, "Well, go ahead and graduate here." And he approved our application.

When we graduated in August 1932, we sent an invitation to Frances' former employer but never heard from him. In the meantime, his business had failed. The irony of the story is that over thirty years later while I was pastor in Oklahoma City we read a tragic story in the *Daily Oklahoman*. The previous day an insurance salesman had committed suicide by walking into one of the city's water supply lakes. It listed his name. It was Frances' former employer!

The following Sunday a nurse in our church told me she had cared for him in the hospital. She said, "He was the most despondent person I have ever known." Also she asked if he would like for her pastor to visit him. He said, "Yes." But she forgot to tell me about it.

Yes, it is true. "Faith is a good thing, but you can't eat it." No, you can't eat it. *But you can live by it*!

4

Those Wonderful "Hoosiers"

Before relating our experiences at the seminary, I want to tell you about our friends in Indiana. In those days, first-year students were told to come prepared to live a year without church work. Most of the part-time churches in Kentucky and southern Indiana had seminary students as pastors. When one graduated, he would recommend a friend. Unfortunately some students were never called to a church while in the seminary.

In my case I was at the right place at the right time. After his first year, my brother-in-law, Henry Lyon, Jr., had been called to two part-time pastorates at Adams and Burney, Indiana. When the pastor of the Hope Baptist Church, Hope, Indiana, graduated, the church contacted Henry. Instead of taking it, he recommended me. So at their invitation, Frances and I visited the church in July 1932. They called me as their pastor, and we moved on the field the middle of August. School did not begin until the middle of September. During that month the Little Blue River Baptist Church in the same association called me. So we had full-time church work before moving to Louisville for our first year in the seminary.

Both churches were composed largely of farming people. They always had their revivals in January when the weather was so bad they could not work outside. Of course, that meant our missing two weeks of schooling. So Frances and I decided we would show those "Hoosiers" when to have a revival—August. Thus, she and I, the song leader Mig Boaz, a retired banker, and the pianist Armyne Wolf, had quite a *revival*. Oh, a few town folks came. But no farmers. Why? Because it was *hay making* time in Indiana! Those Hoosiers taught these two Southerners when *not* to have a revival in Indiana—*August!*

The church in Hope had a parsonage, so in the summer we lived there. Hope is in Bartholomew County, about fifteen miles from Columbus and ninety-two miles from Louisville. Little Blue River is in Shelby County, about seven miles from Shelbyville and 125 miles from Louisville. During the school year we commuted from Louisville. From May until September we lived in Hope, going to Little Blue River as occasion demanded. Each church paid the pastor forty dollars per month. But it took twenty dollars to buy gas and oil for our car.

Yet, in spite of hard times we had bought our first car. Mrs. Jackson had a little money saved up, so she helped us on it. It was an almost-new 1931 Chevrolet coupe, painted blue with cream-colored wire wheels. Oh, it was a sporty vehicle! It also had a rumble (popularly called a "mother-in-law") seat. We bought it in anticipation of having to drive to any church that might call us.

Despite the depression, these Indiana farmers had plenty of food but very little money. They never failed to pay our salary, and they generously supplied us with food. Every year on the Saturday night nearest my birthday when we were at Little Blue River, the church gave us a *pounding* of staple groceries—canned goods, potatoes, sugar, coffee, and the like. We received enough sugar—even for summer canning—and coffee to last for a year.

Speaking of coffee, not a single family at Little Blue drank coffee. Each year in January they wrote on pieces of paper the weekends we would be there. Each family drew a date when we would stay in their home. Knowing that we drank coffee, just before we were due to stay in a home, they would buy a small coffeepot and a pound of coffee. After we left they put them away until the next year.

One weekend we stayed with Ralph and Lola Hester. It was the weekend of the pounding. By that time we had a Chevrolet four-door sedan. We had stacked groceries in the back seat, starting on the floor and filling it up into the rear window. Lola was quite a tease. One time she said that when the coffee got weak we would know that our welcome was wearing out. We had our annual supply of coffee in the car. The next morning before we got out of bed, Lola called through the door, "Brother Hobbs, could you slip me the keys to your car so I can get some coffee? I find I am completely out of coffee." I said, loud enough for Lola to hear, "Hon, let's get dressed and go home. Our welcome is completely gone!"

The parsonage at Hope had a "cellar house" in the backyard. It was cool in the summer and warm in the winter. So we stored our supply of groceries there, taking them to Louisville as needed.

Of course, the people at Little Blue gave us other food during the year. We soon learned never to sit down in our car after Sunday evening services without first feeling on the seat. There would always be a large sack of eggs on the seat from an anonymous donor.

In the winter one man would kill a beef and hang it on the back porch where it was cold enough for refrigeration. Of course, they canned enough of it for summer use. But as long as it lasted, each time we went to Little Blue he would give us enough steaks and roasts to last until our next trip there.

It is no wonder that our first year there my weight went from 145 to 175 pounds! It continued to climb. And I have been fighting the "Battle of the Bulge" ever since! Those Hoosiers had lots of country ham. And I tried to reduce the supply wherever we went. They said my initials, H. H., stood for "Ham Hungry." The irony is that I gained that reputation eating country ham. Through the years I have had to maintain a healthier diet and eat packing house ham, which is not nearly so good.

Clyde and Helen Brown were about our age. Her culinary excellence is attested by the fact that she won the National 4-H Club cooking contest. One of her rewards was a visit with President Herbert Hoover in the White House. She told Frances that she had all of the equipment necessary for canning. At her invitation, we took to their home jars and whatever she wanted to can, and they would can it.

On one occasion when Frances was in Birmingham I spent the weekend with Clyde and Helen. On Monday morning I was in the kitchen shaving while Helen prepared breakfast. She asked, "Brother Hobbs, can you fry bacon?" I said, "Yes. But I can fry ham just as well." When I arrived in Louisville that day, I opened a package she had given me. In it were slices of bacon and country ham. I wondered how she knew that I wanted some ham. But come to think about it, in my usual *subtle* way, I had asked for it.

Ralph Hester had a gravel pit. Each January when the ground was frozen so he could not work, he and his family spent the month in Florida. Since they had to pass through Louisville and Birmingham, Frances rode with them to Birmingham and returned to Louisville one month later. In her absence I ate my noon meals in the Mullins Hall dining room. One year when Frances returned I had fourteen dozen eggs in the refrigerator. For the next month we ate eggs cooked in every conceivable fashion. It was some time before I could look a hen in the face.

I mentioned staying in different homes at Little Blue River, and I must mention the home of Mr. and Mrs. Samuel Phares in particular. They had two daughters, Helen and Beulah. One summer Mrs. Phares was redecorating their home. For the room we used, she took Frances to Shelbyville and let her pick out the colors and materials. Her reason was that this was the "Preacher's Room." Shades of Elisha! But while others did not so designate them, we had lots of "Preacher's Rooms" in that community.

Indiana winters can get very cold at times. When an epidemic such as measles, mumps, or whooping cough occurred, the people would long for a hard freeze to stop it. Farmers liked to have several hard freezes, which killed insects and their eggs, thus avoiding a siege of insects during the growing season. Indiana farmers produce lots of corn. I do not know about now, but then during a hard freeze they "poled" corn stalks. This was done by hitching a team to a long pole. It was pulled sidewise across the corn field. When the stalks broke, they made a loud popping sound much like a rifle shot. One day I was driving along the road and heard what sounded like a battle in progress. It was a farmer poling corn stalks.

Speaking of corn, it caused people in Alabama and Indiana to doubt my veracity. In Alabama most corn stalks produced one, or at most two, medium-size ears of corn. When I told them about Indiana corn having three or four large ears per stalk, they wanted to turn me out of the church for lying. In Indiana they started fires in stoves by placing corn cobs on burning paper. When I told them about using pine kindling in Alabama, they wanted to turn me out of the church for the same reason. On my next visit to Alabama, I brought back a sample of kindling in order to save my reputation.

Often in going to and from our churches, the tires seldom touched the pavement which was covered with snow and ice. On those winter weekends, I preached morning and evening on Sunday. The afternoons I spent visiting the sick and others. We had just bought our Chevrolet sedan, our first brand new car, and I was so proud of it. One farmer made one of the most unselfish wishes I ever heard. "Preacher, I wish I had your car and you had a better one."

In the Little Blue River community there was only one paved strip of road about one hundred yards long. It connected two steep hills. One Sunday afternoon in my visitation rounds I came to it. Snow was banked up unusually thick. Slowly I drove through it as snow piled up in front of the car. Finally, it got so high under the rear axle that the tires were not even touching the pavement. Of course, newer cars were built lower and had wider tires. I had to crawl under the rear of the car and with my cold hands try to rake the snow from under the axle.

While in that undignified posture and process, I heard another car coming. It was a Model T Ford, built high off the ground and with narrow tires. Chug! Chug! Chug! it came. When it came to my new car, it turned off the road into the field, went by and back onto the road, and continued chugging along. I felt it was an insult to my nice, new car. Now preachers don't get mad, but their righteous indignation gets roused up. That day mine was so high it would have made the Rocky Mountains look like mole hills on the plains! Truly, pride goeth before the fall!

On our winter weekends in Hope we stayed in the parsonage. We had moved our bed into the living room, which was heated by a potbellied stove. When we arrived on a cold Saturday afternoon, I started a fire in the stove. The house had had no heat in it for two weeks, so everything in it was cold. As the room warmed, it began to sweat. We could see our wet tracks on the linoleum floor. Even the bed clothes were damp.

It just happened that Anna McKinney was in town. The McKinneys were farmers. She and her husband, Lote, their son, Morris, and their daughter, Mrs. Clinton Calendar, were some of our most faithful church members.

Well, Mrs. McKinney drove by, saw our car, and came in to see us. Seeing the condition of the house, she said, "You children can't stay in this. Put your things in your car and come out to the house." From then on we spent our winter weekends with the McKinneys.

Now Anna had a heart of gold, but she never wanted us to feel that she did something nice because she wanted to, but out of a sense of duty. When we protested that we did not want to impose upon her, she said, "Well, somebody's got to take you!" All the while we knew that it would have broken her heart if we had stayed with anyone else. Each time we left for Louisville, she would give us an ample supply of canned food. When we returned the empty jars, she would say, "Well, I see you brought back some *refills*."

Lote was small in body but big in heart. When he spoke he did so rapidly and with a little jerk in his speech. He liked to kid, though for the most part it was without a smile. In 1938, after receiving my doctor of philosophy degree from the seminary, we drove up to our former church fields for a visit. (For Frances it was the final one.) When we arrived at the McKinney place, Lote came out to greet us. Proudly, I showed him my Ph.D. thesis. He flipped a few pages. Then he asked, "Did you write all of this?" "Yes," I replied. "Did all this come out of your head?" Again, "Yes." "Well, you never know what's in a cabbage head until you cut it open, do you?"

The McKinneys are but an example of how those Hope "Hoosiers" opened their hearts to us. For instance, we had a standing invitation to go unannounced to the Gaither Robertsons' for an evening meal. She was a wonderful cook and their table was always loaded. Also, we were never surprised any morning to find a sack of food left by some anonymous donor. I often told the people that they were a strange but wonderful breed. When a stranger came among them, they stood off and looked at him for six months. If he proved genuine, then they would take the shirt off their backs and give it to him.

We quickly learned that the way to visit farmers was to wear work clothes and spend the day working with them. Frances would help the ladies. She had learned that they thought all Southern ladies were lazy. It probably was a carryover from slavery days when servants did all the work, but in order to disprove that concept, she almost worked herself to death.

I helped the farmers in the field or wherever they were working. As a result I often shocked wheat and made hay. One day I helped Clyde Brown vaccinate pigs. He had a smaller pen in a large hog lot. The pigs were separated from their mothers and driven into the small pen. My job was to hold the pigs by their hind legs, leaving them to stand on their front feet while Clyde vaccinated them. Of course, the pigs were squealing, and their mothers were terribly upset.

There was one big shoat that had escaped the needle the previous year. Taking him by his hind legs as usual, I found him so strong that I had to back up to the fence to brace myself. One old sow hit my hindquarters so hard she almost knocked me down. Had the space between the fence boards been large enough to get her snout through it, she would have bitten a chunk out of my anatomy. That cured me from backing up to a fence.

I remember one day especially. It was at Lote McKinney's farm. We were putting hay in the lofts. The large barn had a hay fork which could lift a wagon load at one time. In the loft it was moved back on a track and dropped where they wanted it. The cow barn had no such contraption, so it had to be handled with pitch forks. One man forked hay from the wagon to the loft. Another forked it back into the loft. At the very back I had to stack it. All day long I had to breath air full of dust.

That night I ached all over. Dr. and Mrs. Reid, Methodists, were our next door neighbors. When I told him about it the next morning, he said I had hay dust fever. After that I turned in my pitchfork.

In those days they did not have wheat combines. Today, using combines, the wheat is cut, threshed, and blown into trucks all in one operation. But then, binders cut the wheat and bound it into bundles which were shocked or stacked, loaded on wagons, and taken to threshing machines.

There would be several of these outfits working in a given area. All the farmers made up the working crews. Each man was paid a certain rate which varied if he only furnished himself and a pitchfork or a team and wagon. At the end of the harvest, each group had a "settling up" meeting; however, due to alternating what each farmer furnished, no one owed anyone anything. But for the occasion the owner of each rig furnished gallons of ice cream and the ladies brought cakes without number. A good time was had by all.

I managed to work at least one day with each outfit, but there was method in my madness. Frances and I were eligible to attend all the "settling up" meetings! More *avoirdupois!*

Now all the seminary students were not as fortunate as we were. Those without churches were at the other extreme. I recall one couple at Howard College and later at the seminary. They had no church work at either place and got by on the proverbial shoestring. At Howard we noticed that they both were putting on weight. Investigation revealed that they had just enough grocery money to buy Irish potatoes. For one month that was their only food. It put on weight but did not provide proper nourishment.

Later in the seminary, this man missed classes for two days. When someone checked on them, they were found in bed too weak to get up. The story came out.

One student made his living by placing ice boxes in the basements of two campus apartment houses for married students. He stocked them with sweet milk, buttermilk, butter and eggs. For instance, when Frances needed a quart of sweet milk, she would write on a tablet her name, apartment number, and the item she had taken. At the end of each month the man would collect for it.

This couple had run out of money. They knew that buttermilk was the cheapest item. So, hoping that some money would come from an unexpected source, they bought buttermilk and signed for it the usual way. That was their sole source of food for one month. But they toughed it out. The last time I heard of them he was pastor of the First Baptist Church, Rushville, Indiana.

To this day my *righteous indignation* is aroused when I hear someone say that preachers are in the ministry just for the money. *I do not know anyone in a religious vocation, who with the same native ability, training, and devotion to duty, could not double or triple his/her income in some other line of work. To say that someone is in this calling for the money is an insult to that person's ethics—and also to his/her intellect!*

As things got worse economically for many students, Dr. John R. Sampey, president of the seminary, and Dr. Gaines S. Dobbins devised a plan to relieve the situation. They established a commissary in the basement of Judson Hall, the apartment building for married students with children. (Rice Hall was for married students without children.) They had monetary cards printed with levels of value from five cents to a dollar. When a student received food, the value amount was punched out of the card. Students with churches were asked to request that their people donate food. Throughout the Baptist associations in Kentucky, churches were asked to collect food at central places. The seminary truck would make the rounds weekly and transport the food to the seminary. This was not done in Indiana since at that time it was solely a Northern Baptist state. However, many members of local churches in Indiana did cooperate.

Henry and Carrie Handly were members of Little Blue River. In addition to working an eighty-acre farm, Henry also sold life insurance for Penn Mutual Life Insurance Company. Year after year he sold more insurance than any other of their agents in Indiana. One day he was driving to Shelbyville and stopped at a farmer's home to try to sell him a policy. He and the man were in the barn. The man's wife came to the barn and told Henry they did not need insurance. So he continued on into Shelbyville.

On his way home he saw many cars parked at that same farmhouse. Upon inquiry he learned that less than thirty minutes after he left, the man was killed when a horse kicked him in the head. Word soon got around that if Henry Handly tried to sell you insurance, you had better buy it.

Well, like many Indiana farmers, the Handlys raised pumpkins. At the harvest season I had seen his entire barn lot covered with pumpkins, waiting for a buyer. Each time we went to Little Blue River we would stack pumpkins in the back seat of our car, reaching from the floor up into the rear window. These were for the commissary. When we drove on campus, word soon spread that the Hobbses had brought in a carload of pumpkins. In short order we would see students' wives carrying a pumpkin to their apartments. And everybody feasted on pumpkin pie until our next trip to Little Blue River.

Thus far in this chapter the emphasis has been largely on extra-church activities, yet they were also a part of the spiritual fellowship between us and the people. Even the days spent working with the farmers were pastoral in nature.

Both of our churches were in the Northern (American) Baptist Convention, yet we had much the same type program as did Southern Baptists. Most of the part-time churches in southern Indiana and in Kentucky had seminary students as pastors, which worked for the good of all. For the most part, seminary students were better prepared educationally than others who would be available to such churches, and it gave the students experience in addition to a livelihood. People in those churches will have extra stars in their crowns for letting us "practice" on them.

Budding young *theologs* usually have more thunder than lightning in their sermons. It is like the two deacons in an Indian Baptist church in Oklahoma. One Sunday the church had a visiting preacher. When one deacon asked another how he liked the sermon, he said, "Heap big wind! Much lightning! Loud thunder! No rain!"

One Sunday in Hope a Mrs. Stewart said to me, "You preach too loud!" I replied, "No, I just need a bigger church in which to preach." It was all in fun, but she never complained again about the volume.

Looking back over the years, I chuckle about some things. I will never forget the first time I was invited to preach a baccalaureate sermon. It was at Hope High School. The president of the senior class wrote me a letter. Just as the buttons on my vest were about to pop off with pride, I came to the following line: "It is customary to have preachers of different denominations to preach the sermon. This is the Baptist year." I was the only Baptist preacher in town! The Lord has many ways to puncture our prideful balloons.

The Methodist and Baptist churches were friendly rivals. On Sunday mornings at nine o'clock, each rang its church bell, calling the people to Sunday School. Each superintendent tried to be the first to ring the bell. Whoever rang the bell first, even if no one came, had a successful Sunday.

Mig Boaz was not only our choir director; he was also Sunday School superintendent. During the week he kept all the literature. At the close of opening assembly he distributed the literature to the classes. At the end of closing assembly, he took it up again. In hard times there was no literature to waste. Also, I suppose it was the banker in him—conserving the resources.

We continued having our revivals in January, and the rivalry between the churches was reflected in them. In a town the size of Hope, few people moved in or out, so prospective new members were few. As for evangelism, we had to wait until babies were born and grew to the age of accountability; then we led them to Christ. The result was that in a revival we usually had about six or eight to make professions of faith in Christ.

One Saturday, Frances and I arrived in town and stopped at the grocery store to buy groceries for the weekend. The owner was a Methodist, and the Methodist church was having their annual revival. I asked him how the revival was going. He said, "Great! We have had fifty conversions already!" I almost passed out. I could see the Baptists firing me the next day. Yes, they spoke of hiring and firing a preacher. However, upon inquiry I learned that the Methodists had had no first-time conversions. The fifty were members who had been *lost* during the past year and were being *saved* again. I slept better that night, feeling that my job was secure—at least until the time for the next *annual call*.

Speaking of baptisms, Little Blue River had a nice baptistry, with warm water heated by a coal-burning stove with a water-coil built in it. One Sunday night I baptized a woman who weighed 320 pounds. The deacons suggested that one of them should be in the baptistry to help me lift her out of the water. I declined, saying that her body would displace water so that she would float; I would need to push her under. I was correct. In Oklahoma City I baptized a tall, heavy man without enough fat on him to fry him. He was dead weight. Afterward I kidded him saying, "I am glad you were saved. But I wish it had happened before you got so heavy."

The baptistry in Hope had rusted out, and we had no money for a new one. In the summer we baptized in a nearby creek, but following our winter revival we had a problem. One year a deacon and I figured out a solution. We borrowed a large horse watering tank from a store that sold them. Then we placed it in the old baptistry. The parsonage was across the street from the church. Each home had its own well with a water pump. By hand we pumped water into a wash tub, carried it into the church building, and poured the water into the tank. We continued until the tank was filled, but we had no way to heat the water.

The baptistry was under the pulpit floor. When used, the podium had to be removed and the floor opened by turning it back on hinges. Thus on Sunday night we were ready to baptize. I did not follow the usual procedure of changing into old clothes.

Following the sermon and invitation, the above procedure was followed. There was room in the baptistry for me to stand alongside the tank. One by one I baptized the candidates, and they emerged from the water sopping wet. Not knowing what we had done, the people thought they had seen a miracle. It was not a miracle, but the result of the ingenuity of a deacon and a preacher. Truly, "necessity is the mother of invention!"

Speaking of revivals, to us Southerners January was a strange time to have them. But not to those Hoosiers. They really came; every night I preached to a packed house. At Little Blue River, fifteen minutes before the service time Frances and I, the janitor, and the church mouse were the only ones there. But suddenly from every direction we would see headlights coming toward the church. At service time the auditorium would be filled. Weather was no problem. I have seen automobiles back up to get a running start to get through snowdrifts on the road.

Psychologically, every pastor lives on a roller coaster. He is with his people in times of deep sorrow and great joy. He must minister to them in both occasions. To do so, he must enter into their experience. Often he will go immediately from the valley of sorrow to the mountaintop of joy—perhaps from conducting a funeral to performing a wedding. If he really fulfills his role at each he must weep with those who weep and laugh with those who laugh. Doing these things takes something out of him.

On one occasion Jesus was on His way to the home of Jairus, whose little daughter was sick unto death (Mark 5:23). He was in a throng of people who, no doubt, were jostling Him. Along the way a woman with an issue of blood for twelve years merely touched the hem of Jesus' outer garment or robe. But in her case she did so in faith that thereby she would be healed. Her faith was rewarded with healing.

Immediately Jesus asked, "Who touched my clothes?" (5:30). The apostles reminded Him that the crowd was thronging Him. But this one woman's touch was one of faith. He felt it above all the jostling, for the healing power went out of Him. "Virtue" (5:30, KJV) translates *dunamin*, power. It drained power out of Jesus to heal her chronic illness. So, I repeat, it takes something out of a pastor if he really ministers to people.

It does so in preaching, if he really preaches. Dr. Gaines S. Dobbins once said to our seminary class, "On Monday morning a pastor feels like a sucked orange." All the *juice* is drained out of him. Dr. W. R. White once told me about a psychologist who wrote a book on preaching. He said that in a thirty-minute sermon a preacher expends as much emotional energy as he would expend physical energy on a fifteen-mile hike. I relate this simply to summarize my pastoral ministry at these and other dear churches where I have served.

Every pastor conducts many funerals, but I often wonder if I can claim one unique role in this regard. In one case I helped the undertaker embalm the body and later conducted the funeral. It was in Hope. The undertaker was Mr. Patterson, a member of our church. A man in our church had requested that at death his body not be removed from his home until after the funeral. When I learned of his death I went to the home. The undertaker was already there when I arrived. Otherwise, only members of the family were present. So I was asked if I would assist in the embalming. Under the circumstances, I agreed.

There are also happy memories—in one case, *humorous*. At Little Blue River there was a young man named Ramsey. He never used two words when one would do. He and his betrothed wanted me to marry them in the church at three o'clock on a Sunday afternoon—just a simple stand-up wedding with a few friends present. Frances and I were there when they arrived.

After the ceremony the groom asked, "How much?" I said I had no set charge, just whatever he thought she was worth. He handed me a five-dollar bill and asked, "That enough?" I said, "Do you think that she is worth that much?" He replied, "If she's not, I'll be back for my change." With that, he took his bride by the arm and they left. I suppose he found that she was worth it. He never asked me for his change.

One of the most memorable weddings was at Hope. It was that of Morris McKinney and Helen Carter. It was a gala church wedding. It was customary after a wedding to make a group picture of the two families and the preacher. In the excitement they forgot to invite me to be in the picture. The wedding took place in July 1935.

Fifty years later I received an invitation to their fiftieth wedding anniversary reception in the Hope Baptist Church. Living in Oklahoma City (Frances had died the previous year), I wrote them the usual letter of congratulations.

But it just happened that during that month I was to teach at Boyce Bible School of the Southern Baptist Theological Seminary in Louisville. My personal plan was to drive from Louisville to Shelbyville, Indiana, on Saturday. The next morning I attended services at Little Blue River. Unexpectedly, the pastor was away that day, so at the invitation of the people, I preached at the morning service.

The reception at Hope was at 2:30 that afternoon. So I drove, arriving about thirty minutes early. I wanted to delay my appearance at the reception until about 2:45, thinking that most of the guests would have arrived. So I drove about town and out into the country to see some familiar places.

Arriving at the church, I got in the line of guests. Helen is a little over five feet tall and just as dainty and beautiful as the day she married. When I shook her hand, she looked up at me and asked, "Do I know you?" I said, "You should. I married you and Morris." She squealed with delight and loud enough to be heard a block away. Turning to Morris, she told him I was there. He yelled for everyone to be quiet and told them. And a good time was had by all! Present was another couple I had married fifty years before.

When time came for Helen and Morris to cut the cake, she asked me to stand with them as a picture was taken. She said, "I have grieved for fifty years over not having you in our wedding picture."

They told me of another couple I had married who lived about a mile from town. He is now an invalid confined to a wheelchair. Before leaving I went out to see them.

(Those visits to Little Blue River and Hope brought back so many happy memories. Two years later I preached in a revival at Hope—in November; at least we compromised between August and January.)

Late that afternoon I drove back to Louisville. It was a beautiful day, and a blazing sunset seemed to make the whole world aglow. I felt a sense of joy and contentment beyond description. As I drove south toward Louisville on Interstate 65, I found myself expressing my feelings by singing "When You Come to the End of a Perfect Day." The only thing that could have made it more so would have been Frances sitting by my side as she had done on so many trips between Louisville and Hope and Little Blue.

As did Frances through the many years—I will always love those wonderful Hoosiers!

5

"The Beeches"

Frances and I first visited the campus of the Southern Baptist Theological Seminary in March 1932. Due to the many beech trees on campus, it is called "The Beeches." The occasion of our visit was the annual March missions conference. This week of lectures gave us a taste of the intellectual fare upon which we were to feast for the next six years. Of course, every faculty member was highly qualified, but taking a span of ten years as a generation, I was fortunate to be in the last generation to be taught by the "giants": Drs. John R. Sampey, A. T. Robertson, and W. O. Carver. Dr. E. Y. Mullins had died four years previously. Though I never got to sit at his feet, I have lived with his books to the point that I feel that I did know him.

It was during this March visit that I enrolled in the seminary to begin my studies the following September. We lived in apartment 310, Rice Hall. On one occasion, Dr. Sampey jokingly said that the first floor of the apartment buildings was the social floor; the second was the intellectual floor; the third was the spiritual floor.

At that time the basic degree was the master in theology (Th.M.). Dr. John A. Broadus, along with J. P. Boyce, Basil Manly, Jr., and William Williams, was one of the founders of the seminary. He had patterned the Th.M. course after the four-year B.A. course of the University of Virginia, but he had devised it into a three-year course. It probably was one of the most difficult courses of study in America. In fact, it was so difficult that some students cracked up under it.

For instance, my first year at the mid-term exam in junior Hebrew, one student was absent. He lived in Mullins Hall, the dormitory for single men. He did not show up for breakfast that morning. When he was absent at lunch, a friend went to his room to check on him. He found him out of his mind, on his hands and knees crawling on the floor muttering the conjugation of a Hebrew verb. Some years later it got so bad that, at the insistence of the medical staff, the Th.M. course was lengthened to four years. A lighter course of three years was substituted for that degree. The new, and present, basic degree is the bachelor of divinity (B.D.).

I recall the day in chapel when, with pride, Dr. Sampey announced that for the first time the seminary enrollment had passed the five hundred mark. At that time Southern Baptists also had Southwestern Baptist Theological Seminary, Fort Worth, and Baptist Bible Institute (now New Orleans Baptist Theological Seminary) in New Orleans. In later years, three more seminaries were founded (Golden Gate, Mill Valley, California; Southeastern, Wake Forest, North Carolina; and Midwestern, Kansas City, Missouri).

At one time Dr. Dobbins was representing Southern at the annual meeting of the American Association of Theological Schools. One by one seminaries of other denominations reported losses in enrollment. Finally, they asked Dr. Dobbins about Southern Baptists. He said, "Well, we have our problems, too, but they are quite different from yours. In recent years we have had to start three new seminaries to care for the men and women preparing for religious vocations." The others almost fell out of their chairs and asked the reason for this. Dr. Dobbins said, "Well, we all believe that God calls people into His service." To which they all agreed. Then with a smile and a twinkle in his eyes, Dr. Dobbins said, "Well, I guess we will have to say that God would rather call Southern Baptists more than others."

While speaking of our seminaries, the following story is most revealing. In 1945-1949 I served as a trustee of Baptist

Bible Institute. It was during that time that its name was changed to New Orleans Baptist Theological Seminary and land on Gentilly Boulevard for the present campus was purchased. Dr. Roland Q. Leavell was the president.

At that time Dr. John Jeter Hurt, Sr., president of Union University, Jackson, Tennessee, was also a trustee. Though many years separated us in age, he and I were kindred souls. He liked to recite Baptist history, and I liked to listen to it. Often at night during trustee meetings he and I would get to ourselves in a corner of the hotel lobby for such sessions. One night he told me the following story.

In 1916 he was on the committee appointed by the Southern Baptist Convention to find and purchase property in New Orleans on which to locate Baptist Bible Institute. The old Sophie Newcomb campus was available for thirty-five thousand dollars! Imagine that! When the committee applied at a bank for a loan of that amount, the banker said, "We'll be glad to lend you the money. The property is worth much more than that. What I can't understand is why you want to invest that much money to establish a school to train black preachers." He knew nothing about Southern Baptists.

In September 1932, we plunged into our seminary studies. In those days Southern Seminary did not grant degrees to women, so Frances did not take a full course, only those subjects she felt would be most beneficial to her as a pastor's wife. Some she took at the seminary and others at the W.M.U. Training School.

But I took the whole load, including "baby Greek." Early in our first year, Frances and I were received as members of the Dodeka Club. *Dodeka* being the Greek word for "twelve," it consisted of twelve couples. Louise and Henry Lyon were also members. It was there that we first came to know Cornell and Ruth Goerner. He was Dr. W. O. Carver's fellow in missions, philosophy of religion, and comparative religions. Later for several years he was a faculty member in those fields. He resigned after some years to become Foreign Mission Board secretary for Europe and Africa.

It was there also that I came to know K. Owen White. Though not a member of the club, he was our guest speaker one night. Years later he succeeded me as president of the Southern Baptist Convention. But I have always remembered him as the one who first introduced me to the richness of Hebrew in interpreting the Old Testament. He was at that time the fellow in junior Hebrew. That night he spoke on Isaiah 40:1: "Comfort ye, comfort ye my people, saith your God. Speak ye comfortably to Jerusalem." He dwelt on the fact that the Hebrew text reads, "Speak to the heart of Jerusalem."

As for my studies themselves, in my first year I studied junior Hebrew under Dr. Kyle M. Yates, Sr. Not only was he a great scholar, but he also had a warm heart. Each year he obtained a list of new students. He learned their first names, from whence they came, and their birthdays. Most of us were homesick. For a professor to speak to us by our first name gave us a lift. On our birthdays we received either a card or a visit from him. Frances was especially blue her first birthday away from home. When our doorbell rang that afternoon, she opened the door and there stood Dr. Yates. What a joy it was to Frances! She and I often said that in our judgment many students toughed out their first year because of Dr. Yates.

Through the years Dr. Yates and I remained close friends. While I was on the "Baptist Hour," few weeks went by when I did not receive a note of encouragement from him.

I recall one letter especially. The previous Sunday I had preached on Moses' experience at the burning bush. When Moses asked God what name he should use, the *King James Version* records Jehovah's response as, "I AM THAT I AM" (Ex. 3:14). But I pointed out that the Hebrew verbs are third person singular and future tense. I had not read this in any book, but discovered it in the Hebrew text. That week in his letter to me, Dr. Yates was ecstatic that a former student of his had caught this as reading, "HE WILL BE THAT HE WILL BE." God was sending Moses as His instrument in redeeming Israel out of Egyptian bondage, so He was beginning to reveal Himself as Redeemer from the bondage of sin.

In English Old Testament, Drs. Sampey and Yates taught on alternate weeks. Through the years Dr. Sampey's students lovingly nicknamed him "Tiglath" after Tiglath-Pileser, one of Assyria's greatest kings.

One day Dr. Sampey's great namesake was in our lesson along with Pekahiah, king of Israel, a rascal of the worst sort. In those days students stood up to answer questions asked by their professors. Dr. Sampey called on a student to identify a king in the lesson. The student stood up, but could not recall the king's name. Dr. Sampey sought to prompt him and said, "Through the years students have called me by his name. I hope it is because they see in me the qualities which characterized this king." The student then replied, "Oh, you mean Pekahiah!" Dr. Sampey roared back, "Don't you call me Pekahiah!"

For years after seminary days I would see this student at the Southern Baptist Convention, ease up behind him, and say, "Don't you call me Pekahiah!" Without looking around he would say, "Aw, Hobbs, shut up!"

Dr. Sampey was from Alabama; we were fellow alumni of Howard College (Samford University). He and I are the only alumni of that school who served as president of the Southern Baptist Convention. He served while I was a student in the seminary; of course, my time came many years later. He was proud of his Alabama heritage. For that reason, if an Alabama student did something wrong he dealt with him severely. But if one did something right, it pleased him no end.

In senior Hebrew we had an assignment to turn in an exegesis by a certain date. It happened that I had a revival at Little Blue River the week it was due. Before leaving for the revival I went to the library and made the notes I would need to complete the exegesis; I also took my typewriter along. During the revival I studied every morning, visited in the afternoons, and preached at night. I finished the exegesis and mailed it in on time.

When he returned the papers, Dr. Sampey said, "Now some of you turned in your exegesis late, so it lowered your grade one letter. An A paper got a B grade. Of course, Brother Hobbs was in a revival, and we understand why his was late." The fellow, Maxfield Garrott, said, "But Dr. Sampey, he mailed his exegesis in on time." The dear old man's face glowed with pride as with a smile he exclaimed, "He d-i-i-d?"

Dr. Sampey's hero was General Robert E. Lee. Instead of an overcoat, in winter he wore a Confederate gray Robert E.

Lee cape. I am told that he was buried in it. Naturally he was quite an authority on Lee. Each year around Lee's birthday he was kept busy lecturing on his life at various clubs around Louisville. Several years after I finished the seminary and after he retired, a student told me the following story:

One year about the time of Lee's birthday Dr. Sampey was asked to conduct chapel at the seminary. He spoke on Jesus. At one point he said, "Jesus was a good man. He was a good man. Good as Robert E. Lee." Realizing what he had said, he shouted, *"Better, better, BETTER!!"* Oh, he was a dear man!

One of the greatest evidences of his greatness is seen in the following incident. One day he was conducting chapel. A lovely lady, wife of one of the students, was the pianist for chapel. And she could really make a piano *talk*! On one hymn she put in notes unfamiliar to Dr. Sampey. So he commented, "It's too bad we can't sing a simple hymn without jazzing it up." A silence fell over the student body as in tears she slipped out of a side door and returned to her apartment.

As soon as chapel was over, students who knew music rushed to tell Dr. Sampey she had not jazzed up the hymn, but had played it exactly as it was written. I will never forget the picture soon thereafter. Dressed in his Lee cape, I saw Dr. Sampey trudging through the snow to her apartment to apologize.

The next day in chapel he sat on the second row. Just before dismissal Dr. Sampey was recognized to make a statement. Facing the entire student body, he said, "A public offense calls for a public apology. Yesterday in my mistaken zeal for our singing I greatly wronged a dedicated, lovely lady. I have apologized to her. She has forgiven me. God has forgiven me. I hope you will forgive me!" With that he sat down, put his face on the back of the pew in front of him, and shook with sobs. Yes, there were *giants* in those days!

Dr. Sampey and Dr. A. T. Robertson had been colleagues since as young men they began teaching at the seminary. They courted the same girl, Eliza Broadus, daughter of John A. Broadus. She married Robertson, but it did not mar their friendship. In fact, Dr. Sampey loved to speak in chapel of their long friendship. One of his favorite subjects was how he and Robertson came to teach Hebrew and Greek, respectively. One of them was to be chosen to teach Greek or Hebrew. Dr. Sampey preferred Greek. But he would say, "I saw the great potential Robertson had in Greek. So I stepped aside and let my good friend be chosen for Greek and I taught Hebrew." And yet through the years there remained a friendly rivalry between them. Later I will relate one incident.

Dr. Sampey's estimate of Dr. Robertson's potential as a Greek scholar was borne out in history. A few years ago I preached in a revival in the First Baptist Church, Stanley, North Carolina. Afterward, on our way to the Raleigh-Durham Airport, the pastor pointed to a side road and said, "If you go down that road a few miles you will come to a small Baptist church where as a young man A. T. Robertson was the janitor." He rose from a country church janitor to become one of the world's greatest New Testament Greek scholars. From sweeping floors and dusting pews he went on to write more than fifty books on the New Testament which were accepted by his colleagues around the world as scholarly works. In producing what he called his "Big Grammar" of almost sixteen hundred pages, he spent sixteen years in research and writing. He knew the Bible lands like the palm of his hand, yet he never visited them.

Dr. Robertson was known to be hard on his students, but he had a purpose behind it all. On his birthday it was customary for the English New Testament class to give him a silver goblet. In my year in that class the fellow, Leslie Williams, appointed me chairman of the committee to purchase and present the gift. The jeweler had to order it, and it had not arrived. His birthday was on Sunday. The committee went to his home on Rainbow Drive to wish him a happy birthday and explain about the gift. He and Mrs. Robertson received us cordially.

As we were leaving, I said, "Dr. Robertson, I must say that it is much more delightful to visit you in your home than in your class." After we all laughed, Mrs. Robertson said, "I've been telling him he shouldn't be so hard on you boys." He replied, "They are going to be preaching the New Testament the rest of their lives. And I want them to know it!" She said, "Yes, but you should not embarrass the boys before the class." His reply, "Huh! That's a part of it. They know they have to face them as well as me!"

Dr. Robertson had a blood condition which at times gave him a purple complexion. If he came to class looking that way—look out! He did not feel well, and we were in for rough sailing that day.

To him an almost unpardonable sin was chewing gum in class. One day he called on a student. His usual custom was to ask two or three simple questions. If the student answered them correctly, he would give him a 10 (perfect grade) and call on someone else. He was looking for those who did not know the lesson. On this occasion the student answered the simple questions correctly, but as he was sitting down he whacked his gum one time. Seeing it, Dr. Robertson asked if he was chewing gum. When he admitted he was, he was told to go to the window and spit it out. Then he added, "Don't you ever again come into my class chewing gum! And I'm giving you a zero for your recitation, sir!" Later Leslie Williams told me that when he got to his office, Dr. Robertson sat at his desk, looked at the grade as he shed a tear, rubbed out the zero, and gave the student a 10. To cap the incident is the fact that he did not know that he was dealing with a future president of one of our seminaries!

We students said that you could fail to get what Matthew, Mark, Luke, and John said, but woe betide you if you missed Dr. Robertson's footnotes in his *A Harmony of the Gospels*.

One day we were studying the birth of Jesus. In the back of his *Harmony* Dr. Robertson had articles dealing with various problems in interpreting the Gospels. One was on "The Probable Date of Jesus' Birth." The one definite conclusion he reached was that He was not born on December 25.

He asked a student, "When was Jesus born?" "December 25," the student replied. With a disgusted look on his face Dr. Robertson asked, "Where did you learn that?" "It's in the almanac," said the student. Dr. Robertson roared, "Brother, do you preach from the almanac?" Throughout the remainder of the year when discussing various views on a passage of Scripture, he would wind up asking this student to get out his almanac and see what it said about it.

Digressing for the moment, "Prof" Inman Johnson taught music and public speaking. They were required courses for every student—one semester each of music and public speaking. Dr. Sampey justified the music course thus, "I know that in your pastorates you will quarrel with your choir, and I want you to do so intelligently."

The student of whom I have just written had a high, shrill voice. One day in public speaking class "Prof" Johnson spent the entire hour trying to lower his voice, but had no success. Finally he said, "I hate to tell you this, but I think you should get into some other type of work. With your voice no one will want to hear you preach." The room was as quiet as a tomb. We felt we were witnessing the death of a man's ministry. Then the student said, "Brother Johnson, when I was young I was awfully wild. Do you suppose that has anything to do with my voice?" Suddenly the room burst into a roar of laughter, and he joined in it with us. Yes, the course of study was hard, but we had fun, too!

But back to Dr. Robertson—in all fairness I should point out that his hardness was not a one-way street. At times some of the students played tricks on him. He was cold-natured, and during the winter he always checked the thermometer on the wall as he entered the classroom. One night it snowed. The window ledges were covered with snow. Several minutes before Dr. Robertson was to appear, some students buried the thermometer in the snow. One stood on lookout. When he saw him start up the steps to the second floor, they ran and hung the thermometer in its place. When Dr. Robertson looked at it, it showed a temperature in the low thirties. He did not say anything. But while the class luxuriated in a cozy room, he almost froze.

He had a sly sense of humor. For instance, pet names for certain types of church members were Sister Sharptongue or Deacon Skinflint. He referred to Pharisees as Rabbi Smellfungus. Speaking of Pharisees, he said, "Theologically they could split a hair six ways and still have some hair left." Whether or not we were listening to him we soon learned when to laugh. When he hit the top of his head with his hand and said, "But-ta," we knew he had made what he regarded as a humorous remark.

I was fortunate in my dealings with Dr. Robertson. Every time he called on me to recite, I knew the answers. There were times when some students did not. Then he would start calling other names to see if they knew, but with the same results. Had he called my name, I too would not have known the answer. I often came out of such a class session feeling like I had been in an electric storm with lightning striking all around me without getting hit.

The nearest he ever came to getting on me was when we were studying the life of Paul. Dr. Robertson asked me, "Where did Paul go to school?" I replied, "He was taught at home by his parents. At five years of age he was sent to the synagogue where the rabbi taught him. At thirteen he went to Jerusalem to be taught by Gamaliel. But scholars generally agree that he did not attend the University of Tarsus. His father, being a strict Pharisee, would not send his son to a Gentile school."

Then he interrupted, "You and the other scholars believe that, huh?" I said, "No sir, I do not include myself." He replied, "Well, Brother Hobbs, I don't agree with that. I think he attended the University of Tarsus." If you corner a dog, he will try to fight his way out. So I said, "Well, Dr. Robertson, all I know is that I have just told you what you wrote in your *Epochs in the Life of Paul.*" The class laughed. I wanted to say, "Shut up. I'm the one on the griddle." The grand old man smiled as he said, "Yes, I did say that in my 'little Paul book,' but I've changed my mind since then. I just wanted to know if Brother Hobbs had studied his lesson. Thank you, sir!" And he gave me a 10!

As noted above, Dr. Robertson referred to his books on Jesus, Paul, John, and Peter as "my little ________ book." Incidentally, Frances typed the manuscript of his book on Simon Peter. The students used to say that Dr. Robertson and I had one thing in common. Neither of us ever passed a water fountain without getting a drink of water. Well, we had another thing in common. We wrote all our books in longhand. Writing rapidly, the result was/is that we had terrible handwriting. He never *walked* but went in what I call a *dogtrot*. One day he was dogtrotting down the hall when he passed the office. One of the ladies was typing something he had written. She called him in to read something for her. He did and then added, "It's easy to read my writing. Just remember that I made my n's,' r's,' and s'es just alike." My typists can sympathize with her.

Well, one weekend snow and ice were everywhere, so Frances did not go with me to our church in Indiana. Instead, she thought it would be a good time to start typing Dr. Robertson's manuscript. When I returned on Monday she was almost climbing the walls from trying to read a certain portion of the manuscript. Fortunately I was familiar enough with what he was saying that I could figure it out. The only consolation I get out of my own *hieroglyphics* is that so great a man as A. T. Robertson did not do any better. Of course, the only similarity I have with him is the quality of penmanship. Compared to his writings, the contents of mine leave much to be desired. But, after all, in one era of time God made only one like him. I will always be grateful for the privilege of being taught by him.

I realize that I am giving a disproportionate amount of space to Dr. Robertson. This is because he was such a colorful person. It is significant that when we old-timers get together to talk about our seminary days we spend most of our time talking about the professors who were the hardest on us. Dr. Robertson heads the list. Time and experience have led us to appreciate what they were doing for us.

So one more incident calls for consideration. Back then we had what were called *coach* classes. The fellow in a given class would spend an hour with us, usually just before exam time, to refresh us on what we had been taught.

The exam questions were given to us in mimeographed form. Through the years it had been discovered that ever so often Dr. Robertson would give the same questions he had used before. Several generations of students had preserved his exams, passing them on to later generations. The idea was that you could *spot* the questions for a given exam. As a result, the voluntary attendance at coach classes in New Testament had become very small.

The particular exam I have in mind was on the life and ministry of Paul. There were only about six or eight present for this coach class. The fellow, Leslie Williams, spent the entire hour dealing with Paul's life in chronological order.

On the day of this exam, Dr. Robertson had only two questions, showing in parentheses the value of each. One was a simple question valued a 20. The other was "Discuss in chronological order and in full detail the life of the apostle Paul from his conversion through his second visit to Corinth." It was valued at 80. There could be no guesswork It had to be right on target.

Those who attended the coach class were ready. As for myself, as soon as I read that question my pencil hit the paper. I wrote as rapidly as I could. All the other students not at coach class stared at that one 80 question. Then they would sigh, look out the window, and finally write something in hopes of some kind of grade. When the hour was up and papers turned in, students gathered about me, asking, "Hobbs, how on earth did you know the answer to that question?" I said, "Coach class, brother, coach class!" At the next coach class the room was packed. Since most of them passed the course, I suspect that Dr. Robertson graded them by *grace*, not by *law*. But he made his point.

Years later, after going to Oklahoma City, I have asked some of my colleagues if they could envision Dr. Robertson in a revival leaving the pulpit during the invitation, walking up one aisle and down another exhorting people to come to Christ. No one could do so. But it happened in the First Baptist Church, Oklahoma City. Shortly after I went there as pastor, an elderly deacon told me about it. Nineteen people received Christ in that service. Dr. Robertson was a scholar *par excellence*. But he also had a thirst for souls.

I related that to one of the older professors at Southern, and he told me "the rest of the story." He was certain that it was the same event. Dr. Sampey was in a revival at the same time. When Dr. Robertson returned to the campus he asked this professor, "Is Sampey back yet?" "Yes, he returned this morning," replied the professor. "Did he tell you how many additions he had?" "No," said the other. "Well, he didn't get many or he would have told you. I had fifty." That friendly rivalry remained.

A. T. Robertson—great scholar, lover of souls, loyal friend—but *he was still just a man!*

Though he did not achieve worldwide recognition as did Dr. Robertson, in my judgment Dr. W. O. Carver was the greatest "brain" on the faculty in those days. I speak in terms of creative thought. He taught missions, comparative religion, and philosophy of religion. So great was his brain that in philosophy, for instance, he would teach all but the last two weeks of a semester. Then his fellow and later associate professor, Cornell Goerner, would take those two weeks to tell us what Dr. Carver had taught us. This was to enable us to pass the final examination.

I will never forget the first chapel service I attended at the seminary. The students had come from all over the United States and many foreign countries. Except for those with whom we had attended college, we were strangers. Yet we must become a community of friends. Dr. Carver was the speaker that morning. His text was Proverbs 18:24. "A man that hath friends must shew himself friendly." It made a profound impression on me. And speaking of chapel, I will never forget the singing. Most of those present were men. Few would qualify as soloists. But those hundreds of men singing lustily made the most beautiful music to be heard this side of heaven.

Though highly intellectual and deeply spiritual, Dr. Carver had a sly sense of humor. Early in the fall session he met a first-year student on the campus. When he asked him how he was getting adjusted to seminary life, the student replied, "Very well, except for one thing. I don't know what to do on the weekend." With a wry smile Dr. Carver said, "Try putting your hat on it." With that he continued on his way.

But then, I know of one joke pulled on him of which he was not aware. In January of our first year in the seminary, a college mate of mine received a letter from his mother. His father was a farmer. She told him his father had broken his leg, and he would have to come home and "make a crop." Dr. Carver heard that he was returning to Alabama, but did not know the reason for it. One day he met this student on campus. Said he, "I hear you are returning to Alabama." The student said, "Yes." "Well," said Dr. Carver, "do you have a field back there?" Again the student said, "Yes." Later he told me about this. Then with a grin he added, "But I didn't tell him a mule was to be my assistant pastor."

Dr. Carver was a member of Walnut Street Baptist Church and almost idolized his pastor, Dr. Findley Gibson. In many ways they were exact opposites. Dr. Gibson's sermons were very simple but warmly evangelistic, and it may have been that very quality which appealed to Dr. Carver so much.

On one occasion I spoke in chapel at a college. My message was a simple gospel sermon. At the close a professor thanked me for the message, saying that it was just what he needed at the time. Then he added, "So many guest speakers in chapel try to impress the faculty with their knowledge. But, you know, we professors need to hear preaching also." The greatest preacher-teacher, Jesus, spoke with simplicity but spiritual depth.

On a Monday morning Dr. Carver asked a student where he went to church the day before. He had attended Walnut Street, so Dr. Carver asked him what he thought of the pastor. The student replied, "Well, Dr. Carver, the man can't preach!"

In reply the wise professor asked if he had anyone there to hear him. The student said the house was packed for both services. "Well," asked Dr. Carver, "did anyone join the church?" The student said there were fifteen additions Sunday morning and ten that night, most of them on profession of faith. Came the rejoinder, "A full house at both services, twenty-five additions, most on profession of faith? I believe that is about what preaching is supposed to do, isn't it? I suggest that you pray about it." With that Dr. Carver walked on. Perhaps he had taught that student one of his greatest lessons.

In my judgment Dr. E. Y. Mullins was the greatest theologian Southern Baptists have ever had. He died in 1928, so I never knew him. But I feel as if I know him from his books. Perhaps his most monumental work was *The Christian Religion in Its Doctrinal Expression*. It was our textbook in systematic theology. It was rich but laborious reading. Its form was detailed outline with full discussion. The outlines ran thus: I, 1, (1), A, (a). The only way to learn it was to memorize it. I did so four times: the night before class, the morning before class, before an expected "pop quiz," and before the final examination. It was tough going, but it has stood me in good stead all these years.

Next to Mullins I would place Dr. W. T. Connor of Southwestern Baptist Theological Seminary, mainly because Mullins taught him. *When they spoke, Southern Baptists listened.*

I cannot resist relating a story coming out of Dr. Connor's class. One day as he was lecturing, a student went to sleep. The student's desk mate nudged him and whispered that he had been called upon to lead a prayer. While Dr. Connor was still lecturing, the student stood up and began praying. After a brief pause Dr. Conner said in his droll manner, "Well, while the brother catches up on his praying I will continue my lecture." Later that hapless student became a member of the faculty at Southwestern. I wonder how many students *he* put to sleep.

Homiletics was another tedious course dealing with the preparation and delivery of sermons. It was learning how to use the *workshop* and *tools* in hammering out the sermonic gems (?) we would one day present to our congregations. Our textbook was Dr. John A. Broadus' *Preparation and Delivery of Sermons*. It was first published in 1870 and still is a classic in the field. A few years ago it was revised by Dr. J. B. Weatherspoon, who was our professor at Southern and later at Southeastern Seminary.

There was no way to make this book palatable. You simply had to *bone* it and *get* it. In the 1930s when many students finished one course they had to sell the textbooks to buy the ones needed for the next courses. I was fortunate enough to not to need to do that. But I did buy a used copy of this book. Judging by the number of names written on the fly page, it had been used by several generations of students. But one brother had expressed his opinion of it by a piece of doggerel poetry penned on the fly page.

If ever again the earth by water is destroyed,
To this book I will fly.
For even if the whole world were totally submerged,
This book will still be dry.
—Author unknown

One day Dr. Weatherspoon gave us a simple assignment. He wanted us to write down a topic, text, and three points for the outline. Mine read:

The All-Sufficient Savior
Text: "Who is sufficient for these things?"—2 Corinthians 2:16
I. He Is Sufficient in Life
II. He Is Sufficient in Death
III. He Is Sufficient in Eternity

When he returned the papers, he had given me a B. I asked him why only a B. He replied, "Too obvious!" It happened that

Dr. George W. Truett was preaching on campus that week. We went directly from this class to chapel. When he stood to preach he said, "I want to speak today on 'The All-Sufficient Savior.' My text is 'Who is sufficient for these things?'" His three points were:

I. He Is Sufficient in Life
II. He Is Sufficient in Death
III. He Is Sufficient in Eternity

Dr. Truett was the greatest of all Southern Baptist preachers. God being my witness, I had never read or heard such a sermon by him or anyone else. After chapel I overtook Dr. Weatherspoon in the hall. I asked, "Dr. Weatherspoon, how did you like the sermon?" With a laugh he replied, "It was very good, wasn't it?" Maybe it was too obvious. But if it was good enough for Dr. Truett, it was good enough for me! However, I still got a B.

Dr. W. Hersey Davis was Dr. Robertson's colleague in New Testament and Greek. He was an outstanding scholar in his own right. I would describe him as an incisive thinker. Like Alexander the Great cutting the Gordian knot, he cut right through to reveal fresh truth. One day he told our class that much Scripture had merely been "harrowed" over, just scratching the surface. For that reason when we read our text most of our congregations knew what we were going to say, for they had heard it before. Said he, "Set your plow to go down deep and turn up fresh soil. There is plenty of virgin soil of truth down there that has never been touched." Not only did he do that, but, speaking for myself, he inspired me to try doing the same thing. I may not have succeeded, but I have tried.

One striking example of Davis' method is Matthew 16:19. The way the *King James Version* reads sounds as if Jesus said whatever His people do on earth they should send a memo to heaven where it will be approved *after the fact*. On this reading the first Roman Catholic Pope, Leo I, based his right, and through the priesthood, to forgive or not to forgive sins. If this be true, then in Matthew 18:18 Jesus gave the same right to every local church!

To my knowledge other versions follow the KJV, except *one printing* of the *New American Standard Bible*. In that one printing the translation correctly renders the Greek text; its other printings strangely follow the KJV. Even Robertson in his *Word Pictures in the New Testament* correctly locates the Greek verb forms, but then translates it from the KJV.

Davis was the *first* and *only* scholar I have heard or read who catches this discrepancy. In junior Greek class he pointed out that the Greek verb forms do not allow "shall be bound . . . shall be loosed." They should read "shall have been bound . . . shall have been loosed." Heaven has given the gospel to the church. It has been decreed that if we bind the gospel on earth by not declaring it, there is no other way by which people can be saved. But it has also decreed that if we loose the gospel by proclaiming it, many will hear, some will believe, and those who believe in Jesus Christ will be saved. What a difference! And as far as I am concerned we owe it to "Big Doc" for reminding us of it.

One day he thrilled us by interpreting a passage. After class I said, "Doctor Davis, why don't you write these things in books?" He said, "Aw, Hobbs, I will some day. But Dr. Robertson and I don't agree on the interpretation of some passages. And out of respect for him I will not write them in books as long as he lives." But he never did. I think he was so absorbed in finding new and better meanings of Scripture that he kept postponing putting them into book form. It is a pity that he wrote only a few books. Through the years in my books I have incorporated many ideas derived from him—simply to keep them alive.

Dr. Robertson died in 1934. But he is still remembered and his books are still being published and used—because he wrote. Dr. Davis died in 1950. Except for his former students, he is scarcely remembered—because with the exception of a very few books, he did not write. Recently in a church I quoted him as having given me his interpretation of a passage of Scripture. Later the pastor who attended another seminary said, "You referred to a man named Hersey Davis. Who is he?" He did not ask me about references to Dr. Robertson.

As long as Dr. Robertson lived he kept his students in line. He always said that one of his callings was "to take the starch out of young Baptist preachers." In addition to his strict discipline he would occasionally ask trick questions. For instance,

"Brother So-and-So, why did God call you into the ministry? Was it because He knew you would grow up to be such a handsome, strapping young Baptist preacher?" One time one of them backfired. He called on a student from Virginia. He asked, "Brother Stone from Virginia, are you an FFV?" (First Family of Virginia). He replied, "Yes sir, I'm a future farmer of Virginia." But his favorite seemed to be "Brother So-and-So, who's the greatest preacher where you came from *since you left?*" The hapless student, trying to think of the most outstanding pastor, did not hear "since you left." So when he would call some pastor's name, it always got a laugh from the class.

For that reason Dr. Davis left the discipline to his colleague while he had fun teaching. But when Dr. Robertson died suddenly, the entire load of teaching English New Testament fell on him. That class had had Dr. Robertson for only one week, so as Davis followed his usual method of teaching, some of the students would *smart-off* to him. It was my last year of undergraduate work, so I was monitoring his class looking toward graduate work in New Testament. Many times as some student would *smart-off* I prayed, "Oh Lord, send Dr. Robertson back just for one more class and let him straighten out this bunch!" But one day "Big Doc," as we affectionately called him among ourselves, had had enough. So he grabbed (figuratively speaking) one of these *smarties* and turned him every way but loose. After that he had no more problems in discipline. He received the respect he deserved.

There were a few "gold-brickers" among us, and he had his own way of handling them. Dedicated as he was, he could not abide deadbeats. For instance, in our class was a fellow who may have had some hearing problem, but not as bad as he pretended. Apparently he did little or no studying. And when he was called on to recite, if he did not know the answer to a question he pretended that he could not hear it. Dr. Davis saw through this ruse. So one day he called on him. In response to the question, he leaned forward with his hand behind his ear as if he did not hear. After repeating the question several times, each time with a louder tone, someone said, "Dr. Davis, he has a hearing problem." In a half-mumble loud enough for all to hear, he said, "I bet he would hear me if I offered him a five-dollar bill!"

Sometimes things happened that were not expected. In our class was a man much older than the rest of us. I suppose he was at least fifty years old. He had just enough gray hair to make him look distinguished, but he was not distinguished in scholarship. In fact he was regarded as the very opposite by other students. Judging by his recitations in class, evidently he studied very little. When called on to recite, most of the time he did not know the answer to a question. The professor would try to prime his pump by saying a word. He would repeat that word only once.

At that time one of the most popular radio programs was "Amos and Andy." Andy played the role of a blowhard. In a conversation he pretended to know everything, when actually he knew nothing. When someone would say something, to cover his ignorance, he would say, "Sho!" Another student and I had a private joke between us. We said this student reminded us of Andy.

One day in junior Greek I sat across the aisle from "Andy," and the other student sat directly behind me. The fellow, Lucius Polhill, later the executive secretary of the Virginia Baptist Convention, was filling in for Dr. Davis. We were reading a passage from the Greek New Testament. Polhill called on "Andy" to recite. He stood in the aisle right by my desk. When he could not read the first word, Polhill tried to get him started by reading it for him. He repeated that word and could go no farther. And so it went through about five words.

Then Polhill put the screws on him. He said, "All right, Brother, I have recited. Let's hear you recite." But he uttered not a sound. Repeatedly Polhill asked him what that next word meant. Still no sound. Otherwise the room was as still as a mouse.

I did not mean for him to hear me, but he did and thought I was trying to help him. I turned my head slightly so the man behind me could hear me. And in a very low tone I said, "Sho!" He blurted out, "It means 'show'!" Polhill told him to sit down.

Years later at the Southern Baptist Convention Polhill and I were talking about that incident. I told him what happened. He laughed until he hurt. Then he said, "I've been trying ever since that day to figure out where he got that translation!"

Up to this point in this chapter it may seem that seminary life was more fun than work. But who wants to read the dull routine of hard study and daily class attendance? I can assure you that these things were the heart of our daily and nightly lives. In our small apartment it was about three steps from the dinner table to my study table. I usually moved directly from the former to the latter. I habitually moved from one to the other about 6:00 p.m. Many were the mornings when, as I was still studying, I heard the tower clock over Norton Hall strike 4:00 a.m. Frances usually slept with my study light on. How she did it I will never know, but she never complained. However, it paid off in the long run.

One day in biblical theology class Dr. Harold Tribble was discussing whether or not seminary students should marry. He said, "Of course we know that single students make the best grades." He was greeted with a storm of protest from the married students. We challenged him to check the grades. Doing so, he admitted his error. Married students made the best grades. Later I told him why. I said, "We married students have found our mates. So we stay at home and study, while the single students are out dating as they try to find theirs."

Incidentally, one day Dr. Davis told a class, "Some of you ask my advice as to whether to get married while still in school. When I discourage it, you argue with me. You don't want *advice* but *encouragement*!" Speaking for ourselves, Frances and I always prized the fact that we went through college and seminary after we married. It prepared her better to be a pastor's wife. And she could appreciate what I went through in preparing for the ministry.

In those days they never told us our grades. Their reasoning was that if an A and a C student were in adjoining pastorates it might make a difference in their relationship. At the end of a course they simply posted on the bulletin board those who passed. We would walk up to the board singing, "Is my name written there?"

Finally, I was ready to begin my final year of undergraduate work. It was September 1934. I had been looking forward to studying senior Greek under Dr. Robertson, but it was not to be. I had only one week with him. On Friday of that week for the last time he called on me to recite. He asked me to give him the twelve rules he followed in his "Big Grammar." I did. When he thanked me I sat down. He marked my grade on my class enrollment card, since he had not yet entered names in the permanent class book. It was a 10.

On that day he gave what was probably his final and greatest testimony concerning the New Testament. "I have been studying, preaching, teaching, and writing about the New Testament for over fifty years. But I never open my Greek New Testament without finding something I had never before seen in it."

The following Monday afternoon was a normal September day in Louisville. It was not unusually warm. I always tried to sit in the front row where, without distraction, I could get the "drippings from the altar." That afternoon I was not more than ten feet from him. When he entered the room I noticed that he did not look well. Early in the class he wrote two Greek words on the blackboard, the last words he ever wrote!

Soon I noticed that he was perspiring unduly. Drops of perspiration were dripping from the end of his nose. He wore a blue shirt. Soon it looked almost black as it became wet with perspiration. Finally at 3:30 p.m. he said, "I don't know what is the matter, but I don't feel well. So I am letting you go." The class moved out. I carried the "Big Grammar" in a small leather satchel. While I was putting it in the satchel, Dr. Davis came in from his class next door. I was the last student to leave the room.

Dr. Robertson never let his class out early. When Dr. Davis heard us leaving early, he knew that something was wrong. He asked Dr. Robertson what was the matter. He replied, "I don't know. I don't feel well." Davis said, "Come on and I will take you home." I followed them out of the room. Had I known what was happening, I would have been like Elisha following Elijah.

About five o'clock word spread over the campus that Dr. Robertson had died. In Rice Hall the four couples living off our landing were talking in hushed tones. I said, "If a tornado had destroyed every building and beech tree on the campus but left Dr. Robertson, it would be more like the seminary than it is with the campus left and Dr. Robertson gone." Later when Dr. Everett Gill, Sr., wrote Dr. Robertson's biography he used my quote to that effect.

His body lay in state in his home. Frances and I went to see Mrs. Robertson. The home was crowded with people on a similar mission. As we viewed Dr. Robertson's body, Frances told me later of a wish I expressed without being aware of it. "Oh Lord, why couldn't he have transferred all that knowledge to my mind?" But, alas, that could not be. What little I have came to me the same way he acquired his great knowledge—through years of hard work and brain sweat.

The workmen die, but the work goes on. Dr. Davis became the head of the New Testament department and taught senior Greek. It was during that year that W. A. and Betty Criswell were married in what then was the seminary chapel. Dr. Tribble performed the ceremony; Cornell Goerner was W. A.'s best man. I drove the get-away car after the wedding because I had a practically new Chevrolet sedan.

The wedding was on Tuesday. The previous weekend it had been raining. The roads on my church field were unpaved, so my car was muddy top to bottom and front to back. We decided to leave it that way since no one would expect a bride to ride in such a muddy car.

Betty was dressed in a beautiful white bridal outfit. When Cornell and I went to bring her to the seminary, she said, "I'm not going to get my dress dirty in that car!" So she got a bed sheet which we spread on the back seat and floor. No one knows what became of that sheet. Betty still says I stole it, but I didn't. Anyway, we got her to the seminary and slipped her in the back way. I parked my car in the faculty parking lot behind Norton Hall.

Jim Middleton, Paul Fox, and another student were planning to mess up the get-away car after the wedding. I could see them prowling around trying to determine *which* car it was. When I figured that the wedding was almost over, I pulled around to the front entrance to Norton Hall and left the motor running. They knew that was the car, so Jim Middleton acted as if he was going to let the air out of the tires. I got out to chase him away, but he ran around the car, turned off the motor, jerked the keys out of the switch, and ran.

Frances was in the chapel with her keys, so I ran to get them. The people were standing as the newlyweds came down the aisle. I got up on the back pew and went from pew to pew until I came to Frances. "Give me your car keys," I said. When she asked why, I said, "Don't ask me now. I'll tell you later!" Then I ran back and started the car. Paul Fox ran up and made a grab for the keys but missed them. I was desperate and didn't even look to see. Instead I got out of the car, put my arm around his neck, and threw him to the ground. He said, "Aw, Hobbs, I don't have your keys!"

Just at that moment W. A. and Betty came out the front door, welcomed by the sight of us scrambling on the ground. W. A. said, "Oh Lord, they're having a fight at my wedding!"

Well, we got away and I drove them to a studio for the official wedding picture. The photographer posed them with both looking into the camera, but by the time he got under the camera cover, W. A. was looking at Betty. After several futile efforts he took the picture—with W. A. looking at Betty.

On their golden wedding anniversary the front page of *The Reminder* of First Baptist Church, Dallas, was a beautiful color picture of them, made against the background of a stained glass window. At the top was a small black-and-white insert of their wedding picture. After fifty years, W. A. was still looking at Betty!

After I deposited them back at Betty's abode, my job was done, so I left. After they had dressed for travel, someone drove them to their car at the opposite end of Louisville. Arriving, they found that all four tires were flat. More than fifty years later I asked Jim how on earth they found W. A.'s car. The only answer was "Heh! Heh!" So I suppose it will remain a mystery until the "books" are opened on Judgment Day.

But hear "the rest of the story." W. A. was pastor of a rural church in Warren County near Bowling Green, Kentucky. In that state on the license tag appears the name of the county in which it was sold. One of W. A.'s deacons had attended the wedding, driving a car exactly like his. It was parked on the seminary driveway right next to Lexington Road, a perfect spot for the get-away car. These "culprits" thought it was the one. So they had put a smoke bomb on the starter. After the wedding excitement was over and all but a few of the guests had departed, this deacon sauntered down to his car. When he stepped on the starter—BOOM!! Smoke boiled from under the hood, and the deacon went running back toward Norton Hall yelling, "Call the fire department! My car's on fire!"

Oh well! *Boys will be boys!* But just remember these are some of the dignified *theologs* whom you have seen in their pulpits looking so pious that their halos hurt. No wonder the world is in such a mess! Paul Fox is with the Lord. But I still love you, Jim! "Heh! Heh!"

We were now in early spring of 1935 with graduation coming early in May. In those days the graduating class had a valedictorian and a salutatorian. To my utter surprise, and I am sure that of the rest of the class, the faculty announced that I was the valedictorian. Millard Berquist was the salutatorian. Years later someone asked Millard if he knew me. He replied, "I should. He kept me from being the valedictorian of my class in the seminary."

As stated previously, they did not tell us our grades in those days, but a professor told a friend of mine what my average was for the three years. Due to my humility (?) I will not tell you what it was—only that it was more than 95 and less than 97.

Three years later, after my doctoral work, I was called to a church in Birmingham. Word of my average grade had spread among ministerial students at Howard College. Those planning to enter Southern Seminary the next year beat a path to my study at the church. They wanted to know how I did it. I replied, "Well, I am not smart. All I can say is that I got up every lesson every day. In college you can loaf for a couple of weeks and then catch up. In the seminary you can't do that. You have all you can handle tomorrow. So you have to get up today's lessons today."

Millard and I had to make twenty-minute speeches at the graduation exercise. I chose to speak on "The Gospel and the Modern Mind"; Millard chose "The Christian and World Peace." Through future years he and I had a running joke between us. He said my speech had in it neither *gospel* nor *mind*. I told him he delivered his speech in 1935, and we have been at war ever since.

We had to get both topic and speech approved by the faculty. Of course, we had to write out the speeches and memorize them. After familiarizing myself with my speech by reading it repeatedly, I memorized it while driving back and forth to our church fields. Frances held the speech and followed me as I said it, prompting me where needed—she knew it as well as I did.

On Monday before I was to deliver it the next night, we had a wreck returning to Louisville. The road was a blacktop, a light rain was falling, and we were on a slight incline. Just before we met an empty school bus, the driver, without any signal, turned in front of us to enter his driveway. Immediately I hit my brakes, locking the wheels, but on the slick road our car was sliding straight toward the bus. I knew that if I hit it head-on it probably would kill both of us, so I whirled the steering wheel and slid into it sideways, thus broadening the impact.

Even so, the force of the impact threw me up so that I hit my head on the door frame and was knocked unconscious. Later a doctor told me that had the blow been an inch lower it would have killed me. My Bible was on the seat between Frances and me. I came down on it with such force as to tear the top leather cover off the Bible. I still have it as a reminder of God's watchcare in danger. In a reflex action my foot was tapping the floor so rapidly that Frances thought I was dying.

Don Myers, another student, was riding in the back seat. Frances said, "Get some water!" The only container he had was his new felt hat. But he ran to a nearby branch, dipped his hat until it was full of water, and brought it to help revive me.

Soon I regained consciousness and asked, "What happened?" Frances said, "Hon, we've had an accident." I kept repeating "what" when I meant "how" it happened. She thought I had lost my memory. So she asked, "Do you remember your speech you are to make tomorrow night?" I started out, "There is no statement today that would find a more ready assent than the assertion that all is not well with religion." She breathed more easily, knowing that I remembered. To this day that opening sentence is all that I remember of the entire speech. As long as he lived Don never let me forget that he ruined his five-dollar hat for me.

Soon my car insurance man arrived. They "totaled" our car. Eventually we continued on to Louisville in a car borrowed from a dealer from whom we later bought a new car.

My mother and sister, Annie Webb, came up from Birmingham for the graduation. When we arrived at our apartment they were already there. That night neither Frances nor I *crawled* into bed. We were so sore that we backed up to the bed and fell across it. My mother, taking us by the feet, turned us to the proper position on the bed.

The next night I delivered my speech without missing a word. Poor Frances! She agonized through it. So familiar was she with it that she said she thought *page one*, *page two*, and so on to the end.

After the ceremony Miss Littlejohn, principal of the Woman's Missionary Union Training School, came to Frances. Said she, "Oh, what a speech! What delivery! Such dignity! Such poise! Not a single gesture!" When Frances told me, I said, "Hon, that wasn't poise. I was so sore I couldn't raise my arms."

When she told me that, however, I was also in a state of shock. From the start she and I had been looking forward to my doing graduate work, and it seemed that everything was falling into place. Cornell Goerner received his doctorate that night. He and Ruth had been appointed by the Foreign Mission Board as missionaries to Romania where he was to teach in the seminary at Bucharest. Dr. Carver had asked me to be his fellow. It paid thirty-five dollars per month. As an undergraduate I had received financial help from the Student Aid and Loan Fund. As a graduate student that would not be available, but the thirty-five dollars plus the salary from my churches would be sufficient. Everything seemed set. In September I would return to the seminary to begin work toward my doctorate.

At the graduation Dr. Sampey conferred the Master in Theology (Th.M.) degrees *en masse*, but the doctoral degrees were conferred individually. After Dr. Sampey had conferred the degree upon Cornell, he said, "Now I have an announcement to make. Dr. and Mrs. Goerner have been appointed as missionaries to Romania, but the trustees have asked the Foreign Mission Board to release them from that appointment. They have elected Dr. Goerner as instructor to assist Dr. Carver. In order for us to pay him a living wage, Dr. Goerner has agreed to do the fellowship work for one year."

Talk about having the rug pulled from under your feet! Or hearing the death knell to your hopes and dreams! For Frances and me that was it! From soaring on eagles' wings over Valedictorian Heights, that one announcement left us falling face down in the mud.

So we packed our few worldly goods on a borrowed two-wheel trailer and headed back to those two wonderful little Hoosier churches which had stood by us so loyally for three years. What we did not know was that our wonder-working God stood in the shadows, keeping watch above His own!

6

Pursuing the Dream

From the time Frances and I entered college, our dream was for me to receive my doctor of philosophy degree from the Southern Baptist Theological Seminary. Someone said that a call to preach is a call to prepare, and we wanted the best preparation possible. I say "we" for from the day of our marriage we had always been a team. We remained such until the day she died. I still think of us as a team because whatever ministry I have had and still have is possible because of the support and encouragement she gave to me through the years.

However, when we left the campus that day in May 1935, pulling that trailer behind us, it seemed that our dream had wound up in the dust. We would return to our Hoosier churches and wait upon the Lord to open the door to whatever our future was to be.

At the final judgment there will be many sins written in "the books" against my name, but at this stage in life I can say that one thing will not be on my record. I have never asked anyone to recommend me to a church, appoint me to a board or committee, or nominate me for an office. I do not take any credit for this; by the grace of God and the kindness of the brethren I have never needed to do these things. We have tried to do the best we could where we have served, leaving matters with the Lord.

The nearest I ever came to violating those things was a letter which I wrote to Dr. W. Hersey Davis. In doctoral work I had planned to major under him in New Testament interpretation. So in May 1935, I wrote him that I could not return to the seminary unless I could get work nearer Louisville; did he know of any possibilities? Some time went by with no reply.

In the meantime, I had been invited to preach a trial sermon in a small county-seat town church in north Alabama. I accepted the invitation for a Sunday in July when we planned a vacation trip to Alabama. We were living in Hope but had been on the field at Little Blue River. On Wednesday afternoon we returned to Hope for prayer meeting that night. The next morning we planned to leave for Alabama where I would preach in that church on Sunday.

Arriving in Hope, we stopped at the post office to pick up our mail. I found three letters which I opened according to their postmark dates. The first was a note from Dr. Davis telling me that he did not know of any work. The second one was also from him. He told me that he had just met Dr. J. B. Weatherspoon in the hall. He had just returned from a trip to the Orient with Dr. Truett, president of the Baptist World Alliance, and Dr. J. H. Rushbrooke, secretary of the Alliance. Howard Colson, Weatherspoon's fellow, had graduated. Since he had been absent at graduation he had not secured a new fellow and asked Dr. Davis if he had any suggestions. In his letter to me Dr. Davis said, "I recommended you, but do not mention it to him unless he contacts you."

The third letter was from Dr. Weatherspoon inviting me to be his fellow. Of course, I wrote him immediately that I was happy to accept his invitation. It was an answer to our prayers. I then called the pulpit committee chairman in Alabama, telling him what had happened. He agreed with me that, in that case, I need not be there on the next Sunday.

The "dream" glowed brightly again, so we spent the summer looking forward to returning to the seminary in September. Of course, we were busy with our churches, and I had an additional chore for the summer. In order to take graduate work every student was required to have at least two years of Greek and Hebrew and two years of Latin and French or German, or a working knowledge of the same. This was required to enable the student, if necessary, to do research in these languages. I qualified in all but Latin. In high school I studied Spanish rather than Latin. In college I took one year of Latin, so I was required to take a reading test in Latin.

Fortunately for me, Beulah Phares of Little Blue River taught Latin in high school. She agreed to be my teacher for the summer. Every two weeks she gave me an assignment on which I had to recite the next time we went to Little Blue River. Following this procedure, I was ready to stand my reading test by September. Dr. Davis let me read about two lines, and then he took the book and read two pages to me. So he and I passed the test together. Thus, I became a full-fledged graduate student. After that I used neither Latin nor French, a little Hebrew, and lots of Greek.

For three years we had lived in Rice Hall, but back of Mullins Hall there were two old brown houses which had been remodeled, with two apartments in each. We were fortunate to get one of these—and it was *luxurious*! We had a small living room, kitchen with a breakfast nook, bath, and a private bedroom! Yes, a bedroom, even if I could hardly get between the footboard and the wall. Yes, and a telephone, so that we did not need to go three floors to the basement to make a phone call. Also we had a small yard where Frances could grow flowers and two pets—chipmunks which had taken up residence in the yard before we moved in.

At last we were settled in and ready for me to begin my graduate work. Or were we? Unknown to us the greatest crisis was just ahead.

The first weekend after moving back to Louisville we were in Hope. Frances scratched a little pimple on her lower lip and wound up with a strep infection. When we arrived back in Louisville, she entered the hospital for a month. This was before we had "wonder drugs," so it was a battle between her constitution and the germ. And the germ almost won.

Later the doctor told us that for two weeks he did not know whether she would live or die. He knew the infection was going to move. If it went up it would hit the brain and that would be the end. If it went down she had a chance. It went down, settling in the pleura. For the rest of her life she had occasional trouble with dry pleurisy. Gradually she won the battle. Before leaving the hospital she had lost so much weight that they gave her the tuberculin test, which proved to be negative.

Back in our apartment the doctor began a program to enable her to put on weight. In addition to her regular meals she had to get down several raw eggs each day. To cook the whites of the eggs, we were told to put vanilla extract into each serving of these raw eggs. The alcohol in the extract was supposed to do this, but this soon lost its power.

It was then that I bought my first and last pint of *whiskey*—on the doctor's order. The seminary is located in the eastern part of Louisville, so I drove to the extreme western end of the city and found a liquor store. Parking my car on a dark street one block behind the store, I walked to it. Seeing no one on the street, I went in. I had no knowledge about brands except that I had seen advertisements of Four Roses whiskey. So I bought a pint and hurried back to my car.

Arriving back at our apartment, according to the doctor's order I mixed a tablespoon of whiskey with two raw eggs. Sure enough, that did the trick. The extra amount of alcohol curdled the eggs so that Frances swallowed them with no trouble. Then I put the bottle in the back of the refrigerator behind everything else. I didn't want some neighbor coming in to help Frances and finding it. Mrs. Jackson came from Alabama to look after Frances, which enabled me to study and do my fellowship work. On her diet Frances put on weight until she weighed 150 pounds. She looked like a butterball. It seemed that we were out of the woods. And then the bomb exploded.

One morning shortly after Mrs. Jackson returned to Alabama the doctor came to see Frances. He told her she could no longer make the weekly trips to Indiana. Neither could I and have her worrying about me. Either I had to get work near Louisville or else leave the seminary. At noon I came home for lunch. When Frances gave me the news it seemed that once again we had reached the end of the road; our dream had gone up in smoke. But unknown to us, God was already at work.

The week before, Dr. Dobbins had led a study course at Highland Baptist Church. It was about two miles from the campus. The pastor, Dr. T. D. Brown, had asked him what he could do to improve the religious educational program of the church. Dr. Dobbins told him to get a seminary student to work part-time as his assistant. Asked for a recommendation, he said it would be difficult for him to select one out of so many. He suggested that Dr. Brown go to the seminary and see Brother *Gohr* (George Gohr, an undergraduate student from Minnesota, who now teaches in a college in that state), let him suggest one student, and Dr. Dobbins then would check him out to see if he could recommend him.

Brother Gohr had charge of directing a teaching program for students who had no church work of their own. Each Sunday these students went into churches, missions, retirement homes, and the like, to teach Sunday School classes and help in other phases of the Lord's work. Now Brother Gohr knew that I had church work and had never been a part of his program. Not in a million years would he have thought of me.

But Dr. Brown misunderstood the name. He thought Dr. Dobbins had said "Brother *Goerner*." Cornell and Ruth, longtime friends, lived in the apartment next to ours. It was on Tuesday morning that the doctor gave Frances the bad news. Shortly after he left, Ruth came to see Frances, who gave her the bad news. (This was the week following Dr. Dobbins' advice to Dr. Brown.) That very morning Dr. Brown called Dr. Goerner. He said he would think it over and call him that afternoon.

When Cornell came home for lunch Ruth told him the bad news, so he said, "Well, that settles it. I'll recommend Herschel." And he did. Dr. Brown called me and made an appointment to see me at the seminary at two o'clock that afternoon. After the interview he asked me to meet with the church's deacons at five o'clock Wednesday afternoon. Dr. Ireland was chairman of the deacons.

Frances and I had agreed that we needed eighty dollars per month, in addition to my fellowship salary of thirty-five dollars, in order to live. But I had said nothing to anyone else about that. In the deacons meeting various questions were put to me. Apparently I answered them satisfactorily, for then Dr. Ireland told me that they had forty dollars per month in the budget for this position. Hearing that, I made up my mind that if the church called me, I would accept. That was too close to do otherwise. Someway, somehow I would borrow the other forty dollars per month.

At that point one deacon asked if I had ever done any preaching. I told him I had been a full-time pastor for over seven years. Then he asked if I would be willing to fill the pulpit when the pastor was absent. (Will a pig eat peaches?) Of course, I said I would be thrilled to do so. That was all. Dr. Ireland said I was free to return to our seminary apartment.

The next morning before breakfast I received a special delivery letter from Dr. Ireland. He said the church had given me a unanimous call and reminded me that the budget contained forty dollars per month for the position. But he added, "We also have forty dollars per month in the budget for pulpit supply, and since you are willing to fill that role, your salary will be eighty dollars per month."

An accident? Not on your life! As the story goes a dear old lady said, "Well, you know what the Good Book says. God works in mischievous ways His wonders to perform." She was slightly mixed up. It is the *hymn* book not the *Bible* that says that. And the word is "mysterious," not "mischievous." But after that experience I believe she was partly right. God does work mysteriously, but in that case His work bordered also on the mischievous. The whole thing turned on Dr. Brown mistaking the pronunciation of a name!

A few years ago when the "God is dead" philosophy (not theology) was going around, I was tempted to write a little book containing this and similar experiences (every preacher could write his own along this line). I would have given it the title *My God Is Alive! Too Bad About Yours!* But this *fad* was so short-lived that before such a book could be published it would have been dealing with a dead issue.

Thus far in this chapter I have related these rather lengthy accounts because they were pivotal points in my ministry. Had I not been able to do graduate work in the seminary I do not know what turn my ministry would have taken. But I do know that the Lord has opened doors which I question would have been available otherwise. I can only praise the Lord and be grateful to my brethren through whom He has worked for the opportunities for service which have come to me.

My work as Dr. Weatherspoon's fellow in homiletics and sociology consisted largely of routine work such as grading exam papers and other written assignments. Only one instance in this regard stands out. It was one exam paper of Clarence Jordan's, who later founded the "Koinonian (Fellowship) Farm" in Georgia. He also translated and published the four Gospels in what he called *The Cottonpatch Gospels*. It was done in language in keeping with the book's title.

In one exam Dr. Weatherspoon called for a discussion of twelve values in having a previously written conclusion for a sermon. Clarence correctly listed and discussed all twelve of them. Then he added a thirteenth. "Besides, if you have a written conclusion you do not have to drag out your holy whine with which to end the sermon." Later I told him if he had missed the twelve I would have given him an A for number thirteen.

The most challenging responsibility was teaching a class in basic English grammar for first-year students who made less than 70 on a placement exam. At least 95 percent of the students were college graduates, but most of them were woefully weak in the fundamentals of English grammar. To this day I cringe when I hear professional speakers such as radio and television personalities using bad grammar. If I am wrong I apologize. But the way I explain this is that grade schools are supposed to teach grammar but do not or not enough of it. High schools and colleges assume that students have already studied grammar, so they do not teach it. Literature? Yes! Grammar? No!

When I would post the list of those who had to take this course, some would come to me mad enough to bite.

It usually went thus: "This is ridiculous! I majored in English in college!" My standard reply was: "You may be able to quote Shakespeare, Byron, and Keats by the hour, but you cannot diagram a simple sentence." The reason for this class was that, as preachers, language was our primary means of communication; we should be able to use it properly. To my knowledge this class was started with A. Ben Oliver as the teacher. He received his doctorate at the time I received my masters. So I inherited the class from him. Insofar as I know, I was the first fellow in homiletics to teach it. Dr. and Mrs. Oliver were missionaries in Brazil from 1935 until they retired a few years ago. He was the founder and president of the Baptist Theological Seminary in Rio de Janeiro until retirement.

Interestingly enough, we had in this class a Japanese student, Sadamoto Kawano. Later he was president of a Baptist college in Fukuoka, Japan. He knew more English grammar than I did. He could quote the rules and tell the page number in the textbook. His purpose in attending the class was to improve his vocabulary.

One day the campus was covered with a deep snow. A narrow path each way had to be shoveled out on the walk between Mullins and Norton Halls. After lunch in Mullins, Sadamoto and I were going to Norton for our class. Coming to this narrow path, I stepped aside for him to go first, but he insisted that I go first. We put on quite an "Alphonse and Gaston" act until finally he said, "In Japan, pupil never walk in front of teacher." That settled it. I led off down the path and Sadamoto followed.

An old saying goes like this, "If you want to teach a dog you must first know more than the dog." I must confess that in that class I learned more English grammar than in all of my schooling up to that time. It has been extremely helpful in both my preaching and writing ministry. So I got more than thirty-five dollars per month out of that fellowship.

In my graduate studies I majored in New Testament interpretation under Dr. Davis. My minors were in philosophy of Christianity and sociology under Drs. Carver and Weatherspoon, respectively. The Bible was not written in heaven, printed on rice paper, bound in leather, and then thrown down to earth. Under the guidance of the Holy Spirit it was wrought out in the hot fires of the arena of history. This meant that we spent equitable time studying the New Testament, ancient history, and textual and higher criticism of the text itself. Of course, except when we met for seminars about once each week, each person studied alone under the guidance of the professor.

In my case the first school year was spent covering the entire field, making copious notes as I read. May to September of 1936 I had planned to spend memorizing the material in my notes.

It was in May of that year that Frances and I met Dick and Lora Hall, Jr. In May 1925, Dick had been scheduled to take his oral exam for his doctorate in New Testament interpretation. He got out of bed with the flu to go for the exam. Dr. Robertson said, "You are too weak to sit up for two hours, let alone endure this exam. Go back to bed and take the exam in the fall." In July he contracted an infection which got into his blood stream. Doctors tried everything in efforts to cure him. One even operated on his shoulder and put maggots in the bone marrow, hoping they would eat up the germs. Dick told me many people walked the floor at night in pain. He ran the streets, but nothing worked.

Finally, a doctor in Miami, Florida, tried an experiment. It was to saturate his blood with iodine, hoping it would destroy the infection. On a graduated scale he gave him drops of iodine in a glass of milk after each meal until he reached thirty-five drops. Then he kept Dick at that level over a long period of time. THAT DID IT!

The seminary had a rule that a graduate student must complete the work within a period of seven years or else forfeit the degree. But due to the circumstances in Dick's case, they made an exception. If he returned to the seminary, reviewed the course, passed the exam in the fall, and wrote his thesis, he would receive his Ph.D. degree. They had returned for that purpose and lived in an apartment near us.

For him and me the situation was perfect. I was to spend that summer memorizing my notes, so we studied together, with him memorizing them, too. Mullins Hall was vacant for the summer months. So daily from eight to five we were in a vacant room boning away. We took one hour for lunch and then went back to the grind.

During his ten-year absence the entire field of *criticism* had been revolutionized. Had he taken his exam with the knowledge of 1925, he probably would have failed. But my notes were up to date, so in October he passed with flying colors. Then he wrote his thesis and received his degree at graduation in 1936. He often said that without my help he could not have done it. But in a very real sense we helped each other. It was much better for me to work with someone than to do it alone.

When our minds got tired we would stop and *shoot the breeze*. One time we were talking about compliments people pay on sermons. He felt the worst compliments were when someone thought they *must* say something to the preacher, but could think of nothing good about the sermon. So, he said, the compliment would come out like, "Brother Pastor, I never heard it just that way before!"

Later on a Sunday night in our church (I was then pastor of the Crestwood Baptist Church in Louisville) we were ordaining some deacons, and I had invited Dick to preach. After the service Mrs. Harry O'Nan, a spicy little lady, came to him and said, "Well, Brother Hall, I never heard it just that way before!" I thought I would explode before she got away so I could laugh. At his graduation I gave him a book, the title of which described Dick to me in light of all he had endured. The title was *The Hero in Thy Soul*.

Years later Dick was pastor of the First Baptist Church in a university city. He and Lora were on their way to New Albany, Mississippi, to visit his father, and they passed through Montgomery, Alabama, where I was pastor of the Clayton Street Baptist Church. When they stopped by to see us, Dick and I sat on the porch talking. Suddenly he said, "Hobbs, I'm glad I have a Ph.D. degree." I said, "I'm glad I have one, too. But why do you say that?" He replied, "Because I have some Ph.D. professors as deacons. At times they oppose me in their meetings. If I didn't have that degree I'd think they knew something. But having one myself, I know how ignorant you can be and have one."

With that I agree. Simply because a person has that degree does not mean he/she knows everything. It means that one knows *more and more about less and less*! Such a person centers in one field. Even if you grant that he/she is an expert in that field (few are), in most cases in other fields that person is as ignorant as the rest of us!

Incidentally, while talking about degrees, Dr. J. B. Gambrell, the great Baptist "commoner" of Texas, once said, "Conferring a D.D. (honorary doctor of divinity) on a pastor doesn't make him a better preacher. It is like curling a pig's tail. It doesn't make any more pork, just dresses him up a little bit."

He had the rare ability to express great truths in homely language. Someone else said, "A preacher with 'D.D.' after his name means that he can go down deeper, stay down longer, and come up dryer than any other preacher in town." Having received two such degrees, I guess I should know.

After Dick Hall passed his oral exam in 1936, my "study buddy" was Jim Leavell. Excuse me, Jim. I mean Dr. James B. Leavell, recently retired as a professor at Houston Baptist University. Each afternoon we went to his room in Mullins Hall. By that time we were looking toward our own oral exams. We were much harder on each other than the professors were in the actual exam. For instance, if one asked the other a question he could not answer, the questioner would hem him up in the corner and let him sweat until he either answered it correctly or else admitted that he could not do it.

It was in the late fall of 1936. One day Dr. Brown of Highland Church called me to his study. He had heard that the Crestwood Baptist Church was interested in me. So after telling me that, he said, "Our people who have heard you preach in my absence tell me that you should have your own church where you can preach regularly. If you choose to stay with us that will be fine. But since you have been here less than a year, you might feel that for that reason you should not leave. All I am doing is removing that obstacle. If they want to call you, and if you feel it is the Lord's will, then you let them do it." They did call me. And exactly one year after going to Highland on December 1, Frances and I moved to Crestwood. It was about thirteen miles from the campus.

Dr. Brown and the Highland people were good to and for us. I learned much from him about how to be a pastor in a city church. Many years after his death I was in a Bible study at First Baptist Church, Maryville, Tennessee. While there I had the privilege of visiting Mrs. Brown, who was in a nursing home in Maryville.

Shortly after Jim Leavell and I began studying together in the fall of 1936, we were joined by a third man. For reasons that will become obvious, I will not give his name. He was older than either of us. A veteran of World War I, he had a lung condition from being gassed in the war. He had been a graduate student at Southwestern Seminary, but for no particular reason switched to Southern.

It soon became evident that his grasp of the material was lacking. No matter what book we mentioned, he had read it. But he did not know what was in it. One day in late December he told us he had set the date for his oral exam, three weeks from then. Of the three of us, he was the least prepared for it. Jim and I looked at each other with the same thought in mind. We had to take him by his collar and the seat of his pants and try to shove him through. So for the next three weeks we reviewed all that we had learned.

One day Dr. Davis met me in the hall. He asked if I was studying with this man. When I told him that I was, he said, "Well, he has set the date for his oral. Is he ready?" I replied, "Dr. Davis, if you will lead him down the middle of the road I think he will be all right. But if you get off into side issues, he is a gone gosling." I suppose he did as I suggested, for the man passed the exam.

The afternoon after he had done so, he dropped by the room where we were going at it. For a few minutes he listened as he rattled keys and coins in his pocket. Then he said, "Well, you boys are on the right track. Keep it up, and you will be all right." With that he turned and left the room. Jim and I could hardly wait until he got out of hearing distance to have a good laugh.

In February 1937, the Ohio River flood hit Louisville. It was worse there than in any other city in the Ohio River system. The eastern part of Louisville is in the highlands. Just down from Cave Hill Cemetery is Beargrass Creek, which normally serves for drainage of that part of the city. Everything west and south of there is flat country. The Ohio River flows around that area. It had been raining for several days so that Beargrass Creek overflowed. All the manholes which normally drained the city were a network into pipes running into the river above the waterline. But the river rose above them, so that each manhole became a bubbling fountain. Thus the low part of the city was flooded.

The call went out for people with boats to help evacuate multiplied thousands of people. A man in our church had a longshoreman's boat. He later told me about an experience at Fourth and Broadway in the downtown area, at least a mile from the stockyards. He stood up in his boat, using his oar to fight off swimming hogs trying to get in his boat.

Southern Seminary is in the highlands. Its campus and buildings were used as the hub for rescue operations. It was the first stop for rescued people where they were ministered to, including certain vaccinations, after which they were sent to areas farther out. Eventually many people were sent to cities and towns all over the state.

This flood produced the first radio network in the nation. WHAS, Louisville, was the flagship station. From there telephone lines went to stations all over the country. Listeners over the nation heard the repeated "Send a boat" to such-and-such addresses to rescue people. In such floods, drinking water is a major need. It was brought in from surrounding areas. Many Louisville warehouses were filled with new empty whiskey barrels. These were used to distribute the water. Imagine the shock waves over the nation when over radios they heard, "Send twenty-five whiskey barrels to Southern Baptist Theological Seminary!"

Knowing that Jim Leavell was soon coming up for his oral exam, I drove to the campus and brought him to our home away from all the confusion. There he could be quiet and study.

Crestwood was one of the first stops away from the seminary for refugees. The high school building served as the hub of our operations. Churches were opened to provide sleeping quarters for many. In the high school gym, cots were placed so close together that one could hardly walk between them. During each day planned activities were carried on in an effort to help people forget their worries.

The pastors in the community decided to hold religious services in the gym. The people sat on the cots or else stood along the walls. Each day the people sang and the pastors took turns in preaching. When it became my turn, the gym was packed, but the flood waters had begun receding. As I was preaching, someone came to tell a man he and his family could return home and start cleaning up. He went throughout the crowd collecting his family. As this family went out, others followed to determine the conditions in their area. By the time I finished my sermon only a handful remained in the gym. After the benediction the Methodist pastor named Grant, with a solemn face said, "Hobbs, that was the most moving sermon I ever heard!" Well, something moved them.

Eventually the flood was over and life returned to normal. Jim passed his oral, so I decided that if he could do it, so could I. I soon set my oral for a day in April.

One day I had a conference with Dr. Davis to determine if I had covered the field. He asked me if I had read anything on the ethnology of the Greeks. At that point I did not even know they had an ethnology. So he assigned me a large, dry book to read. On the exam he did not even mention ethnology. My final preparation by way of review was to read every article on the New Testament in the multi-volume set of *The International Standard Bible Encyclopedia*.

The night before the exam, Frances and I went out to dinner and attended a picture show—just to get my mind off the coming day. Arriving home, we went to bed early so I could get a good night's sleep. I was determined not to take a sleeping pill. One brilliant and well-prepared student had done so. It almost ended in tragedy for him. At ten o'clock the next morning the effects of the pill were still there, so that his mind was sluggish. He barely passed the exam.

As far back as I could remember I had kept a Big Ben alarm clock on the night table by my bed. Its loud ticking had never bothered me. But that night it sounded like a boiler factory. I put a pad on the table under the clock. It sounded just as loud. I moved it to the dresser. It was no better. Then I put it in a drawer. Same thing! I moved it to a room down the hall. The boiler factory was still going. Finally, I put it between mattresses on a bed in that room. I could still hear it, for by that time it was simply in my mind. Finally, through sheer exhaustion I fell asleep. To this day I deplore a ticking clock.

The next morning Frances and I were standing outside the faculty conference room when the examining committee arrived. Of course, it included my major professor, Dr. Davis, and my minor professors, Drs. Carver and Weatherspoon. I was permitted to pick the remaining members: Drs. Powell, Goerner, and McDowell. All but Frances entered the conference room, and Dr. Davis began his one and one-half hours of questioning me. Within five minutes I knew that I was all right. I was relaxed, my mind was clear, and I had no problem answering the questions. But out in the hall poor Frances sweated out the entire two hours.

In fact, I was disappointed in that Dr. Davis would not let me tell what I knew. As soon as he was convinced I was at home in a given field, he switched to another. In the entire time he asked me only one question I could not answer. We were dealing with the fall of the Roman Empire. He said, "One time the enemy almost conquered Rome, didn't they?" I said, "Yes, sir." "What stopped them?" he asked. I said, "I have never read about that." Then Dr. Davis stretched in his chair to his full height, looked around the table, and asked, "Do any of the rest of you know the answer?" For a moment there was silence. Dr. McDowell sat at the opposite end of the long table from me. He had been sitting with his head down and his eyes closed as if he were asleep. Then he mumbled, "Some geese saw them coming and their honking alerted the Romans."

After brief questioning by Drs. Carver and Weatherspoon they dismissed me. When I stepped into the hall, there stood Frances, faithful all the way! In about three minutes they called me back to tell me I had passed. The professors scattered, and Frances and I went our way—rejoicing!

With the oral exam behind me, I turned to the final phase of my doctoral work, the writing of my thesis. I had received approval to write on the theme "Does the Author of the Fourth Gospel Consciously Supplement the Synoptic Gospels?" It is evident that he supplements them. My problem was did he do so *consciously*? Throughout my reading I had been making notes for the thesis, but there remained much research to be done.

One day I met Dr. Weatherspoon in the hall. He asked me the subject on which I was writing. When I told him, he asked what I thought. I said, "I think he did." He said, "Why don't you say 'yes' and be done with it?" I replied, "Well, Doctor, I am trying to do so in a scholarly manner, and it will require about sixty-five thousand words to do it." We both laughed and went our separate ways.

One of my fondest memories connected with my thesis came from Dr. Edward A. McDowell. When Dr. Robertson died he came on the faculty as Dr. Davis' associate. One day I met him in the hall. He asked, "Aren't you writing your thesis on the Gospel of John?" I told him I was and gave him the title. "And aren't you teaching a class in English grammar?" Again I agreed. Then he asked me to do him a favor. Said he, "I am giving my inaugural address on 'The Structural Integrity of the Fourth Gospel.' I would like for you to read it critically with regard to my position and how I develop it and also for its grammatical accuracy." Imagine my thrill that a professor would ask me, a mere student, to do that! I did as he asked, but found nothing wrong with it. But that became a tie of friendship between us until his death.

On the lighter side, I told another graduate student a permanent value of his thesis. It was to keep it on his desk. Some day when he was terribly busy, a deacon drops in just to kill time. After a courteous length of time he could hand his thesis to him just to look at it. He has no interest in it, but to be courteous he thumbs through the pages. Then he says, "I would like to read it sometime." With that he returns it to you and leaves, and you can go back to work.

Speaking of the class in grammar, it helped me in writing my thesis. Every professor on my examination committee had to read and pass on it. The day following graduation Frances and I ate lunch in the home of Cornell and Ruth Goerner. He had the seminary copy of my thesis and showed me the only grammatical error in it. In discussing the first visit Andrew, and presumably John, had with Jesus (John 1), I wrote, "To John it was an unforgetable experience." Note the one "t." I said that I could quote the rule for that: If you add a suffix to a word ending in a consonant preceded by a vowel, you double the consonant. Whether it was my mistake, probably so, or a typographical error, I never checked to see. But, at least, only Cornell caught it, and it became an *unforgettable* experience for me.

Finally the thesis was finished, typed, and bound. I turned in the seminary's copy at about 8:00 p.m. on December 31, 1937. At four o'clock the next morning we were on the highway driving to Birmingham, Alabama, to assume the pastorate of a church which had called us. The following May we returned to Louisville for commencement, at which time I received the degree of doctor of philosophy.

In the meantime we had employed a cook named Fannie. We thought we had *employed* her. But in the typical, loving fashion of an elderly black woman in the South at that time, she had taken us to raise—and I do mean *raise!* Our first morning after returning from Louisville, Fannie came in to serve my breakfast. She said, "Well, well, so you are a doctor now, are you?" I said, "Yes, Fannie, I'm a doctor." She asked, "Well, do you doctor folks?" I replied, "No, I am not that kind of doctor." She said, "Oh! You're one of them kind of doctors what don't do nobody no good?"

And you know, after fifty-four years, I sometimes wonder if Fannie wasn't right after all.

7

"He Gave Some to Be . . . Pastors"

If I had ten thousand lives to live, I would want to be a pastor in every one of them. I have often said that Dr. George W. Truett and I have had one thing in common. We both felt that we could do our best work for God from the pastorate. Like many others, I have had opportunities to go into denominational positions, some rather tempting, but my desire and commitment to the pastorate has held me there. And I am convinced that my life thus far has shown that this conviction is of God. This is not to despise other areas of service. God calls people to fill them. But He called me to be a *pastor*.

Contrary to much thinking, the role of a pastor is not an easy one. Years ago in Oklahoma City we renovated a ladies' classroom—new paint, carpet, drapes, the works. The first Sunday they were back in their room I dropped by to congratulate them. The president insisted that I say a few words. As I was leaving, she said, "We appreciate the pastor coming by. You know, this is his *busy* day." I didn't say anything. But I smiled as I thought, *This is my easiest day of the week.*

Of course, many pastoral duties do not submit to any category. But in Acts 20, Luke relates Paul's speech to the "elders" of the church in Ephesus (vv. 17-35). Paul told them the Holy Spirit had made them "overseers, to shepherd the church of God" (v. 28, NKJV). In the Old Testament elders were elderly men who by virtue of age and experience were able to give wise counsel. Overseers were men who oversaw the work of others to see that they did it properly. To shepherd meant to tend as a shepherd or to do for God's flock all that a shepherd did for his sheep. The Latin equivalent gives us the word *pastor*. Therefore, I see these words as referring to three phases of the office we call *pastor*: counselor (elder), administrator (overseer), and pastor (shepherd).

Some interpreters talk about the *authority* of the pastor. This concept is based largely upon Hebrews 13:17: "Obey those who rule over you" (NKJV). This is not a good translation. The Greek text reads "the ones leading you." (You drive cattle; you lead sheep.) The word for "obey" may also mean "follow"; the context of this verse calls for *follow*. The only *authority* the pastor has is that of example and leadership. In a New Testament church authority is vested in the congregation under the lordship of Jesus Christ.

A church, by vote of the congregation, can make a person its preacher and administrator, but he has to earn the right to be the pastor. He must love the people, and they must know that he loves them. Dr. Robertson once told us that when we became pastors of churches we "must love the people, warts and all." And every church has some warts in its fellowship. Furthermore, the people must learn that they can share with you the innermost secrets of their lives and that you will never divulge them to anyone else. Woe betide the pastor who violates that trust. His wife's health will soon need a change of climate.

Depending upon the size of the church, I have found that it takes from one to five years to become a church's *pastor*.

Already we have sketched briefly events related to our student pastorates. In a sense, Crestwood was a "half-way house" between student-pastorates and post-graduate-days pastorates. We lived on the church field which was about thirteen miles from the seminary campus. The people understood that I was in the closing stage of doctoral work. They were understanding and cooperative, expecting only basic pastoral functions.

Just across a narrow road from the church property is the Louisville and Nashville railroad track. Forty-eight trains went through there every twenty-four hours. There was a double blind crossing at Crestwood where several people had been killed. So the trains went through with their whistles tied down. It just happened that Sunday morning and evening a train went through about the middle of my sermon.

A deacon told me not to try preaching through that noise, for the people could not hear me. I should stop until the train had passed. As Dr. Sampey used to say, just as I got into the "Gee" of "Gee Whiz" here would come the train. After it had passed, all the "Whiz" was gone. So I would simply start all over again.

The pastor's home was between the church and the railroad. We thought we would never get used to the night trains, but we soon got accustomed to them and would sleep right through their passing. One morning about four o'clock I was aroused by a sound like a freight train taking the slack out of the car couplings as it started to move. Not fully awake I kept hearing bells ringing. They were warning bells at the crossings. I kept thinking, *Why don't they turn off those bells?* But finally I went back to sleep.

At seven o'clock I got out of bed and walked down the hall. Imagine my surprise when I saw fourteen boxcars lying in our backyard, with the locomotive lying on its side along the track! We later learned that about a quarter of a mile up the track the locomotive had hit a truckload of cattle stalled on the track. The driver got free, but all the cattle were killed. The body of one was caught on the cowcatcher on the engine's front. It was sticking out to the side far enough to hit a lever which split the switch, causing the wreck. All that noise, and we had slept through it! Which shows that you can become accustomed to most anything.

About a mile from Crestwood was a little hamlet called Floydsburg. During the Indian wars in Kentucky it was known as Floyd's Fort after a fort located there. Floydsburg consisted of a few houses and a country cemetery. Just beyond the cemetery was the Duncan farm. Mr. and Mrs. Duncan had been charter members of our church.

The people like to tell of their son, A. E. Duncan. One day as a young man he was hoeing corn. It was a hot day. He said,

"There's an easier way of making money, and I'm going to find it." So leaving his hoe he went to Crestwood and got a job selling farm machinery. Soon he was employed by the local bank. Eventually he founded the Commercial Credit Corporation. By the time I knew him it was a national concern, and he was a multimillionaire.

One day Mr. Duncan told the few residents of Floydsburg that with their permission he would make the cemetery one of the showplaces of that part of the country. Otherwise, he would move his parents' remains to Cave Hill Cemetery in Louisville. They consented and he did as he had promised. Among other things, he built a beautiful chapel at a cost of half a million dollars, a lot of money in 1937. He erected a rock wall about the cemetery. Fully-grown trees were planted throughout the grounds. I can still see large trucks passing our home hauling those trees to Floydsburg. His only request was that he be permitted to build under the chapel altar tombs for his wife and himself. I am sure that they are now buried there. He expressed the wish that the chapel be used for weddings, funerals, and that appropriate services be conducted there on all national holidays. While not planned, it just happened that I conducted the first of each of these services.

Mr. Duncan had a brother who had provided two lots in the cemetery for his wife and himself. After her death, he married again. When he died he was buried beside his first wife, but there was no place for his second wife. At her request, and at her death she was cremated and her ashes in a brass urn were placed in her husband's grave.

At Mr. Duncan's request I conducted a committal service for her ashes. As befitted the occasion, with all the dignity I could muster, I walked from the funeral director's car to the grave, followed by him bearing the urn. A hole large enough to receive the urn had been dug at the head of the grave. He lowered the urn until it rested on the head of her husband's casket.

I have always said that my sense of humor is such that I can see something amusing on every occasion, even at a funeral. This was no exception. When I arrived home I was chuckling. Frances asked the reason. I said, "I was just thinking what a surprise that man will get on resurrection morning when he wakes up to find his second wife sitting in his face."

C. Oscar Johnson for many years was pastor of the Third Baptist Church, St. Louis, Missouri. In addition to being a great preacher, he was also quite a humorist. One of his stories was about a man married to Tillie. When she died, he buried her on one side of a three-grave lot. Later he married Millie. At her death he buried her on the other side of the lot, leaving the middle one for himself. Then he wrote instructions for his own burial:

I married both Tillie and Millie.
I love both Millie and Tillie.
When I die, bury me equally between Tillie and Millie.
But tilt me a little toward Tillie.

I know this is an oldie for some. But if you never heard it, it is brand new.

Crestwood is located between Anchorage and Lagrange, Kentucky. Someone gave me a two-volume history of Kentucky Baptists. From it I learned that the first Baptist church in Kentucky was organized by a preacher named Hobbs. Anchorage originally was called Hobbs Station. It is the home of "The Little Colonel" who was immortalized in a movie by that name starring Shirley Temple.

At the time I was at Crestwood, the pastor of the First Baptist Church, Lagrange, was T. E. Ennis. He was a stickler for orthodoxy. One day he came to see me. For an hour we sat in his car as he probed my theological beliefs. Finally, he said, "Hobbs, I believe you are all right. I want you to preach in a revival in my church."

He was a "let the women be silent in church" preacher. But, strangely, he had a woman leading the singing for the revival. She would run from one side of the platform to the other, loudly exhorting the people to sing. And they did.

But as I preached he sat on the front pew with a pencil and notebook in his hand. Every once in a while he would make a note in his little book. I soon learned that I had said something with which he did not agree. After lunch each day we would spend half the afternoon in friendly argument about his noted items. Finally one day I said, "Brother Ennis, why aren't you consistent?" That was like stepping in his face. He said, "What do you mean?" I replied, "Well, you say a woman should be silent in church, yet you have a woman leading the singing, running up and down the platform screaming like a banshee." End of conversation.

He was an ardent fisherman. He drove a Studebaker coupe and kept his fishing rod and reel on the little shelf back of the car seat. When driving along the road, if he saw a creek with a likely fishing place, he stopped and made a few casts. I kidded him about wasting time fishing when he should be doing the Lord's work. But one day he said, "Hobbs, in John 21 when the apostles came ashore and found that Jesus had cooked fish for their breakfast, who caught that fish?" That ended another conversation.

On Sunday morning of that revival I preached on 1 John 4:18: "There is no fear in love; but perfect love casteth out fear." In the sermon I showed the difference between this love (*agape*) and most modern concepts of love. Unknown to me in the congregation was the great pioneer movie director, David Wark Griffith. He is still famous in the movie industry for such early classics as "Way Down East"; "East Lynne"; and "The Birth of a Nation," a film about the Civil War. He had retired, had married a Lagrange lady, and was then writing a play.

After the service he thanked me for the sermon and said, "I want to thank you for your *expostulation* and especially for showing us the difference between real love and the mess we have made of it in Hollywood!" *Oh, if he could only see it now!*

Many young preachers move around several times until they find their "nest." It was true with us. From Crestwood we went to Calvary Baptist Church, Birmingham, and then to Clayton Street (now Heritage) Baptist Church in Montgomery. Both were more or less routine pastorates: wonderful people and happy fellowships—but the Lord led us on.

However, four very definite things worthy of mention happened while we were at Calvary. One was immediately evident; the others we learned about later.

The first is that our son, Jerry Marlin Hobbs, was born on January 15, 1939. He was a seven-months baby. At birth he weighed five pounds and four ounces; before starting to grow he lost weight down to four pounds and eight ounces. (He now is almost six feet tall, weighing about 185 pounds.) He spent his first month in a hospital incubator.

The doctor let us take him home on Valentine's Day. His instructions were that we must keep the house at eighty-five degrees temperature and feed him every two hours around the clock. In February we sweated and slept without even a sheet for cover. Every two hours through the night the alarm went off. I threw more coal in the furnace while Frances warmed Jerry's bottle and fed him.

Due to his size, the opening into his stomach was too small for more than a half-feeding. The doctor said he could correct it with surgery, but hated to do it on so small a baby. If we could tough it out for four months, the opening would become larger as he grew. So we toughed it out.

Even so, someone had to be with him all the time. A feeding might stay down; it might come back immediately; it might stay down just long enough for the milk to curdle and then come back. One day Frances had just fed him and returned him to his bed. Not ten feet away she stood combing her hair. In the mirror she saw his little hand up and waving. The curdled milk had come back, closing both his throat and nasal passages. Unable to breathe, he was already turning blue. Frances yelled for her mother. She rushed in, grabbed him by his ankles, held him head down, and began to shake him like emptying a sack. Frances cried, "Mama, you're killing him!" She said, "If I don't get that stuff out, he's going to die anyway!" Suddenly they heard "Waaaaa!" *That was the sweetest music this side of heaven*!

The second experience involved our car. I had been having trouble with the one we had. Every morning for about a week my secretary, Elva Caraway, had to come and push it with her car to get it started. So we went to a dealer to buy another.

Unable to afford a new car, we looked at some used ones. One was a blue sedan—a recent model. The paint was practically new and the speedometer read ten thousand miles. Foolishly I did not have a mechanic friend check it out before buying it. I did the opposite. After checking it, he said, "I hate to tell you, but it has been repainted. It has been in a wreck; I can see where they straightened the frame. And judging by the front wheel bearings, I would say that it has been driven at least fifty thousand miles." In those days that was the limit of trouble-free driving.

After going to Clayton Street we had so much trouble with the car that we traded it in on a new Buick. I told the salesman the history of the car, but he failed to tell that to the man who bought it. He drove it to Florida and had all kinds of car trouble; the transmission even fell out in the middle of the highway.

When he finally drove it back to Montgomery, he went to see the salesman. He asked, "Will you give me the name of the preacher who drove this car? I want to see the person who could so wear out a car in such a few miles." I don't know if he gave him my name, for he never came to see me. That car served one good purpose. I have never bought another used car to this day!

The third instance is of a higher nature. It happened many years later in Mobile. Harold Seever succeeded me at Dauphin Way. On his tenth anniversary there, he invited me back to preach. He and his wife took Frances and me to dinner Saturday evening. As we entered the dining place, we met two couples leaving. He introduced us to them. One man was Bob Norman. The name meant nothing to me, but he said, "You had a part in leading me to Christ."

When I asked where and how he said, "It was while you were pastor at Calvary. I had never been to Sunday School. But some other boys and I knew the inside of every church in Fountain Heights. We roller skated all over that area and would go into the church buildings to get drinks of water. One day I went into Calvary church, roller skates and all. I skated down the hall to a water fountain. You were standing nearby talking to another man. As I turned to leave you asked, 'Son, are you a Christian?' That was the first time anyone had ever asked me that, and it scared me almost to death. So I got out of there in a hurry. But I never got away from your question.

"After you left Calvary I started going to Sunday School there. Finally I was saved, and Dr. John Maguire, your successor, baptized me." Others have told me of hearing him tell this story.

Just a chance meeting both times. But the following week he was moving to Nashville to become pastor of Belmont

Heights Baptist Church. He is now pastor of Clearview Baptist Church in Brentwood, Tennessee. Some years ago he and I shared in a Bible conference. He is one of the most talented and inspiring preachers I know. We never know what God can do with just one seed of the gospel sown in the heart of one lad on roller skates or whatever.

The fourth thing had to do with my voice. I have always had a strong voice, but less than three months after going to Calvary I developed the first and only problem with it. At the outset of a sermon it was as strong as ever, but by the end I was so hoarse I could hardly give the invitation. Had I spent all those years preparing to preach only to have my voice fail me?

Someone recommended a throat doctor. He was a Jewish doctor who had left Vienna, Austria, just ahead of Hitler. He found no *corns* on my vocal chords. Finally, he said, "There are thirteen basic minerals in the body. When they are in balance, the body is healthy. Out of balance, trouble shows up." So he gave me a chart of these minerals and foods containing them.

He told me as I ate to check off the minerals contained in what I ate. Before retiring at night, if I had missed one then I was to eat something which had it. Also, he told me to keep raw peanuts in my pocket and eat them as I went about my work. Within two weeks the trouble was gone and has never returned.

Years later on "The Baptist Hour" I used this story in a sermon on living a balanced spiritual life. It brought a flood of fan mail requesting that chart, the second largest volume of mail ever received up to that time. The staff at the Southern Baptist Radio and Television Commission kidded me about going to jail for practicing medicine by radio without a license. To borrow phrases, all I can say is "If you haven't tried it, don't knock it" and "If it works, don't fix it." And I challenge any one of you in a hog-calling contest!

It was during my three-and-one-half-year pastorate at Clayton Street that the church celebrated its fiftieth anniversary. It was my privilege to write a booklet of its history. Other than my doctoral thesis, it was my first venture into the field of writing books.

In July 1941, I was invited to visit Emmanuel Baptist Church, Alexandria, Louisiana, with a view to a call. Frances and I drove there for a visit. At that time it was the largest troop training area in the nation. Within a few miles of each other were three army camps and two airfields. World War II was raging in Europe, and our nation's leaders were preparing for the eventuality that we would be drawn into it.

Following our visit, our overall feeling was negative. For one thing, the church had no auditorium but held services in a section of the educational building. However, they were making plans to build one. We agreed that if we came we would begin construction of one in the spring of 1942. It was agreed that the pulpit committee chairman, Troy Farrar, would call me the following Saturday at 6:00 p.m. As we drove out of Alexandria on Thursday morning, my feelings were definitely negative. I told Frances, "Hon, if you ever want to see Alexandria again, you should look back right now. I doubt that we will ever be back here."

Exactly at 6:00 p.m. Saturday our phone rang. I knew it was Troy Farrar calling. As I walked to the phone I honestly did not know what my answer would be. The one positive thought was the opportunity to preach to all those soldier boys. Before the conversation was finished I gave him the green light. The next day they gave us a unanimous call, and we were on our way to see Alexandria again. I resigned at Clayton Street that night. One lady came to me after the service. She was thinking of Cajuns, but she asked, "But aren't there a lot of *morons* over there?" I said, "Yes, and soon there will be one more."

When it became known that I had accepted the call of the Emmanuel church, the first letter I received welcoming us to Louisiana came from Dr. J. D. Grey, pastor of the First Baptist Church, New Orleans. That began a warm friendship which lasted until his death in 1985.

We began our ministry in Alexandria in August 1941. On December 7, 1941, not only did the Japanese sink most of our Pacific Fleet at Pearl Harbor, they also sank our plans to begin construction of our church auditorium the following spring. With building material unavailable, all we could do was raise money for the building fund. It became the privilege of Dr. Franklin Sigler, my successor, to lead the church in erecting their beautiful and commodious center of worship.

When the Japanese struck Pearl Harbor we were in Birmingham. Frances' mother was almost at the point of death. Jerry was almost three years old. We had a beautiful young black woman working for us. Her name was Jessie. There was a mutual love affair between her and Jerry. Every afternoon she would make him some delicious pudding. He called it "Jessie pudding." We asked her to go to Birmingham with us to look after Jerry while we were at the hospital.

On Tuesday after Pearl Harbor I felt I had to return home. Mrs. Jackson was improved sufficiently that Jessie could return with me. When she started to get in the back seat of the car I told her to get in the front seat with me. Along the way at gas stations white people looked at us askance. But at Port Gibson, Mississippi, the station owner introduced me to a young black soldier. War had been declared against Japan, Germany, and Italy the day before, so all military personnel on leave were ordered to return to their bases. There was a bus strike on in Mississippi, so the boys were having to get to their bases the best way they could.

I told this serviceman to ride with us. I was going right by his camp just north of Alexandria. I told him and Jessie to get in the back seat, which suited them fine. Along the way we picked up other black soldiers so that the front and back seats were packed with them. As far as Jessie was concerned, the more the merrier. That was the happiest young lady and carload of soldiers you ever saw! The only sad part for Jessie was when we deposited those young men at the gate to their camp. I was happy, too, because I felt that not only had I served my country, but I also repaid Jessie in part for all that Jessie pudding she had made for Jerry.

The greatest challenge facing our church and the entire city during World War II was coping with the deluge of troops in and about Alexandria. The nearby swamps made the area an ideal place in which to train troops for the South Pacific. At one time there were half a million men on maneuvers in central Louisiana. On weekends they were so crowded in the downtown areas I have seen them solid abreast, not from curb to curb but from building to building on Third Street. Located on Fourth and Jackson Streets, our church building became a

Mecca for homesick boys. Our people transformed the church dining room into a social center for them. "Ma" and "Pa" Tucker, as the boys called them, were in charge and were assisted by many of our people. In addition to planned fun and games, food and refreshments were available. Also writing areas with stationery and stamps enabled boys to write to the folks back home.

Many American people have the idea that they should know everything our national government knows about diplomatic and military matters. Had that been true following Pearl Harbor, there would have been a panic throughout our nation. If Japan had been prepared to follow up on that event, their armada could have continued on to our west coast, marched to Washington, and dictated terms of peace in the White House—as later they boasted they would do. Largely their opposition would have come from shotguns and squirrel rifles. It took three weeks for our navy to assemble ships from all over the Pacific Ocean for any semblance of a naval fighting force.

In the early part of the war I drove by training fields and saw soldiers marching with sticks on their shoulders in place of rifles in order to get the feel of carrying a rifle. All available rifles had to be sent to the battle areas. One Saturday night in our social hall I started a conversation with a man in the field artillery. Said I, "Well, I guess you've been firing the big ones this week." With a snort of impatience, he said, "Firing the big ones *nothing!* All we have is a wooden horse with a section of stove pipe for a barrel, just teaching us how to aim it!" All available artillery had gone to the battle area.

Years after the war I read an item in the newspaper. At the height of the Battle of Britain there were twenty-seven battle-worthy fighter planes in England. They flew them at night and repaired them in the daytime. It was of them that Winston Churchill said, "Never did so many owe so much to so few!" We didn't know what he was saying.

At Dunkirk, Great Britain rescued the remnant of her European army, leaving behind all material of war. Hitler had Continental Europe at his feet. In North Africa her army was retreating before Rommel's Nazi forces. Her troops were being driven out of the Singapore peninsula. Once the U.S. entered the conflict we were driven from the Philippines. Never was the free world more on the brink of defeat than at that time! Hitler's generals advised invasion of England, the last bastion of freedom in Europe, but Hitler hesitated. Armed with nothing but words, Churchill held him at bay until the Allied Forces could prepare for counterattack.

In the meantime, we did our little bit in Alexandria. Like most pastors my age (thirty-four), I considered volunteering for the chaplaincy. But military men ranging from officers to buck privates, including veteran chaplains, told me to stay where I was. They said I would minister to more men there than if I were assigned to one unit. These veteran chaplains said that the soldiers were fresh out of civilian life and still looked to pastors for spiritual help. They turned to chaplains only when they boarded ships bound for battle zones. Soldiers said if I put on a uniform I would be just some more "brass" to them. I heeded this unanimous advice. Henry Lyon, my brother-in-law, did volunteer for the chaplaincy and served throughout the war.

With the massive influx of wives, housing was a great problem. People opened their homes to them. In our home we had a young couple with bedroom and kitchen privileges.

The most pressing problem was wives giving birth to babies. They had come to Alexandria to be with their husbands as long as possible. I was chairman of the Baptist Hospital operating committee. One day a general came to me with this problem. He said that their military hospitals were not equipped to deal with it. Even if they built a maternity hospital they could not staff it. We owned a piece of land alongside our hospital. So he asked if we would build a maternity hospital there. I told him we had the land but had no money for it. He said that the government would furnish that.

Well, I immediately thought about the separation of church and state. So I was on the horns of a dilemma: church and state on the one hand and human need on the other. All I could tell the general was that I would present it to our committee. So I called a meeting of the committee.

After presenting the need, I presented the problem. Also I noted Jesus' teaching and actions concerning the Jewish leaders ignoring human need in favor of the institution of the Sabbath.

Were we going to stand on the separation principle while babies were being born without proper facilities and care for the mothers and babies? Then I noted the gray areas in the separation principle on which constitutional lawyers did not agree. The clear facts were that neither church nor state should control the other and that there should be no established church. If we did as requested, we would minister to people on the basis of human need, not on the basis of one's religious preferences.

Furthermore, I pointed out that church and state had obligations to each other. The church should produce good citizens and the state should provide an environment in which churches were enabled to do their work. I recognized the problem of using tax money for religious purposes, but noted that in this case that was not the intent. In this case we had land on which to build and personnel with which to staff the hospital. The government had neither, but could furnish the money which we did not have. So each could help the other in meeting human need, but neither would be subservient to the other. We would be equal partners in a crisis situation.

Dr. M. E. Dodd was a member of our committee. He said, "I am not in favor of accepting any service paid for with tax money." Who was I to question so great and wise a man as Dr. Dodd? Still I replied, "Dr. Dodd, if your church was on fire, would you call the fire department?" "Of course I would!" he replied. "Then would you expect to receive a bill for their services?" I asked. "Of course not!" said he. "Then," I said, "you would be accepting a service paid for by tax money without repaying it." He smiled and said, "Well, I suppose our house is on fire!" And we voted unanimously to do it.

However, to satisfy anyone who might question it, we set up a special set of books. We showed that we owed the federal government the amount of money. Over against that debit we had a credit column. Each time we rendered hospital service to a service man or his family, we did so at a discounted price. The discount was entered to our credit as a payment toward reducing the debt. We continued that until the entire debt was paid.

Since the building was constructed out of concrete blocks it hastened the project and held down the cost to $97,000. The federal government sent me a check for that amount which I deposited in my name as chairman of our committee. I had two attorneys check each bill before I paid it. (I have never desired my mailing address to be Leavenworth, Kansas.) But through mutual cooperation as equal partners, we soon had a fine facility with which to meet this need.

On the purely spiritual side, about half of our congregation on Sunday was in uniform. I baptized great numbers of service men on the profession of their faith in Christ, but we knew there were multiplied thousands of men out in the piney woods about Alexandria. Also, we learned that in every outfit there were men with battery-powered radios. So we purchased an hour's time each Sunday night and broadcast our service over KALB. We were told that all over those woods were groups of hundreds of soldiers lying on the ground listening to our services over a radio placed in the center of the group. The sermons were strictly evangelistic. In the course of the war I cannot tell you how many letters I received from ports of embarkation, on board ships, or in battle areas. One letter was typical. It went like this:

"I . . . am in the war zone fixing to go into battle for the first time, maybe to die. We never met. But I want you to know that if I am killed I am ready to die. I was saved listening to you preach on the radio."

I must tell of two humorous experiences at my expense. One Sunday night trouble developed between the church and transmitter. While they were correcting it they cut us out and played music (?). We were unaware of the problem. The number they played was "Cow-Cow-Boogie." It was really wild, sounding more like throwing empty tin cans back and forth against the walls inside a tin barn. During that time I was leading in prayer. Just at the end of "Cow-Cow-Boogie" the next sound heard on the radio was my voice saying a hearty "Amen." May the Lord forgive me!

In the other instance a man had gotten himself all wound up so that he had not slept for two weeks. He was a patient of Dr. Maunsel Pierce, one of our deacons. They had done everything they knew to do through medication, hot baths, etc., to relax him, but to no avail.

Dr. Pierce said he would die if they could not get him to sleep. One Sunday night during our service he was making his hospital rounds. When he came to this man's room they had the radio on and tuned to our service. When Dr. Pierce entered the room I was preaching up a storm. The man's wife was listening. The man was propped up in bed—*sound asleep!* To me the answer was obvious. While listening to my sermon he had gotten his mind off himself, relaxed, and went to sleep.

When word spread about it, no one accepted *that* version. They said that the vast knowledge of medical science had failed to do what I had done with one of my sermons. Finally, I agreed to accept the credit if the doctor would give me half his fee. I received no fee, so I accept no responsibility. But if I did, I could claim to have saved the man's life. If you have his problem, don't "take an aspirin and I'll see you in the morning." I still have some sermons. Just call me, and I'll come over immediately. Yes, in such emergencies, I do make house calls.

On a more sober note, I received a letter from a mother in Nakina, North Carolina. She lived in a cove on the eastern side of a mountain range, and radio waves from the powerful stations went over rather than into the area. Radio waves are strange things. When they weaken they hit the ground and start bouncing. Wherever they touch down, the station can be heard just as plainly as in the area where the station is located. The waves from KALB came down in that cove. The lady's son was training near Alexandria. Though they were hundreds of miles apart, they worshipped together every Sunday night. He attended our service and she listened by radio. They sang the same songs, prayed the same prayers, and heard the same sermon. We received reports of couples hearing our services in Elmira, New York, and in Utah. The marvels of the electronic age!

Of course, the military wanted to keep it a secret as to when a division of troops was to leave for the war zone, but there were certain evidences which suggested that such was near. A larger than normal number of the men would come to me for counsel and prayer. Hometown sweethearts would come to Alexandria to marry their soldier boyfriends. And soldiers would drive their cars to our home, asking if they could leave them in our yard until some family member could come for them.

At first I did not feel comfortable about the weddings. I had read about women going to various camps and marrying as many soldiers as they could in order to collect their life insurance should they be killed. But it dawned upon me that these were their real sweethearts. The short time remaining might be all the marital happiness they would ever have.

So I married them without a troubled conscience. On Saturdays, beginning about 3:00 p.m. and continuing until about 10:00 p.m., we would have weddings in our home. We allowed forty-five minutes per wedding to get in, get married, and get gone before the next party arrived.

For Frances, the most difficult experience was related to the cars. Our front yard looked like a used car lot. We knew that when the boys left their cars their shipping out was at hand. Frances said she shed more tears in Alexandria than at any other place. She wept when they left their cars and then again with family members who came to drive them home. We loved Alexandria—the people, the deep South culture, and these wonderful boys who went away to fight for freedom, many of whom never returned.

Since retiring from the pastorate, for almost twenty years I have gone throughout the nation in various engagements. Every so often a man will walk up to me and ask if I remember him. Usually I do not. He will say that he attended our church while in training in the early 1940s. There were thousands who *attended*. Back then they were young, with a head full of hair, trimmed down to little more than skin, muscles, and bone, and were in uniform.

About a half century has elapsed since then. Now these former GIs are in *civvies*, bald, paunchy, and in their seventies or more. I don't remember them as they are now. And if they did not know my name by reading the program, they would not know me for most of the same reasons. No, I may not remember them as they are now, but as long as I live I will love them and their fallen comrades because of what they did for me and my family and for our country.

During all this turmoil I received a visit from Dr. Edgar Godbold, president of Louisiana College, just across Red River in Pineville. He told me they were short of faculty in the

Department of Religion. Young men were there preparing for the ministry. Some had small pastorates and others were supplying pulpits, but they did not know anything about interpreting Scripture or preparing sermons.

He asked if I would agree to teach a class two hours weekly in Bible interpretation. I agreed to do it under one condition—that they not pay me for it. I did not want to be accused of drawing two salaries. Since money was scarce, he was only too happy to accept my terms.

For two and one-half years I taught this class, using Romans in the fall and Hebrews in the spring. Each week I would give them a sermon outline, illustrations and all. The fact of the matter is that during the first year I also preached through these books. One day Dr. Godbold said, "If you want to know how much good you are doing, listen to this. Last Sunday I preached in a church. A deacon asked me what was happening at Louisiana College." He explained, "Since our pastor left we have been having ministerial students supply our pulpit. And every one of them has preached from Romans." I said, "You tell that deacon if he will tune in on KALB on Sunday night he will hear another sermon on Romans!"

That was a remarkable class. In it were students who later distinguished themselves in Southern Baptist life. Jaroy Weber later became president of the Southern Baptist Convention. Until he retired, for many years W. C. Fields headed Baptist Press. Until his death, H. C. Brown taught preaching at Southwestern Baptist Theological Seminary. Malcolm Tolbert distinguished himself as a foreign missionary and as professor of New Testament and Greek at New Orleans and Southeastern Seminaries. Billy McMinn taught philosophy and theology at New Orleans Seminary; he now teaches philosophy at a state university. Ray Rust recently retired after many years as state executive secretary of the South Carolina Baptist Convention. Bryant Dean distinguished himself in religious education and music. R. G. Bryant heads a worldwide tract program called "The Planter." And Luther Hall as a pastor served as president of the Louisiana Baptist Convention and as a member of "The Baptist Faith and Message" committee. I have always been proud of "my boys."

I have often chuckled over a remark made by H. C. Brown. One day in class I was stressing the need for more doctrinal preaching. H. C. asked, "But isn't doctrinal preaching dry?" I replied, "The preacher may be dry, but the doctrine isn't." In later years he became one of our greatest exponents of doctrinal preaching and wrote several books on expository preaching.

I hesitate to write the following, but do so to emphasize the value of Bible-centered teaching. On one occasion I delivered a lecture at Southeastern Seminary. Afterward, Dr. Tolbert, in my presence, told Dr. Randall Lolley, "This man is the first person to plant in my heart a desire to know the Scriptures." In 1992, I spoke at the state secretaries annual conference at Charleston, South Carolina. Ray Rust was in charge of the program. In the publicity material he wrote of me that in that class in Louisiana College I opened to him in the Bible vistas of "a world I did not even know existed." After all, that is a teacher's real wages, isn't it? Oh yes! And when we left to go to Mobile, the college did give Frances and me six silver goblets. And I still have them!

I must tell you about one sermon I preached in Alexandria. It was during the darkest hours of the war. On the front page of the *Nashville Tennessean* I saw a cartoon of Uncle Sam kneeling at the front pew in a church. From that I prepared a sermon titled "Uncle Sam at the Mourner's Bench" and preached it on Sunday night where it was heard on radio. I preached against every sin I could think of, saying that unless our nation repented God would not let us win that war. It created quite a stir.

Miss Hattie Strother was dean of women at Louisiana College. In the girls' dining room a black woman waited on her table. On Sunday nights she heard me preach on radio. Each Monday morning she talked with Miss Strother about my sermon the previous night, but on the morning after that sermon she said nothing about it.

Finally, Miss Strother asked if she had heard that sermon. She said she heard a part of it. To which Miss Strother replied, "I thought you like to hear him preach." The woman said, "Yessum, I do." When asked why she turned me off, there came this reply. "Well, Miss Hattie, he was telling the truth and it scared me to death. I didn't want to hear it, so I turned him off."

Since that sermon was so effective I decided to preach it later in Mobile. By that time the war was over. I used the same material but gave it a different application. *It fell flat as a flitter!* To be effective a sermon must have the proper message for the present situation. I did not learn that in the seminary but in the pulpit of Dauphin Way Baptist Church. (At that time a popular radio program was "Major Bowes' Amateur Hour." The contestants were judged by the number of *bells* received. Four bells was perfect; three was pretty good; two was so-so, etc. We had adopted that as Frances' way of grading my sermons. On that particular sermon I don't think she even reached for the rope.)

During all this time the tides of war had turned to favor the Allied cause. American industry and military might were taking their toll on Japan in the Pacific. What Churchill called the "soft belly" of Europe (Italy) had been invaded successfully. An equally successful "D Day" in Western Europe in June 1944 marked the beginning of the end for Hitler. Though much fierce fighting was ahead, it was only a matter of time.

It was in the summer of that year that Emmanuel held a tent revival on the vacant lot where her beautiful auditorium now stands. Dr. M. E. Dodd was the evangelist and Ira Prosser led the music. Each night for two weeks the tent was packed, a large percentage of it in uniform. Many, including service men, were saved.

However, more than we knew was riding on that revival. The next year would be the Southern Baptist Convention's centennial year. Dr. Dodd had been asked by the Home Mission Board to take a leave of absence from his pastorate in order to lead in a Convention-wide Centennial Evangelistic Crusade. He had put out his "fleeces" to determine if God had chosen him for this role. All but one had said "yes." The final one was that we would have 100 additions to our church in the tent revival. But he had said nothing to me, perhaps no one else, about this.

After the service on Friday night of the second week Dr. Dodd returned to Shreveport. I finished the revival, preaching through Sunday night. Dr. Dodd requested that I call him on Monday morning to report the number of additions to our church during the meeting. When I gave him the number as

110, he simply thanked me. Later that morning the lady in our office reported that a double check showed some duplicate cards. The number of additions was *100.* So I called Dr. Dodd and gave him the corrected number, exactly the number on his final "fleece."

His secretary, Alice Prosser, later told me that he came out of his office literally *shouting*. He then called Dr. J. B. Lawrence of the Home Mission Board to tell him he would lead the Centennial Crusade.

In November 1944, I was called to become pastor of the Dauphin Way Baptist Church, Mobile, Alabama. Blended with the anticipation of returning to our native state was the sadness of leaving what Dr. Dodd called "lovely Louisiana" and even more, leaving the *lovelier* people of Alexandria. However, we were in the Lord's hands. We never left a pastorate but that Frances shed tears over leaving. She, along with her husband, loved/love the people among whom we had served.

But in the words of another, "Parting is such sweet sorrow." We did not leave behind the love for *Alex*. We simply moved to another pastorate to enlarge the circle of our hearts as we increased the number of people we love.

8

Our Nest?

Alabama is an Indian word meaning "Here we rest."As natives of that state, when we moved to Mobile we thought we had come home, not to *rest*, but to our *nest*. We even bought a home, our first. I told Frances I was going to put a sign over the front door which said Dun Movin'.

Why not? Dauphin Way Baptist Church was the largest church of any kind in Alabama. The day we went there it had 4,444 members. It was second only to Bellevue Baptist, Memphis, of all Southern Baptist churches east of the Mississippi River. It was a growing church, a beehive of activity. It was only a few hours drive to our families in Montgomery and Birmingham. We loved the climate, the huge live oak trees, the deep South culture, and the abundance of flowers. Mobile is known as the azalea capital of the nation—and camellias galore. There was not a day in the year when flowers were not blooming in our yard. And the people at Dauphin Way were overflowing with love to give to the new pastor and his family. If ever a pastor and people had come together, we had. We thought we had found our *nest*. We learned that God had other plans—but that comes later.

Twenty-one years before, Dr. C. B. Arendall had left First Baptist Church, Troy, Alabama, to become Dauphin Way's pastor. At that time it had about seven hundred members and a small red brick building located at Dauphin and Ann Streets. But there was a large debt on the building. Worse still, the Alabama Baptist Convention was paying the interest on that debt to keep them from losing the property. Dr. Arendall told me that all he had when he came there was the opportunity. But, my, how he used that opportunity! One of the deacons, Will Milling, described him as "a steam engine in britches."

From almost nothing when he became the pastor, when he retired December 31, 1944, he left the largest church and Sunday School in the state. Also, he passed on to me a beautiful auditorium, chapel and parlor, dining room and kitchen facilities—paid for! They finished this building in 1942 and made the final payment on it in December 1944.

Wise friends of mine urged me not to go there. They said Dr. Arendall had built the church, and knowing his dynamic personality they felt he could not turn it loose. But they did not know C. B. Arendall. He taught me how to *work*, and he taught me how to *retire*.

In August 1944, he announced his plan to retire at the end of the year. He urged the church to appoint a pulpit committee and try to have a pastor ready to take over January 1, 1945. His reason: "Let's not have a lull in the work of the church."

I visited the church in mid-November. With my consent the church planned to vote on calling me on a Wednesday night. Dr. Arendall was in bed with the flu. When I visited him he said, "My only regret is that I will not be there to vote for you." The vote was unanimous.

The following Sunday he said to the congregation, "You have called a pastor. He will be on the field January 1. So after December 31 I will neither bury nor marry any member of this church." One dear lady said, "Dr. Arendall, when I die I want you to bury me." He replied, "Well, sister, you had better die before December 31." And he meant it.

Oh, I had trouble with him, but not the kind some of my friends expected. My trouble was that he would have nothing to do with the pastoral ministry of the church. He turned loose at midnight, December 31, 1944. We moved on the field the following week. He told me, "Pastor, I will be out of town preaching most weekends. When I am in the city on Sunday I will worship in some other church. You cannot win the hearts of these people with me hanging around." Each week he came by to visit and pray with me. The first time I suggested that he sit in the chair behind the desk. He said, "Oh, no! That is the pastor's chair!"

His family was active in the church. Mrs. Arendall was one of the sweetest, most gracious ladies you will ever know. Two sons, Charles and J. T., were deacons and supported me all the way. Bob was in the Army. When he returned home he, too, was on my *team*.

Dr. Arendall did not attend worship services at Dauphin Way until Mother's Day. Then he and Mrs. Arendall slipped in after the service started and sat in the balcony. At the close of the service I recognized his presence and asked him to come to the front and pronounce the benediction. Afterward he chided me. "Pastor, you should not have done that!" I said, "Doctor, the people knew you were there. If I had ignored you they would have resented it to no end." He agreed.

As for Frances and me, my first words to the congregation on our first Sunday reassured the people. I said, "Frances and I and our family have not come to take the place of Dr. and Mrs. Arendall. We have come to make a place for ourselves. We do not want you to hesitate to express your love for them. Frankly, if after twenty-one years you did not love them, we would be afraid of you. The fact that you love them proves that you have the capacity to love us also." From that moment on the hearts of the Arendalls and Hobbs and the people beat as one!

As for my *problem* with Dr. Arendall, he would never assist me in a funeral. He said, "Pastor, if I do it one time there will be no end to it." So he always found a reason why he could not do it.

One time he refused to take my place for a funeral when it would have been a service to me. A dear lady died after a long illness. I never saw her except as a bed patient. It was not long after we had come to the church. Nevertheless, the family wanted me to conduct the service. It was set for two o'clock one afternoon. I was scheduled to speak that evening at an associational Baptist Training Union meeting in Montgomery. There was no way I could do both.

So I requested that Dr. Arendall conduct the service. After all, the family scarcely knew me, and he had been their pastor for all those years. When I asked him to do this, he said, "Pastor, I have a time protecting you from yourself! I simply must not do this. Six months from now people will not remember that you were out of town. You and Brother Tucker meet me at the funeral home tomorrow morning at 9:30." James Tucker was our music-educational director.

It was customary for the family to receive guests in the family room at the mortuary. They were all there the next morning, along with Jim and me. At exactly 9:30, Dr. Arendall entered the room talking. As he did so he went around the room shaking hands with the family. His words went something like this: "I wanted to come by to express my condolences about Mother. The pastor has a long-standing engagement this evening to speak to a large group in Montgomery. Many people are depending on him. It will be impossible for him to have the funeral here and get to Montgomery for tonight. He asked me to take the service but I cannot do so. But Brother Tucker will be with you. And he will do as well or better than either of us. Now let us have a word of prayer."

By that time he was back at the door. After the prayer he left, I went to Montgomery, Brother Tucker conducted the service, and the family was pleased—all because Dr. Arendall took the initiative in helping his successor out of a delicate problem.

Unknown to anyone at the time of his retirement, Dr. Arendall had a terminal illness. He only lived fourteen months. I conducted his funeral service. But up until his death we had a blessed fellowship in the Lord. He was my greatest supporter, and as long as I remained at Dauphin Way his family was the same.

I have gone into this at length for three reasons. I want to pay tribute to a noble soldier of the Lord. When I came to the time of retirement from the pastorate, his example helped me to do it, I trust, gracefully. This account may help others in showing how to relate to their successors. But both predecessor and successor should remember that this is a two-way street. I will ever be grateful to Dr. Arendall and his family!

Due to World War II, Mobile, like Alexandria, was overrun with people. It grew from the third to the second largest city in Alabama. People poured into the Gulf Coast area to work in the shipyards. In fact, this influx from inland areas reversed the religious ratio of the Gulf Coast. Originally settled by Spanish and French people, it was predominately Roman Catholic. But shortly after that war a religious census of New Orleans, taken by a professional census-taking company, revealed that the city's population was 51 percent non-Catholic. Whether or not that ratio still holds, I do not know. Mobile is older than New Orleans. Its Mardi Gras, while not as large or as spectacular as the one in New Orleans, ante-dates it.

An interesting item of Baptist history is related to early Mobile. When a small group of Baptists moved to the city, the Roman Catholic authorities told them they could not hold worship services there. Instead they were to go eight miles into the country to do so. Today there is a small community called Eight Mile where these services were held. Some years ago the Mobile Baptist Association erected a monument there to commemorate that event. However, today some of our strongest Baptist churches are located in the city. But back to our story.

When the United States entered World War II, President Franklin D. Roosevelt challenged our nation to produce thousands of planes, ships, and tanks. It seemed like "Mission Impossible." But our industry and ingenuity rose to the challenge and did it. Henry J. Kaiser came up with the idea of building Liberty ships. They could be built rapidly and economically. The Mobile shipyards were involved in this project. Shortly after going to Mobile, I was asked to lead in prayer at the launching of one of the last of these.

In Mobile, and throughout the nation, men and women flocked to work in war industries. A popular song of the time was "Rosie the Riveter," a tribute to women's role in winning the war. In Mobile they spoke of "hot beds." The shipyards worked eight-hour shifts around the clock. So crowded was the city that the beds never cooled. The shift going to work got out of the beds. The one coming off the job went to bed.

A great percentage of these workers came from Mississippi. In friendly jest they were called "Mississippi Pea Pickers."

When Japan surrendered, ending the war, an ad appeared in one of the local papers: "For Sale, one pair of shoes, size 14, slightly used. Going back to Mississippi the way I came." Obviously some wag ran it, but it gave a laugh to all who read it.

Throughout our ministry Frances and I had followed a policy. When we went to a new church we never suggested any significant changes in the program until we had been there six months. It provided opportunity to study the program. Maybe there was no need for change. The old adage is true: "If it's working, don't fix it." I have known pastors who seemed to feel that "all who came before me were fools." Right off the bat they wanted to change everything. People do not change that rapidly. If a program is working, it is better for the new pastor to adjust to it than to seek to revolutionize hundreds or thousands of people. Such an approach often ends in a *revolution*.

Henry Kittrell was a wise man. When he was chairman of the deacons, often I would confer with him about some new program. Many times he would say, "Pastor, I think it is great! It has just one weakness—the human element. Will the people do it?" There and elsewhere on occasion I have found that human element fatal. The pastor should lead, but he should not move so fast and get so far ahead of the people that they cannot follow.

Well, when we came to Dauphin Way we found a sound program and a willing, eager people. Frances and I often said that they reminded us of a fast train going full speed. We just swung on as it raced by. That is one of many advantages of having a new pastor ready to step in as soon as his predecessor steps out.

As previously noted, Dr. Arendall announced in August that he would retire December 31. During that interval many people were joining the Sunday School, but many were waiting about joining the church until the new pastor arrived, whoever he might be. I suppose they wanted to see if he had two heads or just one. I guess they liked what they saw, for they began joining the church.

However, it seemed the elements were against us. It rained every Sunday in January and February. Even so, each Sunday we were running one thousand to twelve hundred in Sunday School. In those days that was great! The first Sunday in March I remarked about that. Then I said, "If we could have just one pretty weekend, what could we do?" Later I learned that one lady said to another, "We'd show him what we could do. We'd go across the bay!" The next Sunday I mentioned that and said, "I have now learned how to pray in Mobile. I do not pray for pretty weather, because you will go across the bay. I do not pray for rain, because you will stay at home. I pray for threatening weather. That will keep you in town, but you can also come to Sunday School and church."

Despite the weather problem, however, we averaged fifteen additions to the church each Sunday morning during January-June. But on the first Sunday morning in July, though we had a packed house, try as I did, no one came forward during the invitation. Not even a ninety-five-year-old woman to surrender as a foreign missionary!

After the benediction people crowded around me to say it was not my fault but theirs. That helped a little bit. But after they were gone, Henry Kittrell came up with a sly grin. He was an automobile dealer. One time he had told me he did not follow his salesmen around to see how many calls they made on prospective customers. He watched the sales board. One month a given salesman would sell cars every day. The next month he would sell few or none. The reason was that the previous month he had been so busy delivering cars that he had not been contacting other prospective buyers. So I got the message when he said, "You've been too busy delivering cars, haven't you?"

In my judgment most people who unite with our churches, by whatever means, have been contacted by someone away from the church building. In this materialistic age people are not beating on our church doors trying to get in. The old adage is true. "When we go, they come." Also, "We visit many people we never get, and we get many people we never visit, but we would not get as many people we never visit if we did not visit many people we never get."

After being at Dauphin Way for six months it occurred to me that Baptists in Alabama might want to know how the church was doing with Dr. Arendall no longer the pastor. So I wrote a letter to Dr. L. L. Gwaltney, editor of *The Alabama Baptist*, giving him a statistical report. Then I added, "I am not foolish enough to think these things are happening because I am here. We are reaping the fruits of Dr. Arendall's labors."

Two weeks later the paper carried a letter from Dr. John Jeter Hurt, Sr., president of Union University. He had read my letter. His went something like this. "Such humility! That man should be endowed by the Southern Baptist Convention and sent all over the country telling preachers how to treat their predecessors!"

A few days later I received a letter from my longtime friend, Chester Quarles. Evidently he knew me better than did Dr. Hurt. He wrote, "Herschel, there isn't an humble bone in your body!" In reply I said, "Ches, you wound me deeply. I am a very humble person. In fact, I have a sermon on 'Humility and How I Obtained It.' My text is Romans 12:3a, 'Not to think of himself more highly than he ought to think.' It has five points:

1. I Am Humble
2. I Am Getting Humbler All the Time
3. I Am Proud of My Humility
4. I Deserve a Lot of Credit for My Humility Because I Have So Much of Which to Be Proud
5. Even When I Am Bragging, I Am Humble Because I Am a Lot Better Than I Say I Am."

I have never gotten the courage to preach it. But if you want to do so, go right ahead. It is not patented. But before preaching it be sure you have a call to another church. You will need it.

And speaking of Dr. Gwaltney, when we left the seminary Frances went to an army surplus store and bought me some golf clubs. They consisted of an old canvas golf bag and four clubs: a driver, a #5 iron, a #9 iron, and a putter. She wanted me to exercise. I played with Dr. Gwaltney each week. One day he said, "Hobbs, through the years I have selected a young pastor, taught him how to play golf, and played with him until he began to beat me. Then I got me another young partner. But in you I think I have found me a lifetime partner."

But the wisest thing he ever said to me was about pastors who did not study. "They are like wasps. They are bigger the day they are hatched than ever thereafter."

One day I received a phone call from Dr. Gwaltney in Birmingham. He said, "It looks like Howard College (Samford University) will have to leave Birmingham. They need more campus space and no one will sell them that much land. Would you all be interested in having it in Mobile?" I told him we certainly would. I called a meeting in my office of Dr. Howard M. Reaves, pastor of First Baptist Church; J. L. Bedsole, chairman of its deacons; and Henry Kittrell, chairman of our deacons. We agreed to make a bid for it. Then we secured the cooperation of the chamber of commerce. We offered them a large tract of land overlooking Mobile Bay and a sizable sum of money. Two other cities, Gadsden and Opelika, entered the picture also. Seeing they were in danger of losing a fine institution, Birmingham got busy.

A called meeting of the Alabama Baptist State Convention was held in the City Auditorium in Montgomery. When the bids were read it appeared that Birmingham and Mobile had made practically the same offer. So Henry and I voted for the Birmingham offer. Everything else being equal, we felt it was better to have the school near the center of the state. They now have one of the most beautiful campuses anywhere.

However, some years later Alabama Baptists did locate Mobile College in Mobile. At the dedication of their first building I was asked to deliver the address. I had just finished my second term as president of the Southern Baptist Convention and assumed that was the basis of the invitation. But when President William Weaver presented me he said it was due to the fact that I was the one who first planted the idea for a Baptist college in Mobile. Great oaks from small acorns grow.

In the fall of 1947 we had Dr. R. G. Lee with us in a revival. He began on Monday night and closed the following Monday night, preaching "Payday Someday" in the final service. In revivals I always tried to get the best pastor-evangelist available and give him a love offering accordingly. And I always had an understanding with the finance committee as to the minimum offering we would give him. If the gifts did not come up to that figure we would make it up out of the general budget account. If it exceeded the amount, the evangelist received that also. But if you get a preacher the people like, you do not need to worry about the offering. In Dr. Lee's case the finance committee and I agreed on a minimum of one thousand dollars. In those days that was a good offering.

As a young preacher I was a little nervous about having the great Dr. Lee. After settling him in the hotel, we ate lunch. And believe you me, I was on my "ps and qs." But after he had finished his meal he asked the waitress for a glass of sweet milk and cornbread. He crumbled the bread in the milk and ate it with a spoon. I relaxed. He was just a man! And I had been brought up on sweet milk and cornbread.

Dr. Lee was a great baseball fan, and it was the week of the World Series. This was before television, but it was on radio. On Wednesday he was to speak at the Kiwanis Club. Dr. Lee was noted for long sermons, but the way he preached they did not seem long. On this day, however, they put him up at 12:45 and the game started at one o'clock. At five minutes until one he was going out the door, headed for his hotel room.

On Sunday we ate the noon meal in one of our most elegant homes. The radio was in the living room which adjoined the dining room. Throughout the meal if the crowd in the ball park roared, he would jump up, run into the living room, sit on a stool in front of the radio, and listen to what had happened. And the people loved him for it. Like I had, they learned that he was just a man—in fact, almost a boy where baseball was concerned.

The church auditorium was packed for every service. I was a member of the Kiwanis Club and learned that they were sponsoring a concert by the United States Navy Band on the closing night of our revival. I feared what it would do to our attendance. They had only a handful for the concert. Our house was packed; the ushers told me there were between three and four hundred people in the church yard who could not get in the building. Later some Kiwanians told me we certainly ruined their concert. Kidding them I said, "Well, some day you fellows will learn to check on what we are doing at Dauphin Way before making your plans."

In the service we said nothing about the love offering, only that we will worship with the evening offering. After the service, when the people had all departed, I went into the church office to find a jubilant finance committee. That evening we had received $780 in loose offering. They said, "Pastor, we are in great shape. We have enough to give Dr. Lee $1,000 and put $500 in the building fund." I said, "Not as long as I am your pastor." When asked why, I said, "The people did not give that offering to the building fund but to Dr. Lee. And all of it must go to him." That ended it. They were good men who simply needed some guidance.

I gave Dr. Lee his check for $1,500. He said it was the largest love offering he had ever received. The next morning he told me the following experience. "When I was in college I worked one summer in Mobile unloading banana boats. From my hotel window I can see my old boarding house across the street. Last night I sat in the dark looking out the window at that house as I held that check in my hand. I remembered back then when I was so tired I could hardly pull myself up those steps after unloading bananas all day. Then I thought of the crowds that came to hear me preach and the souls that were saved. I looked at the check you had given me. And I just sat there crying and praising the Lord for what He had done for and through me!"

Speaking of revivals, Angel Martinez is the only full-time evangelist I ever used. He was with me five times with four years in between each. He is a great preacher. He does not use a pressure invitation, yet visible results are great. He only repeated one sermon in all those years and that was on the Twenty-third Psalm in a weekday morning service.

I have never heard a preacher quote as much Scripture in sermons as he does. Yet I only saw him take a Bible in the pulpit one time, and he didn't open it then. He has memorized the *King James Version*. (He tells me he is now memorizing the Greek New Testament.) The love offerings were always generous with little prompting from me and not one word from him. And he always preached to a full house.

Among the most memorable revivals in which I preached, two were in the summer and fall of 1946. The former was in the First Baptist Church, Ashland, Alabama. Since that time I have preached in another revival there. But the one in 1946 will always be dear to my heart. It had been thirty years since we left Ashland, but still fresh in my memory was hearing people refer to "the Widow Hobbs and her orphaned children." Now the "orphaned" boy was the preacher for their revival. Frances and Jerry were with me.

In those days when one church in Ashland was in a revival meeting, all other churches joined in attendance. Each day at 11:00 a.m. all the stores closed for an hour, and everybody went to church. So I was privileged to preach to a packed house. The local newspaper, the *Ashland Progress*, each day printed my sermons on the front page.

My mother came over from Birmingham for the weekend. She was so happy to see old friends again. They even had a reserved pew for her and her "party." Instead of the "Widow Hobbs," she was "Queen of Ashland" for three days. I can still see her face beaming with joy over the treatment given her and her *only boy*.

On Monday after the meeting, Frances, Jerry, and I spent the morning driving her around to see what few of her old friends remained. We went to the cemetery to visit the graves of family members and friends. We even took her to the very room in a home where my father had put the engagement ring on her finger. Actually it was a gold wedding band which also was the engagement ring when they married. She wore it until her death. These few days in Ashland crowned her life.

This is such a sweet memory to me because two weeks later she had a massive heart attack from which she did not recover. I went to Birmingham to be with her and my sisters.

This was in September, a busy time for churches as they launch their fall-winter program. Her doctor, knowing this, told me he was going to try a new medicine on her. He said it would be thirty-six to forty-eight hours before he would know whether or not it would help. So he advised me to return to Mobile. If necessary, I could fly back to Birmingham in an hour. He told me not to tell her I was leaving, but just to tell her goodnight.

She and I had what was to be our final visit. She said, "They tell me this was brought on by the excitement of my visit to Ashland. But I don't care. It was worth it." As I was leaving, the last words she said to me were "Son, you never said an unkind word to me in your life." *Those words are not for sale!* They will be my personal treasure the rest of my life!

At noon on Friday I called to find that she seemed to be improving. On Saturday about 6:00 p.m. she was propped up in bed. My sisters told her they were going for a bite to eat and would be back shortly. For some reason, Mary, with whom Mother lived, went back to the room. Just as she got to the door, suddenly Mother sat straight up in bed, fell back, and was gone.

In May prior to this, I was in Birmingham on the thirty-sixth anniversary of my father's death. As I drove her on some errands I asked her if she still missed my father. She said, "Yes, I miss him more on certain days such as anniversaries. But there has not been a day in all these years that I have not missed him." When they called to tell me she was gone, the first thought that went through my mind was "I know Mother and Daddy are happy tonight!" Oh, I know that in heaven they are not husband and wife, but their relation is so much sweeter as not to be compared to what they knew on earth.

Hers was the first death in our immediate family since I was old enough to understand. As we waited for the funeral service to begin, I felt as if my chest would explode. But her pastor and my friend, Dr. John H. Buchanan, began the service with words from Isaiah 43:2-3. "When thou passeth through the waters, I will be with thee; and through the rivers, they shall not overflow thee: when thou walketh through the fire, thou shalt not be burned; neither shall the flame kindle upon thee. For I am the Lord thy God, the Holy One of Israel, thy Saviour." Not until then did I really know the comforting power of God's Word!

My father and sister are buried in Marble Valley Cemetery in Coosa County, about sixty-five miles from Birmingham where most of our family lived. But we had no grave site. Years before, Mrs. Jackson had bought a large plot in Elmwood Cemetery in Birmingham. So she said, "Why not bury her in our plot?" We did. On one side of the family monument are sites for four graves. On the far left are the remains of our infant son. Next to him is his mother. On the far right is my mother. One of these days I will be buried between Frances and my mother—*the two dearest, sweetest loves of my life*!

The latter revival mentioned was in the First Baptist Church, Dallas, Texas. It was in November 1946. But there is a prelude to it.

In the summer of 1942, Cornell Goerner and I were at Ridgecrest. Back then, anytime two Southern Baptist preachers talked for five minutes, three of them were spent speculating as to who would succeed Dr. George W. Truett in Dallas. Cornell and I agreed it probably would be someone in our age group, anticipating another long pastorate. Dr. Truett was there for forty-seven years. Then I remarked that Dr. Truett was a *heart preacher*. Whoever succeeded him would need that quality to meet the needs of a congregation that had been accustomed to it. But he must also be a scholar so that he would be his own man, not a *little Truett*. Cornell agreed. And we also agreed that the only one of our age group with that combination was W. A. Criswell.

I never mentioned that to him, but regularly he would write me and ask my advice about some church that wanted to call him. I said repeatedly, "Leave it alone. God has something larger than that for you." In almost every case I would soon hear from these churches. I accused him of declining and then recommending me. I declined also.

In the summer of 1944 after Dr. Truett's death, W. A. called me about a Florida church. I gave him the same answer. He wrote that he had agreed to preach for them in a week of meetings. Every day I sent him a note urging him not to take it. It was during that week that he received an invitation from the First Baptist Church, Dallas, to preach one Sunday in August. On the train returning to Muskogee, Oklahoma, he wrote me a note telling me that he had declined the Florida church. A few days later he wrote that he would preach at First, Dallas, the following Sunday. He asked me to pray that he would have "liberty" to do his best.

The next week he wrote, "Oh, Herschel, I did not do my best. I suppose I will never hear from them again." But he did. And on a Wednesday night they called him to become their pastor beginning October 1, 1944. The next morning in Alexandria I received a *penny postcard* from him. "Dallas First called tonight. Pray that I will have strength to do the work." I replied that he did not decline that one and give me a shot at it.

At that time each year after the Southern Baptist Convention, Dr. J. W. Storer, First Baptist Church, Tulsa, Oklahoma, would write for the Baptist state papers a humorous report of events at the Convention. The news report of W. A.'s call said he was chosen out of a list of sixty-five pastors considered. So Dr. Storer wrote such an account of a meeting of the sixty-four. He said that after comparing themselves with this young man from Muskogee, one of them asked, "What does he have that we do not have?" With one voice the others replied, "*The call!*"

It was against this background that two years later I received a call from W. A. I was then at Dauphin Way. While he was at Muskogee I had preached for him in a revival. (He had done the same for me at Alexandria and later at Dauphin Way and First, Oklahoma City.)

In his call he said that Dr. Truett always preached in the revivals in Dallas. Consequently it had been forty-nine years since the church had had an outside preacher for a revival. So he had to train the church for this new (to them) approach.

"I figure that the first one I invite will be a lamb on the altar, and I feel we are close enough that you would be willing to be that lamb." I told him that I would and would be with him Monday through Sunday. He said, "If you come on Monday, you may as well wait until the following Sunday. They will hardly know you are here during the week." "OK," I said, "I'll give you two Sundays."

The first Sunday I felt like an Alabama country boy playing football in the Rose Bowl. The crowd overwhelmed me. We had great crowds at both services, with lots of additions. During the week we held night services in the Robert Coleman Prayer Meeting Room. It seated about eight hundred and was full each night. That week we had one addition; a little lady joined by letter. But the second Sunday we had great crowds with lots of additions.

Six months later, Dr. Charles Matthews, then at Travis Avenue, Fort Worth, held a two-week meeting there and had a host of additions. I wrote Charlie that it took about six months for my revivals to take effect.

In 1948, with Dr. Lee's permission, I was asked and had agreed to nominate him for the presidency of the Southern Baptist Convention. I guess I was feeling a little cocky about it. But God has a way of cutting us down to size. Also, Dr. Ellis

Fuller had invited me to preach the baccalaureate sermon at Southern Seminary. When he introduced me, he kept on and on. I wondered if he would ever finish. Finally he stopped, turned to me and asked, "WHAT IS YOUR NAME?"

The next day Dr. John H. Buchanan, my mother's former pastor, my friend and fellow pastor in Alabama, told me he had agreed to let his name be presented less than a month later for the Convention presidency. I knew then that I could not nominate anyone against him. So I requested to be released from my commitment, which was done with understanding.

Dr. Lee was elected, though many were unhappy about him being on the board of trustees of a certain university. He showed me correspondence indicating that long before he had severed that relationship.

After the Convention, a mutual friend wrote me that Lee was scheduled to bring the commencement address at that school that year. I suppose he had heard of my previous commitment, for he said I was the only one he knew who could ask Dr. Lee to cancel it. Who was I to make such a request? Nevertheless I wrote him.

After apologizing forty ways from Sunday, I said, "Dr. Lee, prior to your election what you did was yours and Bellevue's business. But as SBC president it was all Southern Baptists' business in that it could create a stir in certain quarters." For this reason I hoped he could find it in his heart not to do it. I had no idea how he would react. But I received his reply in typical Lee fashion:

> Beloved Hobbs,
>
> I appreciate your letter. I have just written to cancel the engagement. God bless you always in all ways!
>
> R. G. Lee

This was typical of his great spirit. And this "peanut and popcorn" preacher breathed a sigh of relief.

The happiest one experience Frances and I had at Dauphin Way was when Jerry made his public profession of faith in Jesus Christ as his Savior. He was nine years old. We had observed him as he advanced through the various departments of the Sunday School. For the first time we realized how effectively the Sunday School literature for the children was designed to lead children gradually to the point where they were prepared for making this destiny-determining decision. When he entered the Junior department it seemed that his spiritual life began to blossom like a rose.

So one day we explained the plan of salvation to him to be certain that he understood it intellectually. We did not tell him he should or should not make a public profession the next Sunday. We simply said that when he felt in his heart that he wanted to do so, he had our permission. Having removed any barrier that might be in his mind, we prayed and waited for the Holy Spirit to do His work.

Several weeks went by. Then one Sunday he sat with his mother in the morning service, with him next to the aisle. During the invitation hymn she looked down and he was not there. Then she looked down the aisle and there he was, going forward. The time had come, and without mentioning it to us he made his profession.

After the benediction I led those who came to shake hands with the new members. This happened on the day we were breaking ground for two new educational buildings. Many people had their cameras to take pictures of the occasion. One young man made a picture of me shaking Jerry's hand, with Frances standing beside me. Later when we received a copy of the picture she remarked at the trust in Jerry's eyes and face as he smiled at me. She said, "If you ever do anything to betray that trust, I'll hit you on your head with a baseball bat!" And she would have, too! Her life was really wrapped up in that young man of ours!

At the other end of the spectrum, the saddest experience of our Mobile days was the still-born birth of our other son. He was a perfectly developed child. Mrs. Jackson said the only thing wrong with him was that he looked exactly like me. It was simply an accident of birth. He *lived*, if only in his mother's womb, but he is a soul, a person. As such we gave him a name—Harold Elbert Hobbs, my middle name and my father's first name. Seared in my mind is the saddest picture I ever saw—Frances holding her dead baby in her arms—one time! She wanted to do it. But the blessed assurance I have! Now they are both alive—"safe in the arms of Jesus!"

I cannot tell you how many times we asked, "Why?," not in rebellion but as a prayer for understanding. Finally the answer came. In our hearts the Lord whispered, "You can use this experience to help others who are passing through this dark valley." God did not cause it for that purpose. It did happen as an accident of nature, but our son has lived on through us as together or separately we have ministered to others in a similar hour of need.

If you have never had this experience but say to a disappointed mother, "I know how you feel," she will not say, but will think, *You have no idea how I feel!* But we could say, "Honey, we know how you feel. We've been through that valley. And here is how the Lord helped us." As we dried the tears of others, we dried our own.

Yes, we thought we had found our "nest" in Mobile, but the Lord had other plans. He said, "Go west!" Come to think about it, that is what He said to Abraham, for there lay his destiny—and ours.

9

Our Nest (1)!

We finally found our "nest" in Oklahoma City, Oklahoma. If my parents' plans had matured in 1900, I would have been born there. As it was it took me forty-two years to find it.

My first visit to Oklahoma City was to attend the Southern Baptist Convention in 1939, and what an introduction it was! Since I did not decide to go until the last minute, I did not have a hotel room reservation. But upon boarding the Rock Island in Memphis, I ran into Jim Dailey who was in the same boat. He had no reservation either, so we agreed to be roommates. Did I say *roommates*—with no room? Well, mates anyway.

Upon arriving in Oklahoma City early the next morning, we found a large crowd at the depot, even with a brass band. I thought, "Boy! They really know how to welcome us!" I was soon to learn that Jim Farley, postmaster-general of the United States, was on the train. He had come to dedicate the new post office building. So the crowd, "Big Jim," the band, and all soon departed, leaving Jim and me standing all alone.

We hailed a cab, telling the driver to take us to a hotel where we could get a room without having a reservation. He took us to the Hudson Hotel, where we soon learned why we could get a room without a previous reservation.

To say the least, it was not the "Ritz." We had a corner room on the second floor overlooking the street. At midnight it was almost as bright as noon due to the street lights. It was next to the streetcar barn. Day and night streetcars were coming and going. The wheels scraping the rails as the cars turned made a terrible noise. The only redeeming features were that it was cheap and only two blocks from the meeting in the city auditorium, now the Civic Music Center.

I had forgotten to give my secretary my sermon topics for the following Sunday, so I wired them to her: A.M.—Report on Southern Baptist Convention; P.M.—"I Have Sinned." When I returned home Ethel Hall wanted to know if the evening message was simply a continuation of the morning message.

Had I known that ten years later I would be in Oklahoma City as pastor of the First Baptist Church, I would have gone and looked at the building. As it was I simply attended the Convention and went home. I've always had the old-fashioned idea that if the church paid my way to the Convention, I should attend it.

Actually, my first contact with the church came that summer by remote control. I was preaching in a revival at Goodwater, Alabama. Jack Boston, former bookkeeper at First, Oklahoma City, led the music.

One day Jack came to my room and said, "I've just written a letter recommending you to the First Baptist Church, Oklahoma City." I mentioned that Dr. W. R. White was their pastor. He said he received a letter that morning telling that he had resigned. So I laughingly said, "Well, that's fine. Your letter will be the first one received. It will be in the bottom of the wastebasket, so they will never get down to it." It took them ten years to do so.

In the meantime, J. Howard Williams followed W. R. White and remained for over five years. In turn, he was followed by Willis Howard who served for two and one-half years. A friend told me that the average length pastorate there was two and one-half years, although some such as T. L. Holcomb, White, and Williams stayed about five years each.

As a result, the church had acquired the reputation of being a church of short pastorates. Much of that resulted from the early years. But I found that if there was any underlying cause, beginning with Holcomb, much of it lay with the Southern and

Texas Baptist Conventions. Each of the above-mentioned men could have stayed as long as he wished. But the SBC called Holcomb to head the Sunday School Board. Hardin-Simmons University elected White its president, and the Texas Convention elected Williams as its executive secretary. Even in my case I could have left there on three or four occasions for similar reasons but felt that my place was in the pastorate and that pastorate was First, Oklahoma City.

I must say that my family went reluctantly. Once there, however, we never for one moment regretted it.

The contacts with the church began indirectly. In October 1948, I received a phone call from a longtime friend, Ira Prosser, a member of that church. He wanted to know if I would be available for a call as its pastor. I declined on the basis that we were in process of building two buildings. In January 1949, I received a call from Dr. Andrew Potter, also a member of that church and executive secretary of the Baptist General Convention of Oklahoma. When I gave him my reasons for not considering the matter further, he said, "Now don't just say 'no.' Pray about it." I assured him I would.

Jasper Barnette of the Sunday School Board was in charge of the Sunday School clinic to be held in Mobile in March. One day he called me about a matter of so little importance that it could have been handled by "mule mail." Just before hanging up he asked, "By the way, are you going to be in your pulpit next Sunday?" Later I told Frances there would be a pulpit committee from Oklahoma City in our service the following Sunday. They were there. It was January 23, 1949, but after the service they said nothing to me. As we ate lunch I said to Frances that seemed to be the end of that. But soon a call came asking if I would meet them at the Battlehouse Hotel. I later learned they were Ray Young, Oscar Davis, and E. V. Mashburn.

When I entered their hotel room my first words were, "What took you so long?" When asked what I meant, I said, "I know for a fact that ten years ago Jack Boston recommended me to you." After a laugh Mashburn said, "Believe it or not, I was the secretary of that pulpit committee. When your name came up this time I remembered that letter, got it out of my files, and read it to the committee." That was largely a get-acquainted meeting. They were back in the service that night, and I was back at the hotel the next morning.

They told me that after each negative report from me they had dropped my name. But when the entire committee met after visiting some other prospective pastor, my name would come up again. So finally the committee said, "Let's send a sub-committee to Mobile and either get him or forget him."

During our conference Oscar Davis received a call from his office. From his words I knew they had asked about our weather. He said, "The sun is shining, it is seventy-two degrees, and flowers are blooming everywhere." I asked him to ask about the weather in Oklahoma City. He said that it was *snowing*.

When I did not give them any encouragement, E. V. Mashburn told me he was chairman of a committee to plan the church's spring revival. The simultaneous revival program was born in Oklahoma City. It was led by Dr. Roland Q. Leavell when he was evangelism secretary for the Home Mission Board. So it has been a tradition there. Mashburn asked if I would preach in their revival for two weeks, beginning the last Sunday in March. I agreed with the understanding that I was not obligated beyond that. At that point, I did not give them a firm yes or no. The committee returned home, promising that they would keep in touch with me.

The committee returned home to find the city streets covered with snow. For six weeks it snowed, melted, froze; snowed, melted, froze, and snowed. Mashburn and his golfing friends played with balls painted red so they could find them in the snow. When I went for the revival in late March, dirty snow was still in the gutters. During that time the committee barraged us with chamber of commerce literature, but not a word was ever said about that snow. And I never let them forget about it!

Compounding our problem was the loss of our baby at birth and the fact that Frances was facing major surgery as soon as she was able following the birth. A move would mean we would be among virtual strangers with doctors we did not know.

But a gradual conviction was forming in my heart that God was leading us to Oklahoma City. We could think of a hundred reasons (excuses?) for not going, but they were all personal, not spiritual. However, overriding all of these was the one conviction about God's will. I didn't want to go. Frances didn't want to go. Jerry didn't want to go. Mrs. Jackson didn't want to go. And the people of Dauphin Way did not want us to go. But God's will overruled all these, so finally I gave the Oklahoma City committee the green light to present my name to the church on the third Sunday in March. It was one week after the Sunday School clinic and one week before I began the revival meeting in Oklahoma City.

I must add one footnote. Before giving the green light I made one request. I had not visited the church, but they had sent me a picture of the pastor's home. It was a large house on a nice corner lot. In a conference phone call I said that in that climate the utility bill would be much higher and we would need someone to do lawn care. Would the church provide utilities and lawn care? For a moment I hear "buzz, buzz, buzz" as the chairman polled the committee. Then he said, "Yes!" They had already named the salary, so I told Frances I received a one-thousand-dollar annual increase before they called me. It took about six seconds. Had I waited until I got on the field it would have required three deacons meetings and two church business meetings to do it. No slam! This is simply the way democracy works in a Baptist church.

After a unanimous call I boarded a train for Oklahoma City. Frances was still suffering from the loss of our baby and did not want me to fly. In Fort Worth I had a five-hour wait between trains, so I went to Southwestern Baptist Theological Seminary to see Dr. Ray Summers, who had been First's, Oklahoma City, interim pulpit supply for almost a year. The church had been through a Gethsemane, and he gave me a detailed report. After the church had called me the previous Sunday he asked some people what they were going to do now that they had a new pastor. They said, "We will wait until he comes and then face him with it." Ray told me, "Only the Holy Spirit can change the hearts of those people."

Had I not been scheduled to begin their revival the following Sunday I would have sent the church a "No" telegram and gone back to Mobile perfectly happy. Why leave a happy going, growing church to go into a situation like that? But that is human reasoning. It seems that with that revival commitment the Lord had hemmed me in. On his second missionary journey Paul wanted to go to Ephesus, but the Holy Spirit sent him to Troas and Europe. He sent me to Oklahoma City.

Sunday morning during the Sunday School hour I made a personal tour. I found a strong adult division, but below that it was very weak. In a beginners department I saw the best equipment money could buy, five workers, and two children. An old brick house was on the corner where the chapel now stands. There I found two young people's departments with the most discouraged workers and pupils I ever saw. Compared to that, I remembered the "live wire" youth departments at Dauphin Way. I recalled that between Sunday School and the worship service you almost had to knock kids out of the way to go down the hall. Yet I knew that God had called me to Oklahoma City.

So with the heaviest heart I can remember, before preaching my first sermon in the revival, I accepted the call to become their pastor beginning May 1, 1949. I have often shuddered since that time when I recall beginning a pastorate with a revival. Just suppose it had been a flop! But God takes care of His own and fools too. And I know I come in there somewhere. In the two weeks we had more than 140 additions to the church, a large number being by profession of faith.

After the opening service, Catherine Butler, wife of an attorney and only child of a preacher couple, said to me, "I want you to know that I took you sight unseen." I said, "Yes, and I took you the same way!" In fact, that was true of the entire church and my family, except for three members of the pulpit committee. We never had an unhappy pastorate, but Oklahoma City was the happiest of all. I suppose it is because we stayed there the longest and had more time to be happy.

During the revival, back in Mobile Frances and her mother were making plans to move to Oklahoma City. She always said that every time we moved I had a revival somewhere in order to get out of packing. I must say, however, that they did not start *packing* until after I had finished *praying* about the matter. Ten-year-old Jerry had a dog with five puppies. On our front lawn he had a sign: Puppies for Sale. I don't think he sold any.

(Neither did he swap two five-hundred-dollar puppies for a thousand-dollar cat.) But he managed to dispose of them.

At that time, going to Oklahoma sounded so far away. I will never forget two western songs which were so popular then on radio. One went like this. "Way down yonder in the Indian Nation, rode my pony on the reservation in the Oklahoma hills where I was born." The other was, "Those far away places with strange sounding names." One lady asked if Oklahoma didn't have lots of Indian names. I said, "Yes. Names like Sylcacauga, Coosa, Tallapoosa, Tuscaloosa, Choctaw, and Kewahatche." All those were Alabama names.

On our drive to Oklahoma City we went through beautiful Arkansas terrain. Then from Fort Smith we took the most direct route. I now know some beautiful routes, but when we crossed the Arkansas River at Fort Smith we were in for a shock. It led through the *Grapes of Wrath* country made famous by John Steinbeck's novel. Where we now have beautiful Interstate 40, then we had a narrow strip of rough blacktop. The only trees were blackjack oaks. They had no beauty and are fit only for fence posts—not even good fuel, since the wood burns so quickly. Just compare them with the giant live oaks in Mobile! Oh! I forgot one use for blackjacks. On the golf course they are good for catching golf balls. If I hit a ball within twenty-five feet of one it seemed to reach out and grab it.

Naturally Frances and Mrs. Jack were looking at everything critically. Noting that all the trees leaned to the north, Frances asked why. I had no idea but ventured a guess. "I suppose it is because the wind blows from the south during the growing season." Bull's-eye! For a while I thought I was going to have to tie the ladies to keep them from starting to walk back to Alabama. But I calmed their fears by telling them we were not going to live where we were at the moment. In Oklahoma City there is an abundance of beautiful trees.

Once we were there everything was fine. They liked the city, trees, home, and church building. The people welcomed us with open arms and hands as they helped us get settled in our new home. On Sunday they took us to their hearts and we took them to ours. Thus began a happy twenty-four-year pastor-people relationship.

However, the following week I was not so sure. On Monday I received an anonymous letter bragging on the writer and airing out the problem which had plagued the church for about two years. I called Harry Canup, chairman of deacons, as to what should be done with it. He said, "Give it to Homer Hurt, who has a file of such." These letters had upset my predecessor to no end. The next day I received another. Harry said, "Oh my! You'll get disgusted and leave us too." (The writer was no longer a member of our church.) I replied, "Disgusted? Man, I was like a kid on Christmas morning. I could hardly wait to open the letter to see what was in it." Harry circulated my reply, and I have not received another anonymous letter to this day! When the writer saw that it did not bother me, he quit sending them.

That same week I received two telephone calls from ladies asking me to visit them. In the first visit the lady talked about the problem in the church. If ever the Lord helped a poor, dumb preacher, He helped me that day. I knew that the success or failure of my ministry there depended upon how I replied to her. So I prayed while she talked.

When she finished I said, "This happened prior to May 1, 1949." She agreed. Then I added, "You know, I am not interested in anything which happened in this church prior to that date. But I am going to be very much interested in everything which happens in our church after that date." She looked at me for a moment, smiled, and said, "You know, that makes sense!"

In the other visit exactly the same thing happened. After that I heard no more about the matter. Those two ladies remained our staunch friends and supporters as long as they lived.

The church had blueprints and specifications for a three-story addition to the educational building. During the revival I told them to get bids and let a contract so we could break ground on our second Sunday there. They did, and we did. I wanted us to hit the ground running, and one of the best ways to solve or prevent church problems is to keep people busy.

I heard about a man who had some prize and expensive fox hounds. One day the dogs got into a fight among themselves. Trying to stop it the man would grab a dog by the leg and throw it as far from the fight as he could. But it would run right back into the pack. In desperation the man saw his valuable dogs destroying each other. Then he remembered that he had a fox in a pen. So he set it loose. Seeing the fox, the dogs forgot their differences and took off after the fox. On that Sunday we turned loose a *fox*.

The Southern Baptist Convention met in Oklahoma City in May 1949. Hotel rooms were at a premium. Some of my friends said that I accepted the pastorate there simply in order to get a room for the Convention. If so, I certainly had a better room than for the one in 1939.

The Southern Baptist Pastors Conference held its meetings in our church auditorium. Dr. M. E. Dodd had started this conference in 1935 and had been its chairman (now president) ever since. Shortly before the 1949 Convention he had a heart attack, so he asked me to preside. The nominating committee wanted to nominate me for chairman, but I refused. It was uncertain whether or not Dr. Dodd would be able to continue. So I told the committee they could make me co-chairman if they wished. Thus if Dr. Dodd could not function, someone would be responsible for preparing a program. It turned out that Dr. Dodd prepared the program for Chicago the next year, but again I presided. He requested that he not be reelected, so I was elected chairman. The next year in San Francisco, Casper Warren was elected to succeed me. In turn the next year Ramsey Pollard was elected. Beginning with me the conference has followed the one-year term.

When I succeeded Dr. Dodd he turned over to me a document which had been adopted when the pastors conference was formed. It stated that the conference was to be a time of inspirational preaching. No vote would be taken except on the election of officers, and the conference would not in any way deal with matters scheduled to be brought before the Southern Baptist Convention. I passed the document on to Casper Warren. Somewhere down the line it was lost in the shuffle. Unfortunately the conference later became a forum for sounding forth on Convention issues. Beginning about 1990 efforts have been made to return the conference to its original purpose. The manager can tell a pinch hitter to take a turn at batting. After that he is at the mercy of the batter. He may strike out or hit a home run. The presiding officer cannot determine what the speaker will say, but to anyone asked to speak he should make clear to him the purpose of the conference. The pastors conference exists by virtue of the Convention. Were the brethren not gathered for the Convention there would be no conference. No speaker at the pastors conference should abuse his privilege by venting his spleen over a matter which only the Convention can handle. The conference is for inspirational preaching and singing, no more and no less. If it gets out of that area it is violating its reason for being.

In San Francisco my total budget was $323, the cost of printing a simple program. At some future time the budget began to rise. One year, to the best of my knowledge, it soared to $14,000. After several offerings the amount was still $2,000 short. Though not legally obligated, the Convention paid this shortage to save its credit.

Part of this increase over the years was due to larger attendance. Since no church auditorium could accommodate the crowd, it became necessary to rent the facilities where the Convention met later. But in some cases the increase came from using "celebrities" from the entertainment world, paying their expenses plus an honorarium.

To me this seemed to be a waste of money, when there were ten to twenty thousand preachers there at their own expense who would give their right arm to get to preach their "sugar stick" at the conference. And any one of them could out-preach the celebrities!

After the Convention in 1949 we settled down to the "nitty gritty" of the local church. When we arrived in Oklahoma City the church had only three regular staff members. Bill Reynolds was minister of music, Mrs. Erma Bay was church hostess, and Bush Walker was a caretaker. The office staff was composed of ladies in the church who had volunteered until a new pastor could build a permanent staff.

(Speaking of Bush, he was half black and half Indian. His real first name was Bushyhead. When he was born he had a large sac filled with fluid under his chin. Johnny Bushyhead was a missionary to the Indians in the Muskogee, Oklahoma, area.

One day he visited Bush's mother. Seeing this sac, he punctured it with his knife; it drained and went away. Out of gratitude, she named her baby after him.)

The first addition was Lucy Gibson, my secretary. Frances and I came to regard her as a member of our family, and she was my "right arm" in the work for twenty-four years. She left a much better paying job with an oil company, but she came to feel called to her work as I did to mine. After my retirement she remained on the church staff until she retired.

The second major addition to the staff was Stanton Nash. He was with me at Dauphin Way for one year. We never discussed it, but I knew that he and his wife Joy wanted to go with us to Oklahoma City. However, knowing the situation there, I felt I must determine if he would fit the need at First, Oklahoma City. After about a month there I decided that he was the man I needed.

So I talked to Bill. I told him what I had in mind. Then I said, "Bill, you have a job, Stanton has a job, and I have a job. If you two cannot get along together, neither of you will have a job, and I may not. Can you two work together?" He was thrilled beyond words. They had been in Southwestern Seminary together and were close friends. I called Stanton and gave him the same talk. His reaction was the same as Bill's. One of the ladies in the Dauphin Way office later told me that Stanton almost did cartwheels across the office after our phone conversation. For I had told him to pack up and come *west*.

Bill Reynolds stayed with us for six years. Then he was in the music department of the Sunday School Board while earning his Ph.D. in music at Peabody in Nashville. Eventually he became head of the department. Bill—oh, excuse me! Dr. William J. Reynolds—is now professor of music at Southwestern Seminary.

While still with us Bill served on the committee to select hymns for the *Broadman Hymnal*. One Wednesday he said, "Preacher, I'm going to Nashville tomorrow to begin selecting hymns for the new hymnal. Is there any particular hymn you would like to have included?" I said, "Yes. The song they sang when I made my profession of faith—'Let Jesus Come into Your Heart.'" It was practically lost, but he searched until he found it in a dog-eared revival song book. It is in our hymnals to this day.

Stanton was with us for ten years, going from us to serve as executive secretary of the Hawaiian Baptist Convention. Later he was vice president of Golden Gate Seminary in charge of development. Since retirement he has served part-time in that capacity at Southwestern Seminary.

In July 1949, Russell Dunbar came on our staff as our bookkeeper. When Stanton went to be the executive secretary of the Hawaiian Baptist Convention in 1959, Russell became our business administrator, a position he held until his death in 1990.

In our staff setup Stanton was over the entire church program, except the pastoral and music departments. With that arrangement, other than Lucy, only two people—Stanton and Bill—were responsible directly to me. We had weekly staff meetings to plan and coordinate the overall church program. My office door was always open to any staff member who needed to see me. However, I operated on the theory that a person can only work for one person. For instance, I never corrected a janitor. If something needed correcting in that area, I dealt with Stanton, letting him handle the matter through proper channels. In the Sermon on the Mount, Jesus might just as well have said, "No man can serve two bosses" (Matt. 6:24).

Speaking of *bosses*, there is no place for such in a New Testament church. The New Testament speaks of such in condemnatory terms. "Diotrephes who loveth to have the preeminence" (3 John 9). John does not say whether he was a pastor or a layman. "Jezebel" (Rev. 2:20) may well be a synonym for a woman who dominated the church at Thyatira.

Not even the pastor is to be the *boss* over the church. While at Dauphin Way one day I was talking to Frances about something I would like to do in the church. Hearing me, Jerry, who was about seven years old at the time, said, "Well, Daddy, aren't you the boss?" I said, "Oh, Son, if you only knew!"

Those who contend for the pastor being the "ruler" of the church should research Hebrews 13:17. The *King James Version* reads, "Obey them that have the rule over you." This version was translated by scholars of the Church of England or as some call it, the English Catholic Church. That is according to their church polity, but contrary to New Testament polity.

To begin with, the Greek text reads "the ones leading you." You drive cattle; you lead sheep. According to Kittel's exhaustive work on the Greek language, the verb translated "obey" (*peitho*) also may mean "follow." This work cites Hebrews 13:17 as an example of this. "The ones leading you" definitely calls for "follow."

A local New Testament church is a body of baptized believers operating through democratic processes under the lordship of Jesus Christ. He is the Head and Ruler of the church. Pastors are undershepherds of the Great Shepherd, leading the flock of God. The Holy Spirit indwells every Christian (1 Cor. 6:19-20a). As He indwells believers so He indwells the fellowship of the local church (1 Cor. 3:16).

As for myself, in churches where I was the pastor, under my pastoral *leadership* we worked with the deacons and other church-elected committees and officers. Insofar as I know in most churches where the pastor advocates pastoral *rulership* he does the same. The more people you involve in planning and promoting a program, the more enthusiasm they will put into seeing that it succeeds.

As for securing staff members, I let each department head do the "bird-dogging" to find the proper person for a given position. They knew the people in their field better than I. Once we had found the proper person, judged so not only by the staff but by the people with whom they would work, I would ask for a personal conference. Putting it in monetary terms I would say, "We want you to have liberty in planning your work. We are not simply buying so many hours of your time and ounces of your energy. We are buying your mind, imagination, ingenuity, enthusiasm, everything about you." I told the person that I would put up with sloppy work to a fault, but would not ignore disloyalty one minute. Said I, "I will be loyal to you, and I expect the same of you. If you and I agree on a program and you get into hot water promoting it, I'll be in there with you up to my neck. But if you go off half-cocked without my knowledge, you are by yourself. I will not endanger my pastoral leadership simply to pull *your* chestnuts out of the fire."

With two exceptions I never had a problem at this point. In both I sought to help the person to learn from his experience. I never *fired* a staff member, but in these two cases, as a friend, I suggested that if opportunity presented itself to go elsewhere and start with a clean slate, it might be best for them to accept it. In both cases they remained my friends through the years.

In the pastor's case, he fills two roles. In a sense he is a staff member's employer and pastor. These two roles must be exercised in proper balance.

It is a waste of money and talent for a pastor to gather about him people who know more about their work than he does and then for him to do all the detailed planning. Delegating responsibility is good for the pastor, staff, and the overall church program.

Before leaving this theme, I must include what was once a painful but is now a laughing matter. At one point during my Oklahoma City ministry, I brought to the church a minister of education from east of the Mississippi. In turn, he secured age supervisors from the same area. Since we had one of the best groups to be found anywhere, I suggested that we price them out of the market salary-wise. We did and told them so. There was only one problem with this. By the time the new budget year began, every one of them had gone back east of the Mississippi. I told the deacons that in the future when I was looking for a staff member, if they saw me looking eastward, please turn me around. In heaven, Texans are not the *only* ones they put in cages to prevent them from trying to go back!

When we went to Oklahoma City the church was reporting seven thousand members. I told Frances that either they had an inflated membership roll or else, judging by their Sunday School attendance and budget, they were not doing much with what they had. I found that the former was true. So the first Monday of my pastorate there I asked one of the ladies in the office to count the cards in the file. There were nine hundred less than the reported figure.

At the next deacons meeting I called this to their attention and proposed that we revise our church roll. There was a mild objection from a few old-timers, so I did not press the matter. If we were going to fight, there were more important things over which to do it. The fact of the matter was that for several years there was a friendly rivalry between the First Churches in Oklahoma City, Dallas, Houston, San Antonio, and Amarillo as to which would be the largest.

Five years later I brought the matter before the deacons again, only with more insistence. I said, "Brethren, there is not a one of you with a sales force who would expect a salesman to produce on the basis of seven thousand accounts when you know that more than half of them are dead. And I am getting tired of trying to produce on the basis of seven thousand members when I know that we have less than half that many." Without one note of dissent, the deacons recommended to the church that this be done and that a lady be employed to do it!

It took about eighteen months to do it. The first result was to find where the nine hundred were. They *weren't* and never had been. In the early days, the roll was kept in a large ledger and each person was numbered. Inadvertently, one church clerk had made an error of nine hundred, going from one name to the next. In the early days, most church clerks were volunteers elected by the church, and some were not too efficient. They might not write for a church letter. If they did, the other church might not remove a name from its roll. In our revision it was discovered that in some cases, when preparing material for the annual associational letter, the total additions that year were added to the previous total. They failed to delete the deceased or those who moved to other churches. One result of such record keeping was that we found a couple still on our roll who had been in several other churches. When we discovered them, they were active members of the First Baptist Church, Carlsbad, New Mexico. This could be but a sample of many similar situations.

The final tally showed that we had about three thousand resident members and a total of almost fifty-six hundred. I told the church we found one man's name still on our roll who was a Catholic priest but that we found no Jewish rabbis. I wonder what the result would be for Southern Baptists if every church did as we did. But don't hold your breath until they do!

In 1949, three of our most immediate needs were (1) to balance Sunday School enrollment, (2) to increase the financial stewardship of the church, and (3) to obtain parking space. As for the first, suffice it to say, that on my sixth anniversary, Stanton announced figures which showed that we had achieved that balance between the adult division and the remainder of the Sunday School.

During these years and beyond, the evangelism results increased along with the Sunday School growth. At a Southern Baptist Convention a friend said, "Hobbs, I read good things about your work in Oklahoma City." I replied, "Well, I write those reports and make them sound good."

In 1948-49, the church budget was $190,000. The 1950 budget was set at $325,000, a substantial amount of which was for the building fund. We used the one-day budget plan which had been developed at Emmanuel Church in Alexandria, as we did each year of my pastorate in Oklahoma City. We continued to increase the budget figure each year until it finally reached $870,000, which was a lot of money in those days. Each year we subscribed the budget in one day. This followed a month of preparation during which I preached on stewardship and tithing. In all my ministry, I never had a complaint from tithers about preaching on tithing, only from non-tithers. The tithers said, "Go to it, Preacher! We need help!"

That first year I learned that the top pledges in the past had been fifteen hundred dollars annually. So I enlisted five people to pledge five thousand dollars. This annual emphasis on tithing paid off. The number of tithers finally passed the nine hundred mark.

Through the years I adhered to the policy of never looking at the giving records of the people. Of course, I knew that some gave more than others. But in preaching, I did not want the devil to say, "That man gives ten thousand dollars a year to the church, so go light on him," when maybe he was the one who needed the sermon the most. Neither did I want old Nick saying, "This man only gives fifty cents a week, so let him have both barrels of the sermon."

Never have I apologized for preaching on the stewardship of money. If you count the verses, Jesus taught more on this subject than on salvation. He knew what are our besetting sins. Paul said that the Macedonian Christians gave generously because they first gave themselves unto the Lord. God never fully gets *you* until He gets *yours*.

I have heard people say, "I'll be glad when the pastor quits preaching on giving and gets back to preaching the gospel." Out of that came the inspiration for my book *The Gospel of Giving*. Because that, too, is the gospel. The heart of the gospel is that "God so loved the world that he *gave*" (John 3:16).

In the final analysis God does not count the money given. He weighs the love it represents. Giving should not be measured merely by what a person gives, but by how much he/she has left *after* giving. Jesus commended the poor widow for her two mites (about one-half a penny), not the rich for their large gifts. The rich went home that night to a sumptuous meal. The widow probably went to sleep on an empty stomach, for she gave all she had, even her living. But she slept the sleep of the blessed, for she had a full soul.

In 1949, one of our greatest physical needs was parking space. On the only available space, we planned to build a large addition to the church. Oscar Davis was chairman of the house and grounds committee. The church authorized his committee to secure additional parking space, so, with the committee's backing, Oscar and I quietly began buying houses across the street south of the church. It was soon in use for parking.

Dr. Chester Swanson, one of our deacons, was superintendent of the Oklahoma City school system. One Friday afternoon he called me. Just south of our small parking area was a vacant tract of land about a block long which was owned by the School Board. The site of a former grade school, it was used as a football and band practice field by Central High School located a few blocks away. Dr. Swanson told me the School Board had just voted to sell this land in order to purchase parking land next to the school. He thought the church might be interested in buying it for parking, and I assured him we were. At that point no one else knew it was for sale.

So I called five men—R. A. Young, Guy James, Billy Atkinson, Oscar Davis, and E. V. Mashburn—and asked them to meet me in my office Sunday morning at nine o'clock. I did not tell them the reason. From my second-story office window, we could see the land. They all agreed that we needed it.

So I said, "Brethren, we cannot yet take this matter to the church. If word got out about this, every business adjacent to the land would want it, and we could find ourselves in a bidding war." I asked Oscar what the land was worth. He said judging from a recent appraisal of property in the area, it probably was worth $135,000. I said, "Why don't we offer them $85,000 for it and then negotiate upward? I want each of you to give me a check made out to the church for $1,000. Then authorize me to offer $85,000, and give them a check for $5,000 as earnest money. Whatever figure we arrive at, we will present it to the church. We have no assurance that the church will buy it, so you may find that you have bought some land." They were enthusiastically agreeable to the idea.

The next day I made them a firm offer of $85,000. Almost two weeks went by with no word from the School Board. Then on a Friday afternoon, I received a call from the president of the board. They had accepted our offer. Then he added, "Of course the land is worth much more. But since you are a church and will use the land for public benefit, we agreed to your offer."

We were in good shape for parking space, even if some of the land was a block and a half from the building. Later we purchased the northwest quarter of the block on which the church building is located so as to have more close-in parking space.

Since my retirement in 1973, under the leadership of my successor, Dr. Gene Garrison, the church continued to acquire property in the block where the church building stands. The crowning of this effort came when R. A. and Verna Young purchased and presented to the church a building on the northeast corner of the block so that the church owns the entire city square block. Through another generous gift from them, the buildings on the purchased property have been demolished, the land has been beautified and paved for more parking, and a much needed all-weather entrance provided for the church building. And the church is *debt free*!

When we came to Oklahoma City, the church already was planning to make a massive addition to the church plant. Preliminary plans had been drawn which included a large rectangular area in the building for a chapel. However, after we studied them with the building committee, it was decided to start all over again.

As background it should be noted that the auditorium and a Sunday School annex had been completed in March 1912, during the pastorate of Dr. Carter Helm Jones, then known as the "Prince of the American Pulpit." Insofar as we know, it was the first church auditorium in the world to be air conditioned. They built a large concrete vat which each Saturday was filled with one hundred-pound blocks of ice. On Sunday large fans drew air over the ice and into the auditorium. In 1962, I read an item in the "Fifty Years Ago" column of the Georgia Baptist *Christian Index:* "They tell me that the new auditorium of the Baptist church in Oklahoma City is air-conditioned. Such a waste of the Lord's money!" How times have changed!

In May 1912, the Southern Baptist Convention met in that auditorium. During the Convention they made a picture of the *crowd* on the Eleventh Street side south of the building. The front row sat on the curb with other rows standing on risers behind that row. During my pastorate, we established a historical room in the church library. (We now have a beautiful archives room.) We were deluged with items of historical value given by our people. One was an original copy of a New York newspaper dated the day after Abraham Lincoln was assassinated.

One day a lady brought us a copy of the Convention picture. The first person I recognized (by his long beard) was B. H. Carroll, sitting on the front row, with the young George W. Truett sitting on his left side. I also recognized many other SBC leaders of the era. The original is in our church archives. But copies were made and sent to various related institutions: Southwestern Seminary; First Baptist Church, Dallas; Southern Baptist Historical Commission; Oklahoma Baptist Historical Society; and, of course, I kept one for myself which eventually will be among my memorabilia in Oklahoma Baptist University Library. At the time Davis Woolley, Jr. was the executive secretary of the Southern Baptist Historical Commission. He wrote to tell me how thrilled he was to see the picture. The first person he recognized was his father standing on the back row.

In 1929-30, a four-story education building was erected just north of the church auditorium. Then, as noted previously, we built a three-story annex in 1949. But we sorely needed other facilities which would be provided in the proposed building.

As it was finally approved, this building provided an office suite, added Sunday School facilities, dining room, kitchen, a chapel and parlor, and a gymnasium. At the time only the auditorium was air-conditioned as described above, so heating and air-conditioning equipment for most of the entire plant was to be installed in the basement beneath the chapel. In the meantime, the remainder of the plant was air-conditioned with sectional units.

While still in the planning stage, we had difficulty deciding where to put the chapel. The church auditorium was Gothic style. With its tower it reminded me of a locomotive with a smoke stack but no coal car. One day I stood in the parking lot looking at the building. Suddenly an idea hit me. Why not put the chapel on the opposite corner with its own tower—a miniature of the auditorium—thus balancing the entire structure? The building committee immediately accepted the suggestion.

I told the architects it seemed that I had spent half my life sitting in church dining rooms behind a post where I could not see the speaker. So I did not want a single post in ours. It is on the first of four floors. To support that weight the dining room ceiling had steel beams so large that only one company in our nation could make them, and the actual ceiling would be placed underneath them. This within itself presented a problem. In a room that large (almost half a block long), psychologically it would seem that the ceiling was touching the top of people's heads. At a chamber of commerce luncheon, I noticed that the room had recessed ceiling lights. The architects said we could do the same. They used chicken wire to build forms around the steel beams, the remainder of the ceiling being higher with recessed lights. Then they blew material (not asbestos) over the whole to form the ceiling. This not only solved the height problem; it also gave us near-perfect acoustics.

The lower part of the walls was made of tile. The remainder was composed of a Japanese wood called *sen.* When it was finished the people kidded me about my "night club." My reply was that I wanted them to feel at home. So we had a night club ceiling and *sen* all around the walls.

When the architects finished the plans, the estimated cost of building and equipment was $1,200,000—a lot of money in the early 1950s. We figured that when finished, our indebtedness would be about $900,000. One committee member remarked, "Pastor, evidently we misled you into thinking we are a rich church. We are a poor church." I said, "Yes, I have found that we have a *rich*membership but a *poor* church."

All members of the building committee were deacons. All but one are now dead. Since Billy Atkinson was one of these, I call his name. A geologist, he was the youngest man in the history of Oklahoma City to make a million dollars. But when the stock market crashed in 1929, he lost everything and wound up $350,000 in debt, a debt he later paid with interest. When he died, he was again a wealthy man.

Billy had been burned by over extension and did not want that to happen to his church. So he said, "Let's build, but not so elaborate a building with such a large debt." But the committee voted him down. When the program was presented to the deacons, he made the same plea, but they voted to recommend the program as presented. He had a policy never to oppose anything presented to the church by the deacons or the pastor. The church voted to proceed with the program.

The following Sunday morning before Sunday School, Billy came to my office. He always called me "Preacher Hobbs." So he said, "Preacher Hobbs, as you know I was opposed to so large a building program, but the church voted to do it. Never in my life have I asked anybody to give me a job in the church. But I've come to ask you to give me a job in our church." I said, "Well, Billy, if I can I will. What job do you want?" He replied, "I want you to make me chairman of the committee to raise the money to pay that debt."

I did. And he did. He and his wife Mattie gave one-tenth of the cost of the building and equipment. Due to him more than anyone else, the debt was paid three years early! The New Testament word for church relationship is not *membership* but *fellowship*. It means having all things in common, privileges *and* responsibilities. Billy's example is *FELLOWSHIP!*

We finally broke ground for what the church had voted to call the chapel and the youth activities building in the spring of 1952. They were ready for occupancy in March 1954.

The best time to raise money for a building is while it is under construction. One day early in that building period, I went to see Mrs. Louise Prichard. Her husband had been one of the founders and was president of Anderson-Prichard Oil Co. (APCO) until his death in 1949, so she was a very wealthy woman. Also she was one of the humblest and most devout persons I ever knew. As an example, one night we had our annual stewardship dinner with a guest speaker. During the meal I said to our guest, "Perhaps the wealthiest woman in Oklahoma is in the dining room tonight. Can you identify her?" He could not. So I said, "Do you see the little lady with the coffee pot pouring coffee? That is she."

I conducted her husband's funeral. She had lost her only son in a tragic accident. Her only daughter died of a heart attack in her sleep. Frances and I were with her through all of these bereavements. Out of these had come more than a member-pastor relationship. It was more like a mother-children one. We had taken her children's place in her life. I mention all this merely as background.

When I visited her that day, I asked if she would give the chapel to the church. I said nothing about naming it for her; had I done so she would have refused. (When it was finished, without asking her about it, the church voted to name it after her. It bears a simple plaque which reads, "The Louise Prichard Chapel, a gift of her love for the glory of God." This pleased her very much.) She asked how much it would cost and when would she have to give it. I told her the contractor's cost was $107,500 and told her she could give it at her convenience. That was all. She agreed to do it. Then I asked if she would give me a letter to that effect and permit me to read it to the church the following Sunday morning. My purpose was to encourage others to give. She said, "On that basis only, I will let you read such a letter." And I did so.

Bill Reynolds wanted a pipe organ in the chapel. To save money the committee wanted to install the best electronic organ available. But Roy and Mrs. Stanton settled it for them.

The morning after I read Mrs. Prichard's letter I received a call from Roy. He said, "After church yesterday, as we drove home, we were talking about the nice gift Mrs. Prichard made, and we decided that we needed a pipe organ to go with that nice chapel. Tell the building committee to buy the pipe organ and send us the bill." The committee told Bill to select the instrument. He chose an eleven-rank organ which has graced the chapel for almost forty years. It bears a small metal plate stating that it is a memorial to the Stanton's little daughter who died many years before they made the gift

A few days later I went to see Ole Olsen, an oil man. His wife Lauretta was the daughter of Rev. and Mrs. Howard. He was a pioneer Baptist preacher in Oklahoma, a native of Kentucky. I said, "Ole, I want you and Lauretta to furnish the chapel in memory of her parents." He asked how much it would cost. When I told him not more than thirty thousand dollars he agreed to do so.

Shortly thereafter, one Sunday morning, as I was going into the auditorium for the service, I met Mrs. W. E. (Grace) Price. Her husband was a builder who had died recently. Standing in the midst of a crowd entering for the service, I said, "Mrs. Price, your husband was very much interested in our new building. Why don't you furnish the church parlor in his memory?" She also asked how much. I said, "Not over twenty thousand dollars." She said, "I'll do it!" Also, she gave me permission to announce it in the service. Yes, money gets money! And I have not seen a more beautiful church chapel and parlor anywhere in the world!

Finally the building was finished, so one week in March 1954, was set for dedication week. During the final phase of finishing and equipping the building, the contractors asked that no visitors enter it. This hastened the work as well as built up anticipation among the people.

For that week we planned to use four of the five former pastors still living. The one exception was Dr. Mordecai Ham. He had been the pastor for one year in the late 1920s. After one year he resigned, saying, "Just two mistakes were made. One was when you called me; the other was when I accepted the call. I am not a pastor; I am an evangelist." It was after that that Billy

Graham and some of his associates were saved during a Ham-Ramsey crusade in Charlotte, North Carolina.

However, that had no part in our decision not to invite him. At the time, he lived in Louisville, Kentucky, and was *eighty-five years old*. We felt it would be too hard on him to make that trip. Anyone is old who is twenty years older than you are. Now that I am eighty-six, I know that a person at that age is just an irresponsible kid. I would not think it an imposition if you asked me to go to the moon.

You can imagine my consternation that Sunday morning when I got out of my car and saw Mr. and Mrs. B. F. C. Morris and Dr. Ham coming up the sidewalk. Dr. Ham's son had married the Morris' daughter, so unknown to me, they had invited him.

I rushed to meet them, welcomed Dr. Ham, and explained why we did not invite him. Fortunately, the Sunday program called for Dr. Willis Howard, my immediate predecessor, to preach that morning and for me to preach that night. So I told Dr. Ham I wanted him to preach at the evening service. It thrilled him so. Later, Mr. Morris told me that as soon as he got to their home after the morning service, he called Louisville to tell his wife. Dr. Ham was known for long sermons. His wife's closing word to him was, "Now, Daddy, don't preach too long!" He preached for one and a half hours, but it was all for the best. We used all the living former pastors. As of now, I am the only former pastor who is still among the earthly living. The others live on with the Lord, and their works on earth abide. As I did, so Dr. Garrison continues to build upon the works of all who came before him.

As for the dedications, Dr. White spoke on Monday night as we dedicated the recreation facilities. On Tuesday night, Dr. Holcomb preached as we dedicated the chapel and parlor. Dr. Williams spoke on Wednesday night at the dedication of the dining room and kitchen facilities. On that night we crammed—and I do mean *crammed*—about one thousand people into the dining room. *And all could see him as he spoke*. We had the *tools*. It remained for us to use them for God's glory.

Two things remain to complete the story. One is about the indebtedness. Insurance companies were eager to lend us the money, only they wanted members of the church to underwrite given portions of the loan. Businessmen were not willing to do this. In case they needed to borrow money for their business, the amount they had endorsed must appear on their financial statement. Finally, the First National Bank of Oklahoma City agreed to make the loan which would be secured by a mortgage on the church property. The banker said that a mortgage on church property was not worth much, for rarely would someone want to buy a church building. It only satisfied legal requirements. Then he added, "We are lending this on the basis of the character of your people."

He only asked me one question. "How long do you plan to stay at the First Baptist Church?" I replied, "Of course that is in the Lord's hands. All I can say is that I have no plans whatever to leave." That satisfied him. He also asked for a list of the members of our finance committee. When I gave it to him he said, "Your finance committee is stronger than ours." Indeed, one member was a director of that bank. Another was a director of another bank across the street.

This loan was to be repaid twenty-five thousand dollars per quarter. If you want to age rapidly, get such a payment schedule. It seemed that we hardly got out of the revolving door at the bank. The church had authorized the use of building fund money to put air-conditioning units in certain parts of our buildings. On one occasion we had a bank payment due on a Thursday, and the building fund was empty. The finance committee met on Wednesday but adjourned with no definite result. That afternoon, I called Mrs. Prichard and told her of the situation. Also, I said that if she could help in any way, I would appreciate it. That night after the church supper, I was on my way to my office. I met her, and she handed me a book. She asked, "Will you ask Lucy to return this book to the library for me?" The library was only a few feet away, and I wondered why she didn't return it. But as I walked away she said, "By the way! When you get to your office, look through the book." When I did I found her check for twenty-five thousand dollars!

After giving the money for the chapel, she told me that she learned how much joy she got out of giving away money. One day I received a letter from her marked "Personal." Opening it,

I found no letter, just a check for the church in the amount of forty-five thousand dollars. I called to thank her. She said, "Don't thank me! I get more joy out of it than anyone else. I just thank the good Lord that He makes it possible for me to do it."

Every time APCO declared a dividend, she would call me to tell me how much money she had to give. After naming an amount to go through the Cooperative Program she would ask where we needed the rest. At the time, Billy Atkinson was chairman of the finance committee. One day he said, "Preacher Hobbs, if she doesn't get to heaven, there is no use for you and me trying."

The brethren said that if we could get that debt below $300,000 they would rest easy. For no matter what happened to the economy, the church could handle it. In April 1963, the figure was slightly above that mark. The finance committee met one day. The twenty-five thousand dollars were due the next day, yes, and we did not have the money to pay it. After kicking the matter around, they finally asked, "Pastor, what do you have to say about it?"

I said, "Well, brethren, I am not worried about tomorrow's payment. I can get that right around this table, for I know you will not let the church default on that payment. What I want is for us to be out of debt by December 31." They almost fell out of their chairs. Then I proceeded to outline a plan.

I gave them the amount we must pay by that date so as to keep on schedule. In buying parking space, we did not want to borrow more money from the bank. The state Baptist Building was across the street, and they used our parking lot adjoining their property. So we got permission to use fifty thousand dollars of their borrowing power at the same bank. We had paid back ten thousand dollars. Then we borrowed the remainder from Mrs. Prichard. This included a sum used when the church purchased a new home for the pastor's family. I said, "Each year, when the principal and interest payment comes due, Mrs. Prichard writes the church telling us to write off the payment. While she has not said so, I am certain she intends to give all this to the church through annual tax credits. If she knew that by doing this now in a lump sum, the church could be debt free by the end of the year, I believe she would do it. As for the Convention, they are already using our parking lot. We will not do it, but as it is, any day the church could deny them that use. If we offered them a written agreement whereby they could use it for twenty-five years in return for writing off the forty thousand dollars, I am sure they would do it. It would be a bargain to them. If the Convention and Mrs. Prichard would do this, we would need to raise only fifty-two thousand dollars extra this year to accomplish that goal."

By this time the committee was really excited. They said if I could get that done, I need not worry about the fifty-two thousand dollars. They would raise it. Both Mrs. Prichard and the Convention agreed.

The church set the second Sunday in August to raise the fifty-two thousand dollars. In my judgment they picked the worst time of the year to do it, but they raised over fifty-seven thousand dollars. The result was a joyful shouting time on January 1, 1964.

To me, the second thing that completes the picture regarding physical facilities is of an aesthetic nature. Frances always shied away from anything which gave the appearance that she was trying to run the church. Yet, as stated before, we were a team. Many of the best ideas for our church programs came from Frances. She would present an idea to me. If I did not like it, she would drop it. In most cases, my reaction was positive, in which case we would discuss and refine it. If finally I took it to the church, she insisted that I not mention her name.

Only one time do I recall when she went, not over me, but around me. And I am glad she did. As we were planning for parking space and the new building, she suggested that we should also make it beautiful. Instead of simply a concrete jungle, we should make the premises alive with growing things such as trees, shrubbery, and flower beds. I agreed wholeheartedly, but somehow I always kept it on a "back burner," favoring the more pressing needs.

Patiently she waited for several years. Then one year Gene Steelman was elected chairman of the house and grounds committee. His wife Opal and Frances were good friends, so she revealed to Opal her long-held dream. Now Opal was one of those people who, if you asked her to do something, you could forget it. It was as good as done.

Gene was a road builder—so the following week, here came Gene and a crew of men. Before the week was over, the flower beds were prepared and planted. The bare area between the auditorium and north educational building was filled with flowers and greenery, and a row of small trees girded the land owned by the church in the block where the church plant stands. These little trees are now tall trees, so beautiful with the blossoms of spring and breathing life into the area for most of the year.

I am happy that this tradition continues into the present on a much larger scale. Through the love, labor, and gifts of many, the First Baptist Church has ample practical facilities located in a garden of delight. God made His earth both practical and beautiful. We should keep it that way for His glory!

10

Our Nest (2)!

More often than not, we use the word "church" to refer to buildings and land. Such as, the First Baptist Church is located at Eleventh and Robinson. That is no more the church than a house is a family. A given church in the local sense is composed of redeemed people. The church building is the place where the church gathers for corporate worship, Bible study, and the like. It is more fitting to refer to the church as *assembled* and *scattered*. It should assemble to worship and plan corporate activities and then scatter throughout the community to live, work, and witness concerning Christ. One of our great problems today is that we spend so much time *assembled* to plan and promote the work that we do not have time to *scatter* and do it.

The story is told of a church which for six months had a meeting every night. Finally it had a night when there was none. So that night the pastor called a staff meeting to find out why they had not planned a meeting for that night. Exaggerated? Yes. But it points up the problem.

In the previous chapter we dealt largely with the physical aspect of our ministry in Oklahoma City. Now I want you to look at the more spiritual side of the church's activities. God blessed the revival in which I preached prior to our moving to Oklahoma City. It was a much needed blessing. For obvious reasons the church needed it. And I needed it to remove any vestige of doubt that this move was in God's will. After those two weeks I never questioned it.

Mention has been made of the church's reputation for short pastorates. Strange as it may seem, though, the church had had some giants as pastors and under their leadership became one of the key churches in Southern Baptist life, yet I was the only one to be elected moderator of the association, president of the state convention and of the Southern Baptist Convention. They were far more capable than I am. The reason is that they did not stay there as long as I did. The church got stuck with me for twenty-four years, lacking four months.

Shortly after our arrival in Oklahoma City, Raymond and Verna Young had several couples at a dinner so we could get acquainted. Among them were John and Catherine Butler. John was a brilliant lawyer with a sly sense of humor. He asked me how long I was at Dauphin Way. When I said five years, he remarked, "My, that's a long time to stay at one church!" Obviously, that was a take-off on the short pastorate idea. So I said, "Yes, it is. When I go to a new pastorate I always choose a verse of Scripture on which to base my work there. For this one I have chosen Jesus' words to Judas Iscariot. 'What thou doest, do quickly.'" From that moment on John and I were kindred souls. When he died, at Catherine's request I conducted his funeral assisted by Dr. Garrison.

We did get into the work "quickly." As previously noted, on our second Sunday there we broke ground for a Sunday School annex. In the fall of 1949, we also broke ground for a new building at Falls Creek, the state Baptist assembly grounds, to replace an old cabin that had seen its day. It cost about forty thousand dollars. When someone referred to it as a *cabin*, I said, "Any building that costs forty thousand dollars is a *lodge*." In 1949, that was a lot of money, and so it has been called ever since. (Recently, it was thoroughly renovated under Dr. Garrison's leadership.)

By the fall of 1949, Stanton had built an educational staff second to none: Hazel Moseley, director of youth work; Dullie Haggard, director of junior work; and Marie Cunningham, director of elementary work. Stanton directed the adult work as well as serving as superintendent of the Sunday School and director of the Baptist Training Union. In the music department we had a strong sanctuary choir. Now relieved of a multitude of duties, Bill was able to develop a graded music program.

We made no major changes in the educational program other than a greater emphasis upon equalizing the enrollment between the adult division and the rest of the Sunday School. This was achieved by my sixth anniversary as pastor. In this process, the enrollment and attendance showed a steady increase. Tom Marshall once said to me, "Pastor, we can average fifteen hundred in attendance without trying." But with "trying" the attendance was running seventeen to eighteen hundred. On special days we would go well above two thousand.

At the same time the Training Union (Discipleship Training) also was growing. Normally, the attendance was six to seven hundred. On special days it would reach nine hundred to one thousand. But I could go back in the records and point out the date it began to fall apart. It was in the early 1950s. That Sunday night I was walking down the hall when the president of an older adult union came out of their room. Seeing me, he said, "Preacher, I've had it! I have pushed and pushed to keep this thing going, but it's no use!" For some reason, a domino effect took place as the entire Training Union attendance started a downward trend. However, it was not confined to our church. It seemed to have been happening throughout the Southern Baptist Convention. Since that time, churches have been struggling to keep it going. Even so, the format is quite different from former years, and in my judgment is not as effective.

I may sound like an old man looking back to the "good old days" that never were, but I have lived long enough to see the products of the two systems. And in my judgment, the products of the old were far superior to those of the new. For example, in churches with which I am familiar, the Discipleship Training program consists of people knowledgeable in certain fields *teaching* various groups. They inform minds but do not develop skills in others by involving the members of the group in actually presenting the *program*.

When we went to Oklahoma City, George Bond, now deceased, was secretary of the Sunday School. He was an expert in dealing with figures, but he was mortally afraid to stand on his feet and speak to a group of people. In the business world he was secretary of a large savings and loan company. One day he told me the following story:

This fear not only held him back in church work but in his business career as well. He had consistently refused to attend Training Union lest he be asked to speak in public. However, finally he was induced to attend Training Union with the promise that he would not be asked to do anything. But as time passed, watching others take part in presenting the programs, a desire was born in him to do the same. Finally, he asked if he might be permitted to present a small part. In his first effort he was like the man who said, "When I stood up my mind sat down." So he read his part, but he had spoken before a group! In due time he could look his audience in the eye and speak without fear. Eventually he began to lead in public prayer.

His victory in these things was followed by his rise in his company as well as in his church. Before he retired he was first, president, and then, chairman of the board of his company. At the same time he became one of the most effective leaders in our church. He credited all this to the Training Union.

Through the years we maintained a strong evangelistic emphasis, keeping in mind that it involved more than winning lost people. One year at Glorieta, I sat in a conference on evangelism conducted by Dr. Gaines S. Dobbins. One day someone asked, "But isn't conversion the end of evangelism?" He replied, "Yes. But which end?"

The Sunday School Board asked me to write a study course book titled *New Testament Evangelism*. In it I defined New Testament evangelism as being threefold: regeneration, sanctification, and glorification. Regeneration is the saving of the soul. Sanctification (being set apart for God's service) involves the saving of the Christian life. (In the New Testament, all Christians were called "saints," sanctified ones, or set apart ones. Though they did not act very saintly, in both of his letters to the Corinthian church, Paul addressed them as "saints.") Glorification refers to the sum total of glory and reward in heaven. The second you were regenerated, you were sanctified as the Holy Spirit indwelt your life. Your degree of glorification will be in direct ratio to your development and service in sanctification. So regeneration is not simply being *saved* and *done* with it. It marks the beginning of a pilgrimage with Christ which looks to its final culmination with Him in heaven.

Thus every phase of church life should be directed toward evangelism in this sense. Dr. Dobbins often remarked that many Sunday Schools simply counted noses and nickels—how many came and how much they gave. Trite but true is the saying that the process of evangelism is not finished until the evangelized become evangelists.

Of course, traditionally, the Sunday School has been the outreach arm of churches. But in evangelism we found the Christian recreation program was also very effective in reaching new people. Even while we were in the planning stage for recreation facilities Dave Prichard joined our staff as minister of Christian recreation. We wanted his input in planning them. The Sunday School Board had recently established a department of Christian recreation with our longtime friend Agnes Durant Pylant as its head. Dave spent much time with her in Nashville as together they pioneered this new area of ministry. He also was in demand as a consultant by other churches planning similar facilities and programs.

One day I was relating our plans to the head of the architectural department of the Sunday School Board. He was not enthusiastic as he noted the failure of such projects in the 1920s. My reply was that it was due to lack of personnel and a program to use them. If a church builds an educational building but has no planned program and personnel to utilize it, it, too, will fail. You cannot simply advertise in the newspaper that you have a beautiful new building, invite people to come, bring their Bibles, and study them. Such will not succeed. You need a plan of outreach to bring people in and a planned program led by the director and volunteer assistants when they come.

In our case every person using the recreation facilities was asked to register. Visitors were asked to fill out a form which gave us a religious census for the entire family. This information was furnished to other areas of the church program in which there was a follow-through. The record speaks for itself. Through almost forty years, people have been led to Christ and/or into the church fellowship by this means, who probably would not have been reached otherwise. Recently, Dave Prichard, now retired, told me that through these years, about one thousand people used the recreation facilities each week.

Another vital part of our church program was music. The sanctuary choir was one of the best. Our choir loft is a balcony over the baptistry, typical of churches built early in the century. One problem with this choir loft location is lack of proximity between the pastor and choir in worship services. To help this situation Dr. Howard had the church to install mirrors on the front of the balcony. In that way, he could at least see the choir. I always said that I had a ricochet romance with the choir.

At times consideration has been given to lowering the loft but has been dropped. For one thing, in my opinion, the music from that level is more brilliant. It hits the ear before being partially absorbed by people's clothing, the carpet, etc. No music was too difficult for this choir. Throughout each year it presented musical programs in keeping with the various seasons.

One year they sang *The Seven Last Words*, with Russell Newport singing the part of Jesus. It was to be sung on Sunday night before Easter.

Imagine my shock during Sunday School when I went to the auditorium to see that, using heavy brown paper painted to look like large rocks, they had built a mountain. It reached from the auditorium floor level to the top of the choir loft. A ramp had been built on which the cast could climb the mountain. Halfway up there was a small platform, but there was no place in the pulpit for me to stand. However, the mountain effect gave me an idea. I had the building engineer to put a chair on the small platform and run a microphone to that spot.

At the appointed time for the sermon, I walked up to the platform and sat down. Then, with as much vocal meaning as I could muster, I read the Sermon on the Mount. It took exactly fourteen minutes. I knew that I had the rapt attention of the congregation but was not sure how it affected the radio audience. Later I learned that it was excellent. After the service, one lady told me it was the best sermon she ever heard me preach. Of course it was! It was Jesus' sermon. I simply read it.

That night for the music program the auditorium was almost in total darkness. When special lighting effects were turned on, the *mountain* looked exactly like one. The bright lights came on in the choir balcony, revealing three crosses. On the end crosses were two men, dressed only in shorts. (The Romans crucified men naked.)

The music began, and we suddenly heard the beautiful voice of Russell Newport singing, "Behold, and see if there be any sorrow like unto my sorrow." As he sang, he entered the auditorium bearing a cross. The sanctuary choir formed the mob following him. As he sang, they went up the ramp into the choir loft. Stripped of his robe and wearing only shorts, he was lifted in place on his cross.

There he sang "The Seven Last Words." At intervals throughout these "Words," the mob uttered "Bah!" Later we were told that they were so moved as they uttered "Bah!" that tears streamed down their faces. It was a moving experience for the entire congregation. This presentation came during Cliff Baker's years as our minister of music.

The graded choir program founded by Bill Reynolds was continued under his successors: Archie McMillan, Bill McGraw, and Cliff Baker. The most memorable performance, and I dare say it was done by no other group anywhere, came from the Chapel Choir composed of more than fifty high school young people.

A former organist in our church, while working for the Sunday School Board, wrote *Good News*, a forty-five-minute musical for young people. Isis Tuel, a sanctuary choir member, is a native Mexican. Her parents, Mexicans themselves, were also missionaries in Mexico. So Isis translated *Good News* into Spanish and taught it to the Chapel Choir. (Isis also taught them to sing gospel hymns in Spanish.)

Their first performance was at the Mexican Baptist Church in Oklahoma City. A Cuban lady in our church heard it. Excitedly, she later told me, "There was not a bobble! And they sang without an *accent!*" Isis had taught them without an accent. And Cliff, who grew up in Rio de Janeiro where his parents were missionaries, speaks Portuguese and also understands Spanish, which helped in his directing the choir.

Then one Sunday night they sang it in our church. I will never forget the thrill I had when Phil Dean, now one of our deacons, cried, "*Que pasa!*" (What's happening or going on?). Then for forty-five minutes those young people sang in Spanish, purely from memory.

Their first tour was to Mexico. Wherever they went crowds of people heard them. The president of Mexico even had them to sing in his home one Sunday afternoon. I was scheduled to preach for four days at the Mexican Baptist Evangelistic Conference in Torreon, Mexico, while this choir was on this tour. They arranged their itinerary so as to spend two days singing at this conference. They were the *stars* of the meeting. Frances was with me, and we got closer to those young people there than ever we could in our church. At home we were just the pastor and wife, and they were the young people. But in Torreon we were a *team* engaged in mission work.

They were to leave on their bus one day before Frances and I flew home. Edna Dunn was one of the sponsors. It was her responsibility to purchase enough sandwiches for their lunch the next day. She spoke no Spanish, and I spoke very little. I was sitting in the hotel lobby when she was on her way to buy the food. Seeing me, she asked if I would help her. So we went to a nearby cafe. With my *jabbering* we let them know what we wanted. In short order we had the sandwiches.

Bright and early the next morning, Frances and I saw them on their way. They left as happy as only young people can be. Frances and I watched them leave, wishing we could go with them. We were filled with joyful pride to have such wonderful people and to know that we were a part of them.

The following year they made their second tour to South America. In the meantime, Isis had taught the choir to witness for Christ in Spanish. Such choirs singing in English were a dime a dozen in South America, but this one singing in Spanish was something else. They took South America like a storm!

Their first stop was in Bogota, Columbia. On Sunday morning the choir sang in the First Baptist Church. That afternoon they sang in a city park. While they were singing, a Catholic priest drove by. Seven years previously he had led a mob in throwing rocks at some of our missionaries. After hearing this choir he invited them to sing in his new cathedral building, which they did.

In Lima, Peru, missionaries had purchased television time for them to sing *Good News*. When the program director had heard them videotaping it, he told the missionaries that the station would not charge for the air time. Also, he was giving the choir a copy of the tape so that other stations on their itinerary could run it. They sang in Santiago, Chili; Buenos Aires, Argentina; Rio de Janeiro, Brazil; across the bay at Nicheroi, and surrounding areas. John Soren, pastor of the First Baptist Church in Rio, later told me that the choir blessed his church with their music, but the greatest blessing was that his young people saw how normal Christian young people in the United States are. It was quite an improvement over the picture they received from movies and television.

They continued their tour up the east coast of Brazil as far as Belem, where the Amazon River flows into the Atlantic. When they arrived in Miami, the parents and sister of Patty Tuel met the plane. She did not tell them how much she enjoyed the trip. She said, "Oh, Mama, Daddy, I witnessed in Spanish about Christ to a boy!"

Upon their return to Oklahoma City, the choir was asked to sing portions of *Good News* in Spanish on a local television station. At the same time they were in South America, Vice President Nelson Rockefeller was on a goodwill tour there. Wherever he went, demonstrators threw rocks at him. The emcee of this television program remarked about that. Then he said, "In the future, we should send this choir back down there for our goodwill tours."

Bear with me for one other word. The next year, this choir toured Scotland, England, Spain, and Portugal. One Sunday night in Spain, they sang *Good News* in a Baptist church. For the first time in history the Catholic-controlled Spanish government permitted a television station to televise a worship service in a non-Catholic church. In addition to the choir, it included a Baptist baptismal service. A Spanish news reporter wrote a brief story about this which appeared in an Oklahoma City paper. His point of emphasis was the government's permission to televise the service. His closing line was "A youth choir from the United States also sang." He reported the *effect* but practically ignored the *cause*.

I realize that it may seem that I have given an unusual amount of space to music, but I feel that the two items with which I have dealt were so unusual as to merit it.

It goes without saying that the church had a thriving Woman's Missionary Union. In every church these dear ladies are the missionary conscience of the churches. Frances taught in Sunday School and attended Training Union but always her first love was the WMU and missions. One year she refused to let the WMU elect her as their director. She had a strong conviction against heading any organization of the church. But at their request she advised and encouraged each director during our ministry in Oklahoma City and elsewhere.

A. T. Robertson used to refer to Luke 8:2-3 to describe the first Woman's Missionary Union. From that small beginning the women have ever led the way in world missions. I cannot speak for other conventions, but, in my judgment, the Woman's Missionary Union, auxiliary to the Southern Baptist Convention, has become the mightiest force for world missions in Christian history. Since 1889, the ladies of our church have kept pace with it. And may it ever be true!

But all was not smooth sailing. During my Oklahoma City ministry we had two major crises. The first came in 1954, in connection with grading the adult Sunday School classes. While the majority favored it, strong opposition came from two couples classes. Even they were willing to grade by age. They opposed grading by sex. Their phrase was that we wanted to "de-sex" their classes. This was not peculiar to our church. In many churches without couples classes, some, mostly women's classes, were opposed to age-grading.

J. D. Grey told of one such class in the First Baptist Church, New Orleans. He went into their class to talk about it. He said, "Now, ladies, we do not need to grade you by age. We just need some standard by which to grade. If you prefer, we can grade your class by *weight*." This produced a storm of protest. As one voice, they replied, "Oh, no! We'll grade by age!"

Speaking of J. D., he was one of the speakers at the Sunday School clinic in Mobile. Most of those present were educational directors, so J. D. said, "I hear that some of you are afraid of grading adults. Well, don't be afraid! We graded adults in our church. Of course, it cost us five educational directors, but I'm still there! So don't be afraid to do it!" He spoke in jest, and it was greeted by a roar of laughter.

But getting back to our church, we began approaching the matter in the fall of 1953, by bringing Lattimore Ewing, First Baptist Church, Lubbock, Texas, to our church for a week. It was planned that for five nights he would spend forty-five minutes explaining the plan and its value. Then for forty-five minutes the people would ask questions about it.

On Monday night a medium-sized crowd was present, mostly those opposed to the plan. Most of those who favored it felt it unnecessary to be there. That night the latter period was spent in making speeches against it, not in asking questions. So those favoring grading got on the phone telling those of like mind they had better be there if they wanted the proposed program. Tuesday night the crowd was much larger, and the debate was from both sides. On Wednesday Stanton Nash and I met with the adult superintendents and the chairman of the church's educational committee. It was agreed that the matter should be dropped for the time being.

That night the auditorium was packed. Both sides were ready to do battle. Instead, I spoke to the group. "We planned this week as a learning experience, but it is clear that you only want to debate the issue. To continue on this course would only harm the fellowship of the church, so we will not consider it further at this time. This is the night for our regular prayer meeting, so I ask that all of us get on our knees for prayer." After the prayer the people sat down and looked at me expectantly to see what came next. I shrugged my shoulders, extended my hands, and with a smile said, "Prayer meeting is over. Good night!" They went home, some happy, some disappointed, and some, no doubt, relieved.

But the matter would not go away. In January 1954, the youth activities building was nearing completion. It provided additional space for adult Sunday School, so the question of grading adults came up again. But the same opposition was also present. Finally the matter was discussed in the deacons' meeting. The leading spokesman against grading finally proposed that we grade the rest of the adults but have a separate department for couples classes, or that we grade throughout but have a graded couples class in each department.

Finally, we had a meeting of the adult superintendents and the educational committee. Frankly, I favored grading but also having a department of couples classes. However, by that time the adult superintendents and some members of the educational committee strongly felt that we should discontinue couples classes. So I finally said, "All right. We will either grade all the way or not at all." The matter was brought before the church with a recommendation that we proceed with the grading program. The church adopted the program but not without some opposition.

(At this point I want to make two observations. One criticism offered against couples classes is that they major in social life. In our case the fact is that these two classes set one night each week to visit prospects and then gather at one home for a social time. The second observation is that in the five years that I was pastor of these two classes, from one of them I baptized more adults than from any other class in our Sunday School.)

By the time the Sunday arrived that we had set to inaugurate this new program, these two classes had arranged to move to two other churches. Our loss was their gain. It was like a blood transfusion. From two small churches they began to grow and are now two of our best churches. Ironically, the following fall, a man who had strongly opposed adult grading in our church was elected superintendent of the Sunday School in his new church. I was told that the first thing he did was to grade adults. Most of those in these classes are with the Lord, but with one or two exceptions they remained my friends as long as they lived.

"Back at the ranch," the other two couples classes went along with the new program. In fact, the man who taught one of these classes taught a men's class for many years until his health no longer permitted it.

In all honesty, I must say that the new program did not produce the anticipated results. Also, in all honesty, I must add that it was not the fault of the program. As Henry Kittrell said in Mobile long ago, "It has one weakness, the human element. Will the people do it?" As a whole they did not do it! I offer Tom Marshall's class as Exhibit A that the program was/is based on sound principles. Following the *plan*, the church elected Tom as a teacher. We assigned him a classroom, six men as members, and a list of prospects. As I recall, in about a year that class had an enrollment of about forty-five men. Had every adult class done the same, you can see the tremendous growth our Sunday School would have experienced.

The history of Sunday Schools shows that the larger percentage of growth comes through new classes. (Statistics show that the greatest increase in church growth and baptisms comes through new churches.) A new class reaches its greatest growth in about eighteen months and then tapers off. Possibly two things are responsible for this. By that time the enrollment is such that if only half attend, it is a nice group; thus, incentive to seek new members lessens. Even more the cause is that looking after absentees and ministering to the needs of class members absorbs so much time that little is left for visiting prospective members.

Furthermore, adults soon lost their enthusiasm for promotion. If a stream continues to flow, the water remains fresh. Otherwise, it becomes stagnant. Long ago someone observed that the Dead Sea is dead because it is constantly taking in but, except for evaporation, is not giving out.

It would be humorous if it were not so tragic. In our church the people in Adult IV had a psychological hang-up about being promoted to Adult V. To them it was the end of the line. In an effort to break up that logjam, Tom Marshall persuaded his class as a body to move up to Adult V, which was the oldest department. But for reasons I need not state they moved back to Adult IV.

When we graded adults, Adult V was the largest department. For years Frances' policy had been to teach for three years in a certain adult age span, then move to another. Thus she was related to all adult ages. But in 1954, she began teaching in Adult V. Those dear ladies would not let her go, so she taught that class for nineteen years. One day she said, "If our class maintains an average attendance of forty-eight, I think we are doing pretty good." Now I dare say that the entire department does not do that. Why? The undertaker has taken them away! Adult IV feared it would happen to them if they were in Adult V. Now that is happening to them. *You can neither fool Mother Nature nor hide from Father Time!*

Recently, I heard that someone said I would not have graded adults had I not been pressured by the Sunday School Board. In reply to such an idea, let me say this. *At this writing (1992) I have been a pastor for sixty-four years. Not one time have I ever been pressured by any denominational agency—national, state, or associational—to do anything! What I have done has been by personal conviction and judgment as I felt led by the Holy Spirit and through the democratic processes of the local church. Being human, I have not always been right. But I have always been conscientious and free.*

Before leaving this matter of church growth, let me tell this true story. When I was a pastor in Montgomery, Alabama, we lived across from a small Methodist church. As far as I could tell, it was drying up on the vine. After we left there, it moved to another part of the city but did not astound the world with its growth. But under its present pastor, it began to grow so as to attract the attention of the entire city and even the nation. It is now one of the most rapidly growing churches in the nation.

People began flocking there from all over the city. Adults and young people were even leaving Baptist churches to go there. So much so that some Baptist pastors asked for a conference with the Methodist pastor to ascertain the secret of his church's growth. He told them he found an old book in a used book store on how to grow a Sunday School. Its author was Arthur Flake. And said he, "We are following it to the letter."

Now it just happened that Arthur Flake was a staff member of the Southern Baptist Sunday School Board. He wrote this book, the greatest ever written on that subject, but some years ago, it was discarded along with the rest of what I consider the greatest religious study course series in the world. I dare say that these young Baptist pastors had never heard of it. The irony of it is that this *Methodist* is taking our *method* and beating us to death with it!

In my judgment, our Sunday School Board could do us no greater service than to republish this book, flood our churches with it, and challenge our churches to have *week-long* study courses, something as extinct as the dinosaur, and teach our people the "nuts and bolts" of how to grow great Sunday Schools. And our churches could do no better than to follow it "to the letter." *Growing* churches are *going* churches.

The other crisis had to do with racial segregation. Our church plant is located less than three blocks from the largest concentration of black people in our city. We had no black members. None had ever requested to be admitted to our fellowship although we had no policy or attitude against black people worshipping with us. A black preacher from Enid often attended our services. When I knew of his presence I always asked him to lead us in the benediction. For a long time a fine-looking black man attended our morning service regularly, but after the event which I will relate he never came again. He apparently did not want people to think he was a party to such.

In May 1961, I was elected president of the Southern Baptist Convention. The civil rights struggle was on. In the July meeting of the deacons, I told them that it was possible that our church could become a test case in the struggle. If a black person presented himself/herself for membership, we should know how to handle it. After discussing it among themselves, someone said, "Well, let the preacher handle it. He'll know what to do." I replied, "Yeah, good old preacher! If that be the case, I'll tell you what I will do. I will follow the church by-laws. Before I came as your pastor you passed a by-law to the effect that if a person came for membership and there was one negative vote, it would be referred to the deacons for study and recommendation to the church. It was done, not to keep black people out of our church, but to prevent certain white people from being received without due study. So if a black person comes forward I will present it to the church as we do with all people. If there is one negative vote, I will refer it to you." Someone asked what if there was no negative vote. I said, "Then you will have a black member." Everyone laughed, and that ended it.

After the meeting one deacon told me he thought it was a mistake to bring up the matter. Perhaps no one would come. This would simply start people talking. But I assured him it would happen, and at least, we knew what we would do. (In another prominent Southern Baptist church the pastor presented this matter; the deacons refused even to discuss it. When it happened they really had a mess on their hands.)

On Friday before the first Sunday in September in 1961, an item appeared in the newspaper. On the following Sunday, black young people, led by the youth director of the NAACP, would picket four churches: Methodist, Christian, Presbyterian, and ours. I told Tom Stevens, our head usher, to have his crew on duty before the Sunday School hour. If they came at that time the ushers should take each of them to the department and class where they belonged by age, just as we did white young people. If they did not arrive until the worship hour, they were to be invited in and seated in the best seats available, just as we did white people.

On Sunday morning, when Frances and I arrived at the church before Sunday School, we were greeted by about fifty black young people marching in front of the building carrying signs. One read "Welcome Negro Haters!" This was obviously an untruth. Also there stood good old Tom on the top step leading into the auditorium. Of course, the press was out in force. A cameraman from one of the TV stations was there. He took pictures of Tom with a big smile gesturing toward the open church door as he invited the young people into the building. Of course, they ignored him.

That night the station carried the story on the evening news. The newsman gave them "fits," because, as he said, these young people did not come to worship but to demonstrate. Newspapers gave much the same comments. The following Saturday the newspaper carried a half-page story with pictures of three black pastors and their criticism of the demonstration.

The first Sunday in October they were back but with a much smaller group. There was a cold rain falling on the first Sunday in November. Only about a half-dozen showed up. On both of these Sundays the ushers were on duty with a warm welcome, which was ignored. On Friday before the first Sunday in December another item appeared in the paper. It stated that on the following Sunday morning one of these young people would try to join each of these four churches. The stated reason was "to keep our movement alive."

In our worship service that Sunday morning, a sixteen-year-old boy was present along with the youth leader. People sitting around them later told me what happened. At the "invitation," the young man did not want to go forward, but the leader pushed him into and down the aisle. I shook his hand as I did for several families who came forward. One by one the family groups were received by unanimous vote. In the young man's case there were only two negative votes, by a man and his wife. Otherwise, the vote was positive.

So I explained to him the by-law and said the matter would be referred to the deacons. In turn they would appoint a committee that would meet with him, but I told him I wanted him to stand in line with the others so that the people could shake his hand and get acquainted with him.

The chairman of the committee told me the meeting would be the next Thursday night. When I told him I would have to be in Nashville that night, he said, "That's fine! We do not want you there. Should the meeting be unpleasant but the church later receives him, you will be his pastor. I think it would be better if you are not involved."

In Nashville, Porter Routh, a former deacon in our church, asked what I thought the church would do. I said I thought he would be received. But when I returned, the chairman said they were recommending that he not be received. Before the meeting the committee favored receiving him. But in the meeting, instead of talking with the committee, the young man gave them a tongue lashing. He said, "I did not come for fellowship in this church but to break a racial barrier." The committee agreed that they would not recommend a white person with that attitude.

At a called meeting of the deacons they agreed to pass this recommendation on to the church. At that point I said, "I will have to administrate whatever action the church takes. As I understand it, this means that the young man is entitled to all the privileges and activities of the church other than being a member of the fellowship." The deacons agreed. The recommendation was adopted by the church with this understanding.

So I asked him to come to see me. I explained the meaning of the action. Then I said, "You are a victim of circumstances not of your making. If you will come and participate in church activities for six months and prove to the church that you have the right attitude, the church will receive you as a member. And I will recommend it. Also, members of our church have established scholarships at Oklahoma Baptist University, and I have authority to assign them. When you graduate from high school I will see to it that you will have a four-year scholarship to that school so that you can be certain of a college education." He agreed. Our young people accepted him as one of them. But after about three weeks he returned to the church of which he was a member.

Now hear "the rest of the story." In August 1965, I received a letter from Mrs. Maud Henderson, a black woman and a retired school teacher. She was a member of another black church. In her letter she said that her church was always in a fuss about something, and she wanted to go where she could worship God in peace. Having heard me on the radio, she would like to join our church. If we did not receive her, she would understand and try elsewhere.

I read her letter to the deacons, and they encouraged me to visit her. I told her we would be happy to have her come, but I could not guarantee that she would be received, even as I could not give that assurance to anyone else. But I said I had every reason to believe that the church would receive her. (In the meantime the church had repealed the by-law about one negative vote.) Also, I encouraged her to ask her husband, a deacon, to come with her. She had already done that, but he had refused. They had a daughter who held a masters degree in education from the University of Oklahoma. Her husband had a doctor of philosophy degree in the same field. And they had two lovely children. I suggested that they come with her. She had already asked them, but they said they wanted to "stay with Papa." I wanted some of her family to come with her so as to make the transition easier for her.

Nevertheless, she joined our church the following Sunday and was received with only a few negative votes. That week she called the church office to learn into what Sunday School class she should go and the name of the teacher. On Sunday she was there and asked to be shown to that class. The departmental secretary was the wife of the department director. When the class secretary brought her class report, she asked, "Why did you bring her into our class?" Her reply, "Because she asked for that class! My husband and I did not vote to receive her, but the church did. As far as we are concerned, she is entitled to the same rights and privileges as any other member of this church." That settled it.

I told some other members I wished all the members measured up to her. She tithed, attended Sunday School, worship services, and WMU. And if she knew she would be out of town on Sunday, she would call and tell me.

But an ironic twist took place in her life. In Oklahoma City is a black nursing home which was in dire need of volunteer workers. They wrote to the president of our Woman's Missionary Union asking if any of our ladies would volunteer. When the letter was read at the monthly general meeting, Maud said, "That is something I can do in my church."

When she showed up among the volunteers, they would not let her help. They told her that if their churches were not good enough for her, she was not good enough to help in their nursing center. She paid a price for a place where she could worship in peace.

She continued to be a faithful member of our church until she died long after I retired from the pastorate. Maud Henderson is now in heaven, and I am proud to have been her pastor!

Speaking of nursing homes reminds me of another ministry of our church during my tenure there—a ministry to patients in nursing homes. This ministry was under the direction of Dr. J. W. Hodges, who was my associate pastor for many years. It finally involved twenty-eight homes. According to the extension department of the Sunday School Board, insofar as they knew, it was the first of its kind on so large a scale.

The administrators of these nursing homes were somewhat leery when Dr. Hodges first approached them. They had had some unfortunate experiences with extremist groups. But he convinced them that our program would be sound. It was well accepted by all of them.

Groups of our people were organized, each being assigned a home. Once each week they went to these homes for a worship service for ambulatory patients. It involved singing, prayer, and Bible study. The *message* was to teach the Sunday School lesson for the following Sunday. Afterward, they would visit and pray with the bedridden patients. So many of these people had no family, at least living nearby.

As often as possible, I would accompany some group. I also would visit the bed patients. One such visit was typical. I asked a little lady how she was feeling. She replied, "Oh, all right I guess. But I am so lonely!" Those little visits let them know that somebody cared. One of our members said to me, "That is the only purely unselfish service we render. They cannot attend our services to swell the crowd. Neither do they contribute financially to our church." It certainly fitted our Lord's words when He said, "I was sick and ye visited me."

I want to close this chapter by mentioning a *breakthrough* in our church's ministry. It is what we chose to call our "Good Shepherd Ministry." It is a ministry to the underprivileged. For years the church had wanted such a ministry to a large area between our location and the heart of the downtown area. Dr. W. R. White said that when he was the pastor he would look upon that mass of people and covet them for the Lord. But they had been so exploited by others that they were suspicious of any effort to help them. It was evident that in order to reach them we must overcome that attitude. And I believe that God put into our minds the idea as to how to do it.

The children in that community attended the same school. When we explained to the principal our proposed program, we obtained names and addresses of the parents. In turn, we received their cooperation. Each Tuesday, at the end of the school day, we had a bus at the school. We brought the children to our gymnasium where they roller-skated for two hours. After refreshments the bus delivered the children at their homes.

This continued for a year. During this time we never mentioned Sunday School. Occasionally, a child would ask where he/she should go if attending Sunday School, and we would tell them. But each child was asked to fill out a card giving his/her name and the names of the parents and others in the family—with their religious preferences. Thus we had a religious census of the families.

After a year, we were ready to try to enlist all these in various church activities, feeling that they knew by that time that we loved them for themselves. At that very time the Lord provided leadership for the endeavor. Susan Miller of our church was chairman of the board for the associational Baptist Rescue Mission. Two of their volunteer workers were Mr. and Mrs. Butch Price. They had expressed to Susan their desire to get into a program for underprivileged people that was sponsored by a local church. She told me about it. So Frances, Susan, and I had lunch with the Prices. They were happy to become the leaders of this new endeavor. They had been trained by the Home Mission Board for such work. We agreed to call it the Good Shepherd Department of our church, with a program which paralleled the total program of our church. They requested that we not pay for their services. Butch worked for Sears, Roebuck Company. Their only request was that room be provided for their own apartment in a two-story building on our block. Since the owner did not wish to sell the house, we had rented it. Later they did sell it to the church. The Prices owned their own home, but would rent it out. They wanted to live on the second floor of this house so as to be available should any of the people need them. The lower floor would be used for weekday activities. For Sunday services they used a portion of the church building. One of our ladies, Manila James, gave the church a bus for use in bringing people to the church.

To begin the work the Prices visited every family we had in our "census." To our delight they reported that never before had they been so cordially received. The skating program had broken down the "middle wall of partition." So the longtime dream was on its way. In a very short time the Good Shepherd program had an enrollment of about three hundred. Volunteers from the "Mother Church" assisted with the teaching. Butch did the preaching. People won to the Lord and His church were received as members of our church. But the Prices warned against trying to mix these people with the "Mother Church." "If you try, you will lose them," said they. "If one is ready for that, we will tell you."

I recall one young man who also is named Butch. He was saved, baptized, and later called into the ministry. He attended

Hardin-Simmons University. I am sure he is a pastor in his own right now.

One day Butch Price came to me with a problem. Some of the young people wanted to get married. Though he was not ordained, he was the only *pastor* they had ever known. Well, we took care of that; we ordained him. And I trust that the couples are living happily ever after.

This ministry is now at least twenty-five years old. Only eternity will reveal its fruits. Under Dr. Garrison's leadership, this work continues to grow and to expand its ministry. In addition, the church now has a similar ministry for Hispanics, Koreans, and Vietnamese. Each Sunday morning in our building, we have five Sunday Schools and worship services. The language groups have their own native pastors.

Our church is engaged in bearing witness for Christ "in Jerusalem [city missions], and in all Judaea [associational missions], and in Samaria [Home Missions], and unto the uttermost part of the earth [Foreign Missions]" (Acts 1:8). Also, it has it in embryo under the roof of our building in Oklahoma City. And so may it ever be!

No record of our ministry in Oklahoma City would be complete without brief mention of the annual "Gridiron." It may be going from the sublime to the ridiculous, but I know of no better way to show the wonderful fellowship we enjoyed as pastor's family and people. We worked hard together, but we also had fun together.

Due to bad weather, January usually saw a drop in Sunday School attendance. In order to counteract this, the two youngest adult departments had an attendance contest. In February they had a dinner with the loser paying the bill. After the dinner a cast from both departments put on the Gridiron. It was a takeoff on staff members and highest elected church officers. They wrote their own script, including words adapted to popular song tunes. Dick—oh excuse me, Dr. Richard Clay—was the principal script writer.

After each Gridiron they immediately started working on the one for the following year. As the pastor, I was the principal target. Emzy Saul, a dentist, always played my part. He studied me like a book—for instance, how I carried my Bible, any pulpit mannerisms of which I was unaware. Naturally, he overdid it in his takeoff of me, but that was where the fun lay. I use myself as an example, but all came in for a ribbing.

Each Gridiron had a different theme. For instance, in 1955, Frances and I made our first trip to Europe and the Holy Land. That year a feature song was "How You Gonna Get Heem Back een the Pulpit After He's Seen Paree?" It was sung to the tune of a World War I song, "How're You Gonna Get Them Back on the Farm After They've Seen Paree?" Nita Lee was cute as a button. She sang it dressed in a costume of a Parisian girl.

During the song, she left the stage, came to me, and ruffled up my hair as she sang. Of course, I entered the fun by swooning at the attention of such a beautiful girl. That really brought the house down. To this day I call her "my Fifi." That gives you some idea of the format. It became such a popular event that finally they had to put it on for three successive nights to accommodate all who wanted to see it.

One night one of our ladies brought a lady from another church of a different denomination. She was shocked beyond words that a church would treat its pastor so. But Frances and I loved it. The rest of the year they treated me with the utmost respect as their pastor, but that night everyone let his/her hair down and had fun. Each year I had less hair to let down.

As for the woman's reaction, it would have worried me had they stopped it. For it formed a bond of love between us and the entire church that I dare say could not have been done any other way. I am sure that it deepened our mutual love which continues until this day.

I must relate a far-reaching service rendered, not by me, but by Frances. One day she was with Mrs. Prichard. She asked Frances, "Honey, I am rewriting my will. Do you have any suggestions?" Frances said, "Yes, I have one. When Herschel and I were in college and our money ran out, there was a fund at the school from which we could draw a few dollars to tide us over until payday. I have long wished someone would establish a fund at OBU for scholarships for ministerial students." Mrs. Prichard said, "I like that."

Frances was thinking of a few hundred thousand dollars. But when finally Mrs. Prichard's will was read, she had left all of her estate, except a few family bequests, to OBU for that purpose. It amounted to five million dollars! Eventually, the sum will be about seven million dollars. I understand that as a result OBU has more ministerial students than any other Baptist college or university.

Both Mrs. Prichard and Frances are with the Lord, but they will continue to serve the Lord until He returns.

Precious memories! And how they bless my soul!

Jerry was ten years old when we moved to Oklahoma City. But as kids will do, he grew into a fine man. In 1966, he married Jennifer Fields. She is a wonderful Hoosier from Bloomington, Indiana. When she was born, a lady visited her mother in the hospital. Seeing the baby, she said, "She's a beautiful cookie!" And "Cookie" she is to this day—the sweetest Cookie you will ever see. They presented us with two lovely granddaughters—Sheri and Brandi. Space does not permit me to list their superlative qualities! They all live in Houston, Texas, and are the crowning joy of my declining years.

Many states have "Halls of Fame." Many induct people only after they have died. Oklahoma inducts the living. To read the membership makes one proud to be an Oklahoman. It includes people of national and international fame. A person does not know that he/she is being considered, and one negative vote disqualifies the candidate. Inductees are elected in April and inducted at a large banquet on Statehood night, November 16.

One Saturday morning in April 1963, I was reading the morning newspaper. In passing, I noticed a headline "Five Elected to Oklahoma Hall of Fame." I did not read it but thought, "How nice!"

At a brunch that morning, ladies kept saying to Frances, "Congratulations!" She smiled and thanked them. Finally, one lady said, "You have no idea what we are talking about, do you?" Frances said, "No, I don't." The lady said, "Your husband was elected to the Oklahoma Hall of Fame last night!" (A letter had not had time to reach me to inform me officially!)

Well, Frances called me. I read the article, and there it was! It was the last thing I ever expected to happen to me, especially since I was not a native of Oklahoma. I was inducted the following November. Each year thereafter, as Frances and I drove home after seeing who had been inducted, I asked her, "Honey, how did I ever make it?" And, you know, I still ask myself that.

While on the subject, in 1964, I received the second "E. Y. Mullins Denominational Award" from Southern Baptist Theological Seminary. Dr. Duke McCall presented it to me at the Southern Baptist Convention in Atlantic City, New Jersey.

Lest I be accused of bragging, I quote the lovable TV character Will Sonnett, "Not bragging! Just facts!"

I retired from the pastorate January 1, 1973. But thanks to the Lord and the brethren, I have been busier than ever before. When the Lord calls me home, I hope I am so busy I will run a block before I fall.

But that is getting ahead of the story.

11

Fellow Laborers Belonging to God

In his first letter to the Corinthian church, Paul dealt with the problems which plagued its fellowship. One of these was divided loyalty to preachers (1 Cor. 1:11-12). Using himself and Apollos as examples, he showed they were not men over which to fight but laborers in the Lord's work (1 Cor. 3:4-7). "For we are laborers together with God" (3:9, KJV). The *New King James Version* reads, "For we are God's fellow workers." When I read these translations I see us working with God as His equals, but this was not the intent of the translators. The Greek allows a better rendering. "For we (Paul and Apollos) are fellow-laborers belonging to God."

In John 17:22, Jesus prayed for all who believe in Him as Savior: "That they may be one just as We are one" (NKJV). This is seen by many as a proof text teaching ecumenicalism (see v. 21), the ultimate end of which is one super church. However, Jesus was not thinking of the eleven apostles being one man the size of eleven men. The key is "just as We are." The Father and Son are two distinct Persons in the Godhead, but they are one in spirit and purpose. It is an anachronism to speak of denominations in the New Testament. They are later developments which have emerged through the centuries. Each has its own polity and program. The oneness for which Jesus prayed is not in *body* but in *spirit* and *purpose*. (I am assuming those individuals who truly have believed in Jesus Christ as Savior are committed to evangelizing the world in His name.) John Wesley said, "If thy heart be as my heart, give me thy hand." This is not *organic union* but *Christian unity*.

Thus, like most other Baptists, through the years I have worked alongside other believers of other bodies in matters of mutual interest which did not involve a compromise of my own faith. At the same time, I have always been, and still am, a committed Southern Baptist. I have not always been, neither am I now, in full agreement with everything Southern Baptists have done. The old saying is true. "If you get two Baptists together you will have three opinions." That's the fun of being Baptists. But as a part of the Southern Baptist fellowship, I have always tried to cooperate in whatever we do. I am like the Irishman who when asked if he were not an Irishman what would he be, said, "Faith, and I would be ashamed of meself!"

Many years ago in Oklahoma City, Don Powell was one of our deacons. He is the son of Dr. Sidney Powell, a leader in the American Baptist Convention. He often visited his son and family. One Sunday night he preached for us. On one occasion we ate lunch together. In the course of our conversation he said, "In the American Baptist Convention, we meet annually and adopt programs, but we seem to go home and forget about them. In your Convention, you adopt programs, and then go home, roll up your sleeves, go to work, and carry out the programs." Then he asked, "What kind of pressure do you put on your people to get their cooperation?" I replied, "In the thirty-five years as a pastor [at that time] I have never felt the pressure of anyone's little finger to get me and my church to cooperate. The only pressure I feel is the obligation to cooperate with my brethren in accomplishing the Lord's work. We believe that we do best that which we do together."

Southern Baptists are a mystery both to the world and to themselves. With no organic connection between Baptist bodies from the local churches through the Southern Baptist Convention, Southern Baptists carry on a program across our nation and throughout the world.

The financial heart of all this is the Cooperative Program plus the Lottie Moon, Annie Armstrong, and state missionary offerings. Wherever Frances and I have visited mission fields around the world, we found one thing in common. The missionaries point out new stations, missionaries, and equipment, and say that it comes through "Lottie" and "Annie." But with the same breath they would add, "But don't forget the Cooperative Program, for it is our lifeline." It is not either/or but both/and. In times of recession, when many other Christian groups have been forced to close mission stations and recall missionaries, Southern Baptists have been able to enter new mission fields and appoint more missionaries.

Dr. M. E. Dodd's committee, which presented the Cooperative Program to the Southern Baptist Convention in 1925, was composed of brilliant people, but I do not believe they were smart enough to concoct such a program. I fully believe that it was revealed to them by God through His Holy Spirit!

The statement I am about to make is mine and mine alone, but I fully believe that one of the most dangerous things to come out of the extended controversy since 1979 is the plan to alter the channel through which our missionary giving flows. The adage is ever true. *"If it's working, don't fix it!"*

When I wrote "11" at the top of the first page of this chapter, it was/is my purpose to write about my privilege to serve in the Convention outside the local church. Instead, I have thus far written in more general terms. I have sound biblical grounds for this digression. In Ephesians 3:1, Paul started to pray, but he digressed to discuss another matter. Thus in 3:14, he returned to his prayer. So now, having digressed, I return to my original purpose. I suppose it is natural that every person aspires to be recognized in his profession and/or calling. However, there is a great difference between *aspiring* and *conspiring* to achieve it. I have never conspired.

In my first pastorate after seminary days, I felt that if I were appointed a member of the associational obituary committee, I would have it made. Well, I have never been a member of any obituary committee, so I suppose that I will have to wait until I am a part of some such committee's report. But by the grace of God and the goodness of the brethren, I have been privileged to serve in almost every other capacity in the Southern Baptist Convention, state conventions, and local associations. I have often said that if I had received one dollar for every hour spent sitting on boards and committees I could tell the Annuity Board and Social Security to remove my name from their check mailing list. But, brethren, don't do it, for like everyone else, I served *gratis*.

Oh yes, one year, without my knowledge, I was nominated for president of the Baptist General Convention of Oklahoma. It was on a Thursday afternoon, which was my day to play golf. Thinking that nothing much would happen, I must confess that I was on the golf course. They elected the pastor of a rural church. Stanton Nash said that I might have made it if I had known how to milk a cow. Later, I was elected for one year, the limit in Oklahoma.

It was in San Antonio in 1942 that I received my first Southern Baptist Convention responsibility as a member of the resolutions committee. Dr. J. Howard Williams was its chairman. In those days it was very simple, consisting largely of resolutions of appreciation for the hospitality of the city and to the local committee. Later, I served as chairman of this committee, twice, as a favor to friends who were presidents of the Convention. By that time the number of resolutions had increased enormously—so much so that someone remarked that members of the committee did not have time to attend the Convention. At that time, a live issue was whether or not to change the name of the Convention. Many suggestions had been offered. In one of my reports, I added another, the Resoluting Baptist Convention.

At the San Antonio meeting, I also was elected as the Louisiana member of the Foreign Mission Board. When Dr. C. E. Maddry retired, I was appointed to serve on the commitee to nominate his successor. We readily agreed not to consider anyone then connected with the foreign missions work. Due to World War II, there was no meeting of the Convention in 1943. For about a year we considered a number of people but interviewed no one. In each case one thing or another blocked us from doing so.

In 1944 the Convention met in Atlanta. We held a pre-Convention meeting at the Biltmore Hotel. Dr. and Mrs. M. Theron Rankin were staying in that hotel. At the time, he was the secretary for our mission work in the Orient. The chairman of our committee was a lawyer from Knoxville, Tennessee. When our meeting started, he noted the difficulties sustained thus far. Then he said, "I wonder if we did not make a mistake in our decision not to consider anyone then connected with the Foreign Mission Board."

We all agreed. Then he added, "Without mentioning any names, I want us to have a season of prayer for the Lord's leadership. After which I want each of you to write on a piece of paper the name of the person you feel we should choose." When the secretary read the names, each of us had written the name of M. Theron Rankin! This was one of the most outstanding experiences I have had as to the leadership of the Holy Spirit. I realized more clearly that, as He directed the spread of the gospel in the first century, He is still doing it today.

When the chairman called his room, he found Dr. Rankin there. At the chairman's invitation, he soon arrived at our meeting place. He much preferred remaining in his position in the Orient. But, like the committee, he could not deny the leadership of the Holy Spirit. So, he was nominated and unanimously elected by the Foreign Mission Board. History records the Spirit's blessings upon his leadership.

Upon moving to Dauphin Way in Mobile January 1, 1945, I automatically went off the Foreign Mission Board. Soon thereafter I received a request from Dr. Duke K. McCall, then president of Baptist Bible Institute, to allow my name to be presented for election to fill a member-at-large vacancy on its Board. During my term of service there, three significant things took place. The name of the school was changed to New Orleans Baptist Theological Seminary. Dr. McCall became the executive secretary-treasurer of the Executive Committee of the Southern Baptist Convention and was succeeded by Dr. Roland Q. Leavell, then pastor of First Baptist Church, Tampa, Florida. And the site of the present campus was purchased. The last calls for special comment.

This site was the last large tract of land in New Orleans without crossing a body of water. It was located on U.S. Highway 90, then the main traffic artery running east and west along the Gulf Coast. The Roman Catholic archbishop had his eye on that land on which to build a cathedral with a Catholic community around it.

In the meantime, the Southern Baptist Convention had authorized the trustees of the seminary to locate and purchase a new site for the school, even appropriating whatever funds necessary for the transaction. So one morning the trustees voted to purchase the land. That afternoon Roland Leavell closed the deal, paying cash. As I recall, the amount was $260,000.

The next morning, two representatives of the archbishop appeared to buy the land, only to be told that the Baptists bought it the day before. There was no rivalry involved. It was simply a sequence of events. Incidentally, it was about that time, or a few years later, that the non-Catholic groups paid a professional census company to take a religious census of New Orleans. It showed that for the first time, non-Catholics outnumbered the Catholics by a few percentage points. Through the years, New Orleans Baptist Theological Seminary has been a major factor in the continued growth of Baptists along the Gulf Coast and throughout the Deep South.

Already I have related how my going to Oklahoma City involved me in the leadership of the Pastors Conference. This ended in 1951, at San Francisco. At that convention, Dr. Henry G. Bennett, president of Oklahoma A & M (now Oklahoma State University), was elected as an Oklahoma member of the Southern Baptist Convention Executive Committee. However, he never attended a meeting because he and Mrs. Bennett died in a plane crash in Iran. The Executive Committee requested that the Baptist General Convention of Oklahoma nominate a replacement for Dr. Bennett. I was their nominee.

At my first meeting with the committee, I was appointed to serve on the finance (now the program) committee. I served on this committee for twelve years. When I became a member of this committee, Louie Newton was chairman. When he rotated off the Executive Committee, Douglas Hudgins became chairman. Through the same process, I succeeded Doug as chairman.

In my judgment, this is one of the most important and hardest working committees in the Convention. In addition to its regularly assigned duties such as allocating funds for the budgets of all the Convention agencies, this committee serves as a "catch all" for matters assigned by the Convention to the Executive Committee, which naturally did not go to some other subcommittee. Whenever problems arose between agencies as to which one had responsibility in a given area, it was this committee's responsibility to work with these agencies in solving the problem.

Finally, so many such problems were arising that the Convention voted to publish an *Operations Manual*. It was assigned to the Executive Committee, and, you guessed it, in turn it was referred to the program committee. Albert McClellan was the staff member who worked with this committee. At the time, I was its chairman. Although I was chairman, I came without a thought as to where to begin. It was like trying to pick up an elephant, and I did not even know where to take hold of it.

When we entered the room where we were to work, on the conference table at each committee member's place, there was a stack of mimeographed paper more than a foot high. Albert and his staff had gone through every Southern Baptist Convention Annual from 1845 to the present (at that time) and put on these mimeographed sheets every action of the Convention assigning to each specific agency its responsibility. All we had to do was examine them and arrange them in their proper place. In short order, we had the copy ready for typing and being turned over to the printer. Without that preliminary preparation I am not sure we would have ever completed our job, certainly only after much time elapsed.

I have often said that if you start out to shoot all the fools in the SBC, don't shoot Albert McClellan until just before sundown. Southern Baptists will never know their debt to him. Neither can they ever repay it.

Shortly after I retired from the pastorate, I was elected a trustee of the Southern Baptist Theological Seminary. Due to conflicting engagements, I was unable to attend the first two meetings. I wrote Duke McCall to send me future meeting dates so that I could protect them. He sent me the dates through 2021. I wrote him that I was not sure about the other dates but that I would do my best to be there in 2021.

While on the board, I was asked to be national cochairman of two fund-raising campaigns. One was for $500,000 to fund the Billy Graham Chair of Evangelism. We raised about $750,000. The second campaign was for endowment and campus improvements. The goal was $10 million. We raised about $12 million. More recently (1990-1991), I served for one year as national chairman to raise needed funds resulting from the SBC Executive Committee freezing allocations to agencies. I do not recall the amount raised, but it was sufficient for the need.

In 1955, Frances and I, son Jerry and nephew Henry L. Lyon III, made our first of many trips to Europe and the Holy Land. In Egypt, on a visit to the giant pyramid at Gizeh and the nearby Sphinx, I got my first lesson in a tourist trading with the Arabs. A small boy offered to sell me for one dollar a *scarab*, the sacred beetle of ancient Egypt. He said it had come from the tomb of one of the ancient pharaohs. I bought it, thinking that when I got home I would really have something to show the people. When we returned to our hotel in Cairo, I turned on a light to examine it. When I looked on the underside, I was greeted with the words "Made in Japan!"

Well, at least it prepared me for other visits to the Holy Land, so I suppose it was a dollar well *lost*. I am like the little boy, who on the way home from church, was listening to his family criticize the pastor's sermon, the choir's singing, and the organist's playing. Finally, they asked the youngest son's opinion. He said, "I thought it was a pretty good show for a nickel."

After this first trip, Frances and I agreed that the biblical events had to have been as the Bible records them. On later trips, my primary interest was to see how archaeology has vindicated the Scriptures where their accuracy had been questioned. Archaeology has been and is one of the greatest friends the Bible has. My faith in the Bible has never wavered, but it is gratifying to see tangible evidence which verifies faith.

In 1959 the Foreign Mission Board requested that Ramsey Pollard and I represent Southern Baptists at the seventieth anniversary of the beginning of our mission work in Japan. People in our churches made it possible for our wives to accompany us. At the time, Ramsey was president of the Convention. No one knew that in 1961, I would succeed him, but that, plus our friendship, made it a happy combination.

Baker James Cauthen told us that if we could take the extra time, it would be as cheap to go on around the world as to return the way we had gone. We agreed to do so. I hope we helped the missionaries, but I know that they helped us to gain a greater perspective of our total foreign mission work. Since then, I have been able to tell people over the Convention that we get full value and more for every missionary dollar we spend.

In 1965, I was elected North American vice president of the Baptist World Alliance. Dr. William R. Tolbert, Jr., vice president and later president of Liberia, was elected president of the Alliance. Since the Alliance's headquarters are in Washington, D.C., and he lived in Africa, he asked me to serve as his "deputy." This involved me more in its work so that I gained a greater appreciation for our world Baptist fellowship.

In 1957 in Chicago, I was privileged to preach the annual Convention sermon. We met only a few blocks from the White Sox ball field. The game began at 1:30 p.m., and a large portion of the messengers had tickets. I knew they would leave shortly after noon. The sermon was scheduled for 11:00 a.m.

As often happens, the Convention became embroiled in a debate which lasted until long after 11:30. I was in a huddle with Casper Warren, president, and Porter Routh. I wanted Casper to shut off the debate so I could preach. J. D. Grey was sitting with Frances. He knew what was happening, but he said to her, "Now isn't that sweet. Casper and Porter know how much this sermon means to Herschel, so they are down there praying with him." I can assure you that it was not a prayer meeting!

Finally, I got to preach about noon. It probably was a better sermon by cutting it short. Anyway, we got out in time for the "national past timers" to get to the game.

I did not want any future preacher to go through that experience. So at the Executive Committee's next meeting I proposed that it offer at the next Convention a recommendation that all business cease in order to hear the sermon when the time came for it in future Conventions. Such was adopted at the next annual Convention. Since that time, that has been done.

A good example of that took place in Indianapolis in 1992. At exactly 11:00 a.m., right in the middle of a lengthy business session, President Chapman called a halt. And in a worshipful atmosphere we heard the sermon.

Two phases of my denominational ministry were the "Baptist Hour" and my writing ministry. Both opened to me in a somewhat unexpected manner.

In the spring of 1958, I received a telegram from Paul Stevens, head of the Southern Baptist Radio and Television Commission. He asked me to record my sermon the following Sunday morning and send the tape to him by Tuesday morning at the Brown Hotel, Louisville, Kentucky. He said nothing as to his purpose for this. I told Stanton Nash that I supposed Paul was teaching a class at Southern Seminary on religious broadcasting and wanted my tape to show how not to do it.

I told Stanton that the sermon I planned for the following Sunday was of such nature that I did not want to accede to the request. Later he called me. "Pastor," he said, "why don't you let me record the sermon. Then you can listen to it. If you still feel as you stated, we can forget it. If you change your mind, I will mail the tape as requested." I agreed. The sermon sounded better than I expected, so he mailed it.

On Wednesday afternoon I received a call from Ed Arendall, chairman of the "Baptist Hour" committee of the Commission. They had asked forty-eight pastors to send tapes. In order not to prejudice anyone for or against any preacher, they numbered rather than named them. Of course, they kept a list matching numbers with names. Tuesday and Wednesday had been spent listening to the tapes. By the process of elimination they had chosen one. It turned out to be my tape. Ed called to ask if I would preach on the "Baptist Hour" for three months beginning in October. Of course I agreed to do so. Ed suggested I use sermons already preached from my pulpit, but I rejected that idea on the basis that the two audiences would be different. So I would prepare separate sermons for the "Baptist Hour."

Parenthetically, at this point, let me sketch briefly the beginning of the "Baptist Hour." Dr. Samuel F. Lowe, pastor of the Grant Street Baptist Church, Atlanta, Georgia, had a vision of the possibilities for a Southern Baptist radio ministry. At the outset it was a vision shared only by a few people, but prodigiously and persistently he finally led Southern Baptists to establish the Radio Commission. (With the emergence of television, it was finally expanded into the Radio and Television Commission.) Dr. Lowe was its first secretary, even as he remained in his pastorate. Its first annual allocation of funds was the handsome figure of twenty-five thousand dollars. It remained at this figure until after Paul Stevens succeeded Dr. Lowe as executive secretary of the Commission. Ramsey Pollard was the first chairman of the Radio Commission and became Dr. Lowe's great ally in selling this program to Southern Baptists.

I will never forget the consternation of the program committee of the Executive Committee when Paul made his first budget request for seventy-five thousand dollars, up from twenty-five thousand dollars. Many negative reactions were expressed. Finally I said, "Brethren, the Commission led Paul from a good church in Ada, Oklahoma (First Baptist) to lead in this work. I think we should grant this request to enable him to do the job he was asked to do." The committee granted it. *And he did the job!* (Now the Commission's allocation runs into the millions of dollars annually.) He was soon on a first name basis with the top moguls of all the networks in New York. During the years he was with the Commission, through working arrangements with the three major networks, Paul and his staff annually secured *gratis* many millions of dollars of television time for Southern Baptists.

At the outset the Commission was headquartered in Atlanta. After Paul Stevens assumed its leadership, the Commission was moved to Fort Worth, Texas. For several years it was located in a building on Camp Bowie Boulevard, which had been remodeled for radio and television production. Later, the Commission moved to West Freeway in Fort Worth where they built the present facilities, the only building in the world built especially for religious radio and television production.

I always told Paul that if he were boiled down to a half pint it would be a half pint of imagination, an absolute necessity in that work. The following event illustrates this. When ground was broken for the West Freeway building, Paul said, "We are in the space business. So we are going to use it to break ground." A firm in Fort Worth was connected with NASA, so Paul asked them to help do this. They told him to bury a bundle of sticks of dynamite a safe distance from the people attending the groundbreaking. They ran a wire from the dynamite to a telephone line which would be connected to a machine in their plant. This machine would be aimed at a spot where light from a distant star would shine directly into this machine at the exact time Paul wanted the ground broken. This light would generate a spark of electricity which would go through the wires and detonate the dynamite.

Being the preacher on the "Baptist Hour," I was asked to be the speaker for the occasion. We were running a little ahead of schedule. He was in touch with the downtown firm by telephone. So he told me that wherever I was in my speech, whenever he pulled on my sleeve, I was to stop for a few seconds. When he pulled my sleeve, I did as instructed. After a pause of about two seconds—*BOOM*! Not a second early or a second late! Southern Baptists will never be able fully to repay the debt they owe to Paul Stevens!

Now back to my part on the "Baptist Hour." At the Southern Baptist Convention in 1958, Ed Arendall asked me how I felt about my forthcoming time on the "Baptist Hour." I said, "Fine, except for one thing. Three months is not enough time. It will take that long to get my audience. Then you must start all over with another speaker. I think it should be for six months." By the time I began in October 1958, they had extended the time to six months. After three six-month periods, I was invited to become the "permanent" preacher for the program. Someone asked me what "permanent" meant. I said, "It is the same as being the permanent pastor of the First Baptist Church, Oklahoma City. I may be on for years; I may be fired the next business meeting." I was on the program for eighteen years through September 1976. I gave it up to have more time for other writing.

During that time, the peak was appearing weekly on six hundred stations all over the world. Incidentally, I served free, *gratis*. It was a *privilege*, not a *job*. When I retired from it, the Commission gave Frances and me a banquet and a week's trip to Hawaii. We had been there before, but no one ever tires of Hawaii. At the banquet, Paul said that I had preached to a potential audience each week of 100 million people. But no one will ever really know. For instance, Porter Routh told me of two Baptist women in the Ukraine of Russia who spoke English. They said they heard the "Baptist Hour" each Sunday, broadcast out of Monte Carlo. For several years it was on the "Voice of the Orient" out of Manila, beamed to India, the second most populous nation in the world. Due to the long British influence, English is the nearest to universal of all languages in India. Back then in India, television was in its infancy. But when Frances and I traveled through India, we noticed that almost every hut had a radio antenna. We were told that the people listened to local stations, BBC out of London, and the "Voice of the Orient."

I have always tried to do expository preaching, so I followed that method on the "Baptist Hour," but had to adapt my style of delivery to radio. In the pulpit, the preacher has many points of contact with his listeners—gestures, voice inflection, pauses, facial expression, etc. But on radio you have only one, the voice. For one thing, I learned that a whisper is more effective than a shout.

In a book along this line, a psychologist said that if a person is in a crowd, listening to a speaker, he expects the speaker to speak loud. But if he is alone, it makes him mad. According to statistics, about 85 percent of listeners to radio are alone, many in their automobiles. When someone wrote that it seemed that I was sitting in his car as I spoke to him, I felt that I had succeeded.

A friend asked me how I could sit alone in a soundproof studio, talk into a microphone, and put so much feeling into my voice. I told him that I read selected portions of the mail and could feel the listeners' presence, their needs, and problems.

Speaking of mail, the sermon that produced the greatest amount of mail in the history of the "Baptist Hour," was called "A Sermon Long Overdue." Coming at the close of a June series on courtship and marriage, this sermon dealt with divorce. It majored on marital problems, their prevention and cure. Mothers requested enough copies of the sermon to give each of their children. The response was not due to the excellence of the sermon but rather, the enormity of the need.

While speaking of letters, let me tell of two. One came from a woman in Knoxville, Tennessee. It started with this sentence: "I want to thank you for saving my life." She had been in a hotel room preparing to commit suicide. Just to have some noise, she turned on the radio with the volume up high. Said she, "You came on the air with a question which caught my attention, so I sat down and listened. By the time you finished I had gotten hold of myself."

Those in the know say that unless you catch people's attention in the first two or three minutes, you lose them. Also, we felt that if we came on the air with religious music, many would switch stations. So I began using what I called a "hook." It was a brief question or statement designed to hook on to people's attention before the music began. So I checked to see what the hook was for that message. I had come over the "dead air" with the following question: "How have things gone for you lately? Pretty tough, eh? Why don't we talk about it?" The Holy Spirit works in mysterious ways His wonders to perform.

The other letter came from a man in Mexico City. He understood English. On a Sunday morning, he listened to our program while driving south of Mexico City. It was a simple message on salvation by grace through faith. It brought him under conviction. That afternoon he was returning to Mexico City and stopped at a filling station for gas. The owner introduced him to a young man also bound for Mexico City, so he asked him to ride with him. Upon learning that the young man was a Baptist missionary, the driver asked if he ever listened to the "Baptist Hour." He replied that he did when he could. The man told of his experience that morning and asked if he would tell him how to be saved. While parked on the side of the road, the missionary led him to receive Christ as his Savior.

The man wrote us relating this experience. Then he said, "I want you to pray that I may lead my wife to Christ." Some weeks later we received another letter from him. He had led his wife to Christ. Then he asked us to pray that they might lead their children to Christ. We never heard from him again. But I still hope and pray that they did so.

Authorities in the field say that for every letter received, good or bad, fifteen hundred people wanted to write but did not. The people who work for the Southern Baptist Radio and Television Commission are a dedicated group, but only eternity will reveal the fruits of the ministry by means of electronics!

One further word needs to be said about my "Baptist Hour" ministry. For years the Commission put out a monthly magazine called *The Beam*. The last section of each issue was composed of my sermons preached the previous month. At one point, the editor decided to scatter the sermons throughout *The Beam*. This brought a flood of protests from pastors. They wanted the sermons kept in a body. Since they were expository in nature, these pastors took them out as a body and placed them among their commentaries. Later, when *The Beam* was suspended, a plan was substituted whereby the sermons were printed quarterly and mailed to subscribers. This resulted in a large subscription list.

Often young preachers would say, "I am preaching your 'Baptist Hour' sermons. I hope you don't mind." My answer was, "Brother, I try to preach them and can't. If you can, then go right ahead."

Another beneficial use of these sermons was that both the tapes and printed copies were sent to our mission stations around the world. The missionaries used them in teaching classes in English, one means of reaching people. As the students listened, they followed my printed words. Also, many missionaries said they used the programs in their personal and group worship services in English.

I might add that I possessed a complete set of the tapes for my eighteen years on the program. Along with my library I have given them to the library of Oklahoma Baptist University. They have made them into cassettes for their audio library. Professors in the Department of Religion tell me that instead of assigning books for parallel reading, they give an assignment for students to listen to a certain number of these tapes. Also, these tapes are entered into the nationwide library computer system.

To my dying day I will be grateful to Paul Stevens and his staff and to Ed Arendall and the entire Commission for this tremendous privilege afforded me!

Through the years I have been able to develop quite a writing ministry. Beginning in 1951, up until now (June 1992), I have had 141 books published, with a number of manuscripts now awaiting publication. I am told that I have written more books than anyone else in the history of the Southern Baptist Convention and have written more for the Southern Baptist Sunday School Board than any other person. This does not include chapters written for many books compiled by others or innumerable articles for various publications. Since October 1961, I have written a weekly column called "Baptist Beliefs" for Baptist state papers. For years it was carried by most of these and is still used by several of them—"not bragging, just facts."

I am often asked, "With a large church and the denominational work you do, how do you find time to write as much as you do?" My reply is manifold. I have had a sympathetic wife who did not begrudge me the time, an understanding church, and a staff that has taken much of the load of details off me. And for most of these years, I have had my study in my home. In that way I do much of my writing at night. For instance, if Frances was doing something that did not involve me, I would go into my study and write. I would not leave her to go to the church to do it. Since Frances' death, I find relief from loneliness by staying busy. And writing has been my way of studying. Writing for publication makes me study more carefully. The product may not be worth publishing, but I try. All in all, I have written for seven publishers, the reason being that I have written books faster than any one publisher would want to publish books by the same author. I am grateful to each one of them.

More than forty of these books deal either with Baptist doctrine and heritage or with expositions of the books of the New Testament. At present, I have written on all the New Testament books except Acts and the pastoral and general epistles. If the Lord allows me time, I plan to write on these. One book, *The Origin of All Things*, is on Genesis.

As an aside, I might add that this writing ministry has been good for my health. In 1981, I preached on Sunday in my former pastorate, the Dauphin Way Baptist Church in Mobile. Dr. and Mrs. George Mitchell took Frances and me to lunch.

He asked about my age. I told him that the following October I would be seventy-four. He said, "You don't look that old. Do you know the reason why?" I said, "I take my vitamins." He said, "That isn't it. You keep your mind active. When people stop using their minds, they become senile."

One writing project, *Studying Adult Life and Work*, calls for special treatment. I am writing this in my hotel room during the 1992 Convention in Indianapolis. I mention this because when I return home I will finish the last chapter of the July-September 1993 volume. That will mark twenty-five years that I have been writing this book. As of June 10, 1992, ninety-six books in this series had been published.

Recently, a friend of mine told me the following event. Sometime before William Barclay died, this friend had visited him in Edinburgh, Scotland. He told Dr. Barclay about my writing ministry, including this Sunday School series. Dr. Barclay remarked, "That is most interesting! For years I have written Sunday School lesson helps for the Sunday School teachers of Scotland." My book is only for teachers, but I am told that in some classes, at the request of the pupils, a copy is furnished for each one.

How did this book get started? When we were using the Uniform Series, our teachers in Oklahoma City felt that *Broadman Comments* was too simple, so they would buy some other such as *Peleubits*. As we discussed whether or not to use the new *Life and Work Series*, their concern was about lesson helps. I told them that I had not seen such but was sure the Sunday School Board would provide them. They voted to try it for six months.

Finally, I secured the volume provided for that purpose. Then I told Wallace Parham, our minister of education, that our teachers would not accept it. If he wanted to stay with the new series we would have to do something. I added, "I have more than I can do. But if you and the teachers asked me, I would write lesson helps, give each teacher a copy, and teach them each Wednesday night." They wanted it, so I did.

Sometime later, Wallace met with about twenty-five other ministers of education. They were talking about their teachers' unhappiness with the lesson helps. (Later these helps were "beefed up" considerably.) Finally, they asked Wallace what we were doing. When he told them, they wanted us to send them enough copies for their teachers.

Later, when he told me, I said, "The first thing is to get permission from the Sunday School Board. Then we will send each church one copy. If they will not reproduce it, they do not deserve it. We're not in the literature business." When I called A. V. Washburn, he was happy to grant permission since they were getting some *flack* about it. We thought we would be sending out about twenty-five copies. But soon the number was about 250 per week, including some of our largest churches. We learned that in one case a deacon in a church that received the material was in the printing business. He was printing enough for all the churches in his association. A good thing was getting out of hand.

Some time later, Wallace was in Nashville. A group was talking with Jim Sullivan, president of the Sunday School Board. He and I were in the same graduating class at the seminary and have been friends ever since. He said, "Though we gave Herschel permission to do what he is doing, it is really a violation of the copyright." When I heard this, I called Jim. "Jim, I have worked with the Convention too long to start working against it. You gave me permission to do what I'm doing. All you need do to stop it is to tell me." He said, "I wish you would. We have about a million dollars tied up in this, and the only way we can get it back is to sell literature." I agreed to write the churches and explain.

About two weeks later Jim called me. Said he, "In all my years in this office, I have never received such mean mail as in response to your letter." You see, it was lay people telling it like it is, not pastors using nice "preacher talk." Then he asked if I would do him a favor. Would I write three months of the material? Then the Sunday School Board would put on a crash effort, publish it in a book and sell it. I told him I would if they would let me write it the way I wanted to do it. He said, "You write it, and we will publish it." So I agreed.

Then he asked a second favor. "Will you write these churches and get them off my back?" Again I agreed. Now a third favor. "Will you continue to send out your lesson helps until we can get the book published?" Gladly I agreed. So the first book was for October-December 1968. Jim later told me he hoped I would continue to write it as long as I can push a pen. (I assured him that I hope it will be longer than he does.) Thus began a long and happy relationship.

Any kind of writing ministry calls for discipline on the part of the writer. It is especially true of this *Life and Work* book. I have always liked to push my work, but I never like my work to push me. To avoid the latter, I must write at least one chapter per week. In fact, I spend more time on this book than on most.

In writing biblical exposition in other books, I do so largely with pastors in mind. So I assume that they possess a knowledge of the Scriptures greater than that of most lay persons. In *Life and Work* I try to give a thorough treatment of the historical setting. The same is true of interpretation. For instance, if my interpretation varies from others, I insert in parentheses the key Hebrew or Greek word with its root meaning to show why I so interpret it. Most teachers have no knowledge of these languages, but many express appreciation for this. They say, "I don't know their meaning, but I know that you do and that gives me confidence." Even some seminary professors express appreciation for some new shade of meaning. Even a blind hog will root up an acorn now and then. Through the years I have been able to root up a few.

The people at the Sunday School Board tell me that they sell between 90,000 and 100,000 of these books each quarter, mostly to teachers. Multiply that by the average attendance in adult classes throughout the SBC. This shows how many people I would lead astray if I give a wrong interpretation—hence, the care I exercise. Through the years, critical mail is almost nil, which leads me to conclude that my theology must be acceptable to most Southern Baptists.

Southern Baptists have never been extremists in doctrine to the right or left; they have been in the center. I agree heartily with Albert McClellan. At a Peace Committee meeting he said to me, "Herschel, I don't want to be known as a Conservative or a Moderate. [They both have political overtones.] I just want to be known as an 'old-time Southern Baptist.'" I said, "Amen." At the 1992 Convention in Indianapolis, I said, "I am a Southern Baptist—an old-time Southern Baptist. I have been a

Southern Baptist since the day I was immersed in Montevallo Creek just outside Montevallo, Alabama, into the fellowship of the Enon Baptist Church. I will be a Southern Baptist until the day I die!" The Convention responded with a standing ovation. I judge that was their way of saying, "AMEN!"

Through the years I have faced many Southern Baptist Conventions. With two exceptions, they have been pleasant experiences. One was in St. Louis in 1980. I spoke against a motion and a few people booed me. Later, I was told that in the press room, Marse Grant exclaimed, "Listen! They are booing HERSCHEL HOBBS!"

But the meanest Convention I ever faced was in Denver, Colorado, in 1970. A motion had been made to withdraw from further publication volume 1 of *The Broadman Bible Commentary*. There was strong opposition to the material on Genesis written by an English Baptist, Dr. Henton Davies. Other than James Sullivan, president of the Sunday School Board, and Clifton Allen, general editor of the commentary, I was the only person to speak in opposition to the motion. Each speaker was allowed three minutes. I felt that this was unfortunate. In open-heart surgery you do not set a time limit for the surgeon. In a sense, we were doing open-heart surgery on Baptist polity, but I said nothing about it. On the podium were three lights to enable the speaker to keep track on his time.

I had three points to make. The third and strongest I saved for last. Suddenly some messengers began to holler "time" as though I had exceeded my time. The lights showed I still had one minute left. It soon became a chant throughout the crowd. W. A. Criswell was president of the Convention that year. He held up one finger to indicate that I had a minute left, but they paid no attention. I started to ask him to call the Convention to order and to give me that time, but I knew it was useless. They were not open to reason and would vote as they wanted to vote. So I left the podium without making my third point.

At that time, I knew that only about ten thousand copies of the volume had been sold. There were many more messengers than that present, so either there had been much lending of the book or else many had not read it. I am sure the latter was true. Later, a friend of mine told me that he sat toward the back in a nest of those yelling, "time." According to this friend, they were literally frothing in their mouths. He asked, "How many of you have read the book?" *Not one of them had done so!*

It was a psychological situation much like the "Barking Dog Revivals" on the frontier of Kentucky. The pioneers lived under the constant threat of attack by Indians; some endured actual attacks. Due to that and other hardships, they lived with pent-up emotions. Once each year, they had two-week camp meetings. Under the spell of preaching and singing, they let out all these emotions. Many went down on their "all-fours" (hands and feet) and ran around barking like dogs—hence, the name.

Strangely, as soon as the motion to withdraw the volume passed, messengers rushed from the meeting and soon bought every volume 1 in the book exhibit hall. When word of the action went across the country, there was a rush on Baptist Book Stores to buy it, so much so that the Sunday School Board had to send out instructions not to sell any more of that volume. A Baptist state paper editor, in an editorial about it long before the Denver Convention, had closed the editorial by saying, "Don't buy it. It's a waste of money." He was later asked if he would sell it. His reply, "I would not take a thousand dollars for it." I told a friend I wish someone would attack certain of my books. They were not selling so well.

Oh yes! And what was my third point? "The motion is contrary to the Constitution of the Southern Baptist Convention. Even if this were a motion to *approve* of one of *my* books, I would oppose it. According to the opening paragraph of the Constitution, the purpose of this Convention is not to approve or condemn books. It is to harness the power of the churches for evangelism and missions."

As strange as this seems, equally interesting things happened later. That afternoon I opposed a motion to change the wording of one article in "The Baptist Faith and Message" statement. The Convention vote supported me. The next morning, a request to the Convention initiated by Ramsey Pollard and me, and signed by all but two of the Convention's former presidents (one refused to sign it, another told me later that he would have signed it but we could not find him) was received with approval by the Convention. The request was that the Convention not take up a matter concerning a seminar held in Atlanta by the Christian Life Commission; it would only do harm.

Later, I reasoned through the unfortunate volume 1 experience. My conclusion was that it was not really aimed at me personally but in an entirely different direction. I will not say more. But in 1972, I was the guest at a breakfast given by "The Baptist Faith and Message Fellowship" of Orlando, Florida. I did tell the whole story there, and they agreed with me. I will only say that that was also a misplaced blame.

One young man present told me he owed me an apology. When I asked him why, he said, "I was one of those yelling 'time' at you. I thought you did not believe the Bible"—that despite the fact that I had chaired the committee which drew up the 1963 revision of the 1925 Statement on "The Baptist Faith and Message" with its strong statement on "inerrancy" of the Scriptures. In addition, I had written many books dealing with the exposition of the Scriptures in which I come out loud and clear on my faith in God's Word. I could only conclude that this conscientious young man had not read them. But I assured him that he did not owe me an apology! (Incidentally, with all the writing I have been privileged to do, the only negative reaction I get is when I touch on someone's pet doctrine such as election or speaking in tongues.)

At this Denver Convention, W. A. Criswell said to the messengers, "We are a bunch of speckled birds!" W. A. hit the nail squarely on the head! But that is the fun of being a Southern Baptist! And I close this chapter by saying that I love and appreciate Southern Baptists for the privilege of serving. "Speckled birds" we may be, but let us keep on flying for the Lord!

12

The Presidential Years

Every two years for six years someone asked me to permit them to nominate me for president of the Southern Baptist Convention. Each time I refused. In 1960, Ramsey Pollard was eligible for election for a second term. Just before time for nominations I asked him who was going to nominate him. He said, "I don't know." I replied, "Well, I'll do it myself."

After his election, in a taxi on the way back to the hotel, I said to Frances, "As you know, I have been refusing for six years to allow my name to be placed in nomination. Next year, if anyone wants to do it, I will permit it, for I feel that the time has come to do so." That was in May. I did not mention it to another soul.

In January of 1961, I received a call from Wayne Dehoney. He said, "Some of us have been talking about who should be the next president of the Convention. We agree that you are the one, and I am calling to ask if you will permit your nomination." I agreed. Then I told him what I had told Frances, but I said that I would do nothing to be elected. He said they did not want me to do anything. All they wanted me to do was to say whom I would like to have nominate me. After thinking it over, I said, "Carl Bates." A few days later I received a letter from Carl asking permission to nominate me. I agreed. That was it!

No one else talked to me about it. With one exception, I talked to no one else. Since I was chairman of the program committee of the Executive Committee, I felt I should tell Porter Routh. But I said, "That does not mean that I will be elected, but I felt that you should know." He replied, "Well, I believe you will be elected. From my position, through the years I have noted that there are many nominated but never elected. But there are those who go on doing the work assigned to them by the Convention, neither seeking nor expecting to be elected president. But suddenly things begin to fall into place for them, and that is their year. I see that happening to you, and I think it is your year."

Normally, back then when a new president was to be chosen, there would be many nominees. At the close of my second term there were thirteen! But in 1961, in St. Louis, there were only three, and one of them withdrew. The only reason I can give for that is that at that time I had been on the "Baptist Hour" for almost three years, and my name would be known throughout the Convention. So any others passed it by for that time.

This was prior to computer ballots. Each messenger simply wrote his/her choice on a piece of paper and dropped it in a basket passed like a collection plate. Usually, the vote was taken on Tuesday morning, and the electee was announced that night. But that day, in about ten to fifteen minutes, it was announced that I had been elected. Everyone, including "yours truly," was surprised about the time element. The following week one editor of a state paper even wrote an editorial about it, but later the chairman of the teller committee explained it to me.

Since there were only two nominees, the committee began its work by placing the ballots into two piles. Mine was so much the larger, the committee knew the result and reported it. Then they actually counted the ballots for the record.

That was followed immediately by a most frightening experience. One minute you are an anonymous Baptist. You know that you are simply one of millions of Southern Baptists. But within a matter of minutes, with no time for preparation for it, you face a secular press that plays "hardball." You and the Baptist Press know better, but to the secular press you are "Mr. Southern Baptist," and every word you say they treat as official and *ex cathedra*. Frances sat by helplessly but lent moral support. W. C. Fields, head of Baptist Press, gave what help he could, but he was like a manager of a baseball team: he can put you up to bat, but after that, you are on your own.

The big issue in 1961 was race relations. That very week the "Freedom Bus" had been burned while passing through Alabama. Knowing that I am a native of that state, these "hardball" reporters went to work on that and other facets of the racial struggle.

I have never had any serious problem concerning race. As a child, I played with black children. As an adult, I have many friends among black people, especially among preachers. I have often said I wish God had given white preachers the ability He gave black preachers to see biblical truth as vividly as they do. The best answer I ever heard to the God is dead philosophy (not "theology") came from a black preacher.

He said, "They tell me that God is dead. I want to ask them some questions. When did He die? Of what did He die? Where is He buried? When did they have His funeral? Why wasn't I invited? I'm a member of the family!" For me, all the theological folderol cannot equal that one.

But back to the press conference. In answer to their probing questions, I stated my personal view. I was/am in favor of integration, but I felt that the current method was moving faster than people on both sides were able to go. You can gain *rights* by legal means, but the ultimate solution must be found on a person-to-person basis. Jesus never sided with one group or person against another. He preached to both as either sinners saved by grace or outside God's grace due to personal choice.

In Jericho, Jesus did not man a picket line carrying a sign which said "Unfair to Taxpayers." He went to the home of Zacchaeus and won him over. Instead of a crooked tax collector, He presented to the people a redeemed tax commissioner.

I related an experience I had had with a *white* lady. She called to needle me about the churches' slow progress in this area. She said that with all the progress of medical science, religion was lagging behind.

In reply, I said that the gospel is doing its work in racial relations. Give it time and the goal which she and I desired would be achieved naturally and spiritually. Then using her own illustration, I said that with all the progress of medical science, it still required nine months for a baby to be born naturally. To try to force it could well end in an abortion. I want the baby to be alive and well at birth.

Also I was asked questions about theology, mostly by Baptist state paper editors. My answers were middle of the road ones, the traditional position of most Southern Baptists. Later I learned that the religion reporter for the Louisville *Courier-Journal* wrote an article calling me a "fence-straddler." C. R. Daley, editor of the Kentucky *Western Recorder*, wrote an editorial in my defense, saying that I answered every question forthrightly in keeping with my convictions and traditional Southern Baptist theology. Thank you, Chauncey!

Someone sent me a clipping of a front page story in the *New York Times* in which it called me a "gradualist" on the racial issue. I like that! In every other press conference while I was in office the racial question was raised. To every such question I referred to the title given me by the *New York Times*. To a newsman that was like quoting the Bible to a Baptist preacher!

On the closing night of the Convention in St. Louis, Frances and I took a cab to the convention hall. The driver asked when the meeting would close. Frances said it would end that night. And proudly she added, "My husband has been elected president of the Convention!" His response: "Then I guess he will be good for a big tip." Since that was all it meant to him, I set a record. I gave him the *smallest* tip I suspect he ever received.

At the close of the session, Della Pollard pinned a beautiful orchid on Frances' dress, and Ramsey handed me the historic Broadus gavel. I only held it for a few minutes. Before the final "Amen" had ceased to be heard, the Convention secretary took it, and I did not see it again until just before the opening session the next year in San Francisco. They guard that gavel like it was the gold in Fort Knox.

Upon arriving home the next day, our people gave us a fitting airport welcome. The church staff insisted that we go by the church before going home. Arriving there, we found a red carpet made of red paper running from the entrance to the office suite to my office. Among other humorous things in my office was a color picture drawn by Paul Hunt, then one of our members. It shows a large dog running away with a bone in its mouth. The bone has a tag on it which reads "SBC." The president a *dog*? Oh well! To this day, it hangs in my home study as the centerpiece for a wall filled with other precious memorabilia. Some day, if the Lord delays His return, it will grace the collection of such in the section of the Oklahoma Baptist University in which my library has found a permanent home.

I must add that before leaving St. Louis I received a long telegram from Dr. John H. Buchanan, who had been my mother's pastor until her death in 1946. In essence, he spoke of my mother's pride in her *only* boy—had she lived. And, you know, believe what you will, but I believe that she and Mrs. Jack stood together, looked down, and said, "Well, we worked hard at it, and it seems to have turned out all right."

The following Sunday morning, E. V. Mashburn, a faithful deacon and pastor's friend, asked if he might say a word just before dismissal of the morning service. To a packed house, he said, "The Southern Baptist Convention has honored this church along with our pastor. It has also placed on him and us a great responsibility. So I move that we release the pastor from all duties necessary for him to meet his responsibilities and that we pledge ourselves to renewed dedication in taking up the slack, so that the Lord's work here will continue unabated." Everyone present stood to accept that added responsibility. And they did. In fact, the work went so well that it worried me. I feared the church would decide that it did not need me.

At this point I want to pay a special tribute to Lucy Gibson, my secretary for almost twenty-four years. She was already shouldering the normal duties of a pastor's secretary. In addition, she typed a "Baptist Hour" sermon each week and the manuscript of every book I wrote until I retired from the pastorate. I always said that she fought a typewriter like she was fighting bees.

When I was elected president of the Convention, Porter Routh told me the Convention would furnish the salary for an extra secretary to handle secretarial duties related to that office. When I mentioned it to Lucy, she said, "Well, let's wait and see." She simply *fought bees* a little harder so that we never spent one dime of Convention money for extra secretarial help! Indeed, she felt as much called to her work as I did to mine.

Well, after the celebration, reality set in. Long before the Convention, I had agreed to be the Bible teacher for a tour of the Middle East. The tour was largely built around me and Bert Lackey, our state secretary. But I debated as to whether I should go in light of developments. Finally, Frances and I decided to make it a missionary tour. So we arranged ahead to meet with our missionaries wherever we went.

In Jordan, Bill Hearn arranged for us to meet their prime minister. He said it would help the mission work if we did. However, two weeks prior to our meeting, the prime minister was assassinated. When we arrived in Amman, they had hidden his successor. On the day we were to see him, they would not tell us when or where. Finally, the tour leader said the tour must continue. Bill said that if I did not see the prime minister, it would be regarded as an insult. So I told the group that Frances and I would remain in Amman until we saw him and would join them at either Mt. Nebo or the Dead Sea.

Finally, we were told we could see the prime minister. One lady, Catherine Butler of our church, chose to remain with us. After going to half a dozen houses in different parts of Amman, we finally reached the one where the prime minister was staying. We had to wait about fifteen minutes. In walked the tallest, biggest Arab I ever saw. On a small tray he had demitasse cups and a pot of Turkish coffee. It was green and tasted like medicine. Bill Hearn had told us that to refuse their coffee was also an insult. Frances finally finished hers and handed back the cup. He filled it again. What Bill had failed to say was that if you did not want anymore you turned the cup back and forth as you returned it.

Just as Frances finished the second cup, they told us we could see the prime minister. After introductions, here came the big Arab and his coffee. Frances had to drink a third cup. Later, as we went on our way, she and Catherine got the giggles. I asked what was the matter. Bill said they were *drunk* on that coffee! He said that after a day of visiting Arab homes, for the same reason he could hardly walk from his car to the house. But

I suppose it was for a good cause if it helped our missionaries. One thing is for sure. We never got addicted to that coffee.

Unknown to me, while on this tour, my first major problem as president was brewing. Back at home, Dr. Dale Moody was teaching at a summer pastors school at Oklahoma Baptist University. After lunch one day, in an informal discussion, Dale and Sam Scantlan had a hot discussion on the subject of apostasy, meaning that a person can be saved and lost again. For the most part, Southern Baptists reject the idea. Dale, a professor of theology at the Southern Baptist Theological Seminary, believed it. Sam, who worked for the Baptist General Convention of Oklahoma, did/does not. Dale was of a disposition that he would rather debate than eat. We were good friends even though we had gone around and around on this theme. I once told him I imagined that each morning, as he greeted his wife, he went into a boxing stance and said, "Good morning!" He laughed and replied, "Well, I don't turn my tail!" Sam is of the kind who will fight a buzz saw, holding a wildcat under each arm. So the ingredients for a real donnybrook were present.

Bert Lackey first heard about it in London through a letter from Albert McClellan. In the British Museum he told me, and we had a good laugh over it. Had I known the future I would not have laughed.

On Monday morning, after returning home on Saturday, I was in my office, where my desk was literally piled with mail. I had no intention to attend the pastors conference, but Max Stanfield, Putnam City Baptist Church, called. He said that on the previous Monday the pastors had agreed on charges to bring against Dale. A committee had put them in writing. Since the matter might wind up in the Southern Baptist Convention, he thought I might want to be present.

So I went. The question before the group was not what charges to make but what to do with the charges on which the pastors had agreed the previous week. Some wanted to call a press conference. But Duke McCall, president of Southern Seminary, was the speaker that week at Falls Creek Baptist Assembly in Oklahoma.

A motion was made that the committee go to Falls Creek on Friday to present the charges to McCall, and he could decide how to handle the matter: administratively or through his trustees. That was the proper procedure, so I voted for it.

On the following Wednesday, I received a call from Erwin McDonald, editor of the Arkansas Baptist state paper. He had received a story written by the assistant editor of the Oklahoma *Baptist Messenger* and released through Baptist Press about the *charges* against Dale. It said that "Herschel Hobbs, president of the Southern Baptist Convention, was present and voted for the resolution," or the charges. This compromised the office of the presidency and was an embarrassment to me personally. I was in the Middle East when the event at OBU occurred. I was in England when the pastors conference agreed upon what charges to bring. So it made me look foolish.

I told this to Erwin and said I hoped he would not run the story. Of course, he was correct that he had to carry it since the other papers would run it. It created quite a stir that the president of the Convention would make such charges. I wrote an article telling the true story, and it soon died down. But error dies a hard, slow death. Two years later, following the Kansas City convention, one editor wrote an editorial complimenting me on "The Baptist Faith and Message" of 1963 and how I presided over that session of the Convention. But it closed with the following words: "It was quite a different Herschel Hobbs than the one who two years ago voted to bring charges against Dale Moody." I wrote him, again correcting the error, but he did not reply. In September 1961, Dale and I got together; he understood what had happened. But I suppose such things go with the office. As Harry Truman said, "If you can't stand the heat, get out of the kitchen."

Even as this was happening, the storm clouds were gathering for the really great crisis of my presidency—the Elliott controversy. At the time of my election in 1961, I had not even heard of Dr. Ralph Elliott's *The Message of Genesis*, but by the time my two years were over, I certainly knew about it. At the time he wrote it, Dr. Elliott was professor of Old Testament at Midwestern Baptist Theological Seminary. The book was published by Broadman Press.

The crux of the matter was that he identified Melchizedek as a priest of Baal. I was told by someone that another professor of Old Testament said that most Old Testament scholars rejected this position, saying that at the time of Abraham, Baal worship had not penetrated this far south in Palestine.

With the storm clouds growing darker, I invited the presidents of all six seminaries to be my guests at breakfast during the Executive Committee meeting in Nashville in September 1961. I told them that, if invited, I would visit with their faculties. They agreed. My purpose was twofold: (1) to interpret Southern Baptists to them, (2) in my president's address in San Francisco in 1962, to interpret the faculties to Southern Baptists. These meetings lasted from two and one-half to four and one-half hours, depending on the size of the faculty.

In the usual format I talked to the faculty for about an hour and a half, trying to interpret Southern Baptists to them. Some objected when I said they were out of touch with the people. One said, "Why, we are preaching somewhere every Sunday!" I replied, "Yes, you fly to an engagement. Someone takes you to a hotel. Sunday morning and evening you are taken to the church just prior to the service, then back to the hotel. The next morning someone takes you to the airport and back to the seminary you go. Have you been with the *people?* Hardly!

"One problem comes from the terminology some of you use. For instance, the word 'myth.'"

I knew that when I asked for discussion who would be the first to speak and that it would be about "myth." I was right. He said, "Dr. Hobbs, you mentioned the word 'myth.' Now the Greek word *muthos* means—." I interrupted him by saying, "I know what *muthos* means. I also know what 'myth' means to European and American theologians. But I also know what it means to the average Southern Baptist. It means 'fairy tale.' When you speak, you are not saying what you think but what others think when they hear you. When you speak of the myth of creation, you mean a literary vehicle for speaking truth. But to the average Southern Baptist you say, 'The fairy tale of creation.'"

The professor asked, "Well, what word would I use?" I replied, "What about 'epic?'" He said, "Well, now, 'epic' means—." Again I interrupted him. "I know what 'epic' means, but it is better than 'myth.' But what is wrong with the good old cornbread and buttermilk expression 'the account of creation in Genesis?'" Then I added, "You can continue to use the word 'myth' if you please, but as long as you do, you can be prepared to be in hot water up to your ears with Southern Baptists."

Then he said, "I have a book at the publisher with that word all through it. What can I do?" I said, "You might call him tonight and tell him to stop the presses." Later, I bought a copy of the book. The word "myth" was not in it!

I have gone into detail about this for one reason. When the meeting ended, I was deluged by other professors, thanking me for what I said to this man. They said, "We have argued with him until we were blue in the face, but it was simply one colleague arguing with another. But when the president of the Southern Baptist Convention looked him in the eye and said what you did, it is the first time we have seen him set back on his heels." My point is that simply because one professor says or teaches something contrary to Southern Baptist consensus does not mean that all of them are doing it. "Shotgun" accusations are not only unfair; they are untrue. All of us need to heed the words of John R. Sampey. When he called on a student who was unprepared and who blasted forth a generality, hoping to hit something worthy of a grade, he would say, "All right, brother! Put up your shotgun, and get out your rifle. Aim at something definite!"

The Elliott matter did not become a Convention problem officially until the 1962 session in San Francisco. In the meantime, Dr. Baker James Cauthen had requested that I visit some of the foreign mission fields. Friends in our church made it possible for Frances to accompany me. We decided to visit Central and Latin America, West Africa, and Western Europe. Incidentally, I was the first Convention president to visit our African mission fields while in office.

United States Senator Robert S. Kerr was a deacon in our church. One day I told him of the plans for the trip. I said, "In the United States, I am just plain Herschel Hobbs. Where I am going, I will be the president of about twelve million people in our country. And there the term 'president' has a political connotation. I will be interviewed by the press and will be making public addresses. In doing so, I could put my foot in a bear trap about some delicate diplomatic matter which is not public knowledge. Would it help if I sent to Washington and let the State Department brief me on anything I need to know?" He said he would open any door in Washington that I wished to enter. Would I like to see the president? I thought, *Why see the boys when I can see the man?* Bob arranged it and went with me.

After a forty-five minute visit, President Kennedy called the State Department to tell them that he was sending me over there. He requested that they assign me an assistant secretary of state to help me. Later, Bob said, "Pastor, I could have sent you, but it would be one of 100 senators sending one of 240 million citizens. But when the president says, 'I am sending him,' they will have the red carpet out to the middle of the street." They did.

But an event back at the president's office is the reason I am telling this. It started more than twenty years prior to that day. While pastor in Montgomery, I had need to see Mayor Gunter, who had held that office for twenty-five years. He was the last of the "city bosses" of that era. After concluding my business with him, I asked if we might have prayer together. When I finished, tears ran down his cheeks. At prayer meeting that night, a deacon said, "I was in to see the mayor after you left. He told me about your prayer. Then he added, 'Through the years, multiplied thousands have come to my office asking for everything under the sun. Your pastor is the first one to ask if he might pray with me.'"

That moment I vowed never to enter the office of a government employee without asking if I could pray with them. As a result I have prayed with such, prime minister on down—Jews, Moslems, Protestants, Catholics, pagans, even animist tribal chiefs in Africa. Never have I had one to refuse my request or fail to thank me.

However, as I talked with President Kennedy, the thought kept running through my mind, *Should I presume to ask him, my own president?* But then the thought occurred to me, *He is just a man, but perhaps the most powerful man in the world. Before nightfall he may have to make a decision that will affect the future of mankind. Surely if any man needs prayer, he does.* So as we started to leave, I asked, "Mr. President, may we pray together?" Of course, he said, "Yes."

I stood between Bob and the president with my arms about their waists. I prayed for Bob. Then I prayed for President Kennedy, for his health, strength, and wisdom, and for his family, including his father who was seriously ill. When I finished he thanked me. Then he said to Bob, "You know, that is the first time anyone has ever done that."

I thought of the ministers who had been in his office. Perhaps they had the same questions I had. If I had not formed that pattern over twenty years prior to that day, I probably would not have done so. Especially in light of future history, I am grateful for having prayed with my president.

The only other time I was with President Kennedy was on the occasion of Senator Kerr's funeral. When we learned of his death, Frances and I were with the William Hinsons and Jess Moodys at the Orange Bowl, watching Alabama beat Oklahoma. It was Joe Namath's final game at Alabama. Across the stadium, President Kennedy and his party were also watching the game. It was on Tuesday. Frances and I were scheduled to visit President and Mrs. Kennedy on Thursday in Palm Beach where they were spending the holidays.

I told Bill Hinson he would have to cancel that; we had to go home. They soon announced that President Kennedy planned to attend the funeral. In fact, just about everybody who was anybody in government was there.

It was on Friday, January 4, 1963, with a light but cold rain falling. The head of the security force told me that when the president arrived he would introduce me to him. I said that I knew the president, but he added that such was customary. But when he arrived, President Kennedy opened the car door, got out, and came straight to me. Shaking my hand, he said, "Hello, Dr. Hobbs, it's good to see you again." I replied, "It's good to see you again, Mr. President." We had been asked to prepare a small room near the entrance to the auditorium where the president could wait until time to enter for the service. We were only there for about five minutes. Unknown to me at the time, I stood in the midst of history. For I was in that room with

President Kennedy, Vice President and Mrs. Johnson, and Governor and Mrs. John Connally—the things which happened to them the following November!

In the funeral service, I was assisted by Dr. John W. Raley and the chaplain of the Senate. In my eulogy, I quoted "A Prayer for My Pastor," written by Senator Kerr.

After leading the casket to the hearse, I ran down the sidewalk to get my hat and overcoat. Seeing me, Vice President Johnson lowered his car window and motioned to me. When I approached the car, with tears streaming down his face, he said, "Could you get me a copy of that prayer? I must have it!" I told him I would send it to him. Actually, I sent it to Carter Bradley, a member of Senator Kerr's news staff and asked him to deliver it in person. I feared that otherwise it might get lost in a pile of mail. Later, the vice president wrote me a note of thanks for it.

Had President Kennedy returned immediately to Air Force One and flown back to sunny Florida, people would have been pleased that he had attended the funeral. But he and Vice President Johnson went the second mile. They had their limousines placed in the funeral procession and went to the cemetery where Senator Kerr's body was placed in a mausoleum while his permanent burial place was being built near Ada, Oklahoma. After a brief committal service in the mausoleum chapel, the president followed me in shaking hands with the Kerr family. As I waited at the door for the family to leave, the president stopped to thank me for the eulogy. Then, as if I needed to be reminded of it, he said, "You know, you visited me in my office." I said, "Yes, Mr. President, and I enjoyed it very much." "You must come again," he said. Then after shaking my hand, he ran in the rain to his car and was on his way to Air Force One. It was the last time I saw him.

Now, let us go back to 1962. By the time Frances and I returned from the mission tour, the Elliott matter was beginning to boil. Dr. K. Owen White's article, "There Is Death in the Pot!," had been carried in most, if not all of the Baptist state papers. (At this point I want to say that I knew K. O. White from 1932 until his death a few years ago. He had one of the sweetest spirits I ever knew. Some pictured him otherwise. He was not an ignoramus. Instead, he had a Ph.D. in Hebrew Old

Testament and was fellow in junior Hebrew. He was a strong conservative in his theology. He succeeded me as president in 1963 but declined being nominated for a second term due to his wife's health.)

There was a widespread feeling that an explosion was possible in San Francisco in 1962. At my invitation, Porter Routh and Albert McClellan came to Oklahoma City, where we met in my office for an entire afternoon. The purpose was to seek a way to avoid an explosion to give us time to solve the Elliott problem.

Finally, Porter said, "Some people feel that Southern Baptists are becoming more liberal in theology. If so, we should know it. It seems that the best way to determine that would be to have a committee study the 1925 statement of 'The Baptist Faith and Message.'" Albert and I agreed.

This raised the question as to who should be on the committee. It was agreed that we should get as close as possible to the "grass roots" of Southern Baptists. (The best way to do this would be to appoint persons who had been elected state convention presidents the previous fall.) It naturally followed that the chairman of the committee should be the president of the Southern Baptist Convention. Also, we felt that in such an undertaking, the theological community should be represented. So we agreed that the presidents of the six seminaries should be on the committee.

To broaden the base of input in preparing the proposal, it was agreed that I would appoint an *ad hoc* committee to work with us. Neither we nor they had any authority. That rested in the Convention. It was simply an unofficial effort to propose a procedure which we felt would be helpful in that present situation.

In San Francisco, the night before we were to present this proposal to the Executive Committee, some of the state paper editors met me in the hotel lobby. Speaking for the group was E. S. James of the Texas *Baptist Standard*, who said, "We have supported you and wish to continue to do so. But if you recommend putting the seminary presidents on this committee, we will have to oppose you. If the *Baptist Standard* were being examined, I, as the editor, should not be on the committee.

Whether right or wrong, in the minds of many people, the seminaries are a part of the problem. Therefore, the presidents should not be on this committee."

Of course, the purpose of this committee, in our thinking, was not to examine any institution. It was to study the 1925 statement of "The Baptist Faith and Message" in light of the condition in 1962-1963. However, I saw their point. So I said, "Brethren, you are right." At a breakfast the next morning I told the *ad hoc* committee about this and suggested that we not include the seminary presidents. They agreed.

The Executive Committee was favorable to the recommendation that we brought. In turn it presented to the Convention the following:

> Since the report of the Committee on statement of Baptist Faith and Message was adopted in 1925, there have been various statements from time to time which have been made, but no overall statement which might be helpful at this time as suggested in Section 2 of that report, or introductory statement which might be used as an interpretation of the 1925 statement.
>
> We recommend, therefore, that the president of this Convention be requested to call a meeting of the men now serving as presidents of the various state Conventions that would qualify as a member of the Southern Baptist Convention committee under Bylaw 18 to present to the Convention in Kansas City some similar statement which shall serve as information to the churches, and which may serve as guidelines to the various agencies of the Southern Baptist Convention. It is understood that any group or individuals may approach this committee to be of service.

A motion was made from the floor to add the six seminary presidents to the committee. It was defeated overwhelmingly. This showed that the editors knew the temper of the messengers. The original motion was adopted.

It is well to note the wording of the purpose, for the product of this study showed it be adopted by the 1963 Convention. It "*shall* serve as information to the churches, and . . . *may* serve as guidelines to the various agencies of the Southern Baptist Convention" (italics mine). To the framers of this motion and the action of the Convention it is clearly stated that the resultant statement was never to be considered as creedal. This became the guiding principle for the committee throughout its work.

It was at the first miscellaneous business period that the Elliott controversy was brought before the Convention officially. Dr. K. Owen White presented the following motion which received a second.

> I move that the messengers to this convention . . . reaffirm their faith in the *entire* Bible as the authoritative, authentic, infallible Word of God, that we express our abiding and unchanging objection to the dissemination of theological views in any of our seminaries which would undermine such faith in the historical accuracy and doctrinal integrity of the Bible and that we kindly but firmly instruct the trustees and administrative officers of our institutions and [other] agencies to take steps as shall be necessary to remedy at once those situations where such views now threaten our historic position.

It was at this point that, insofar as I know, I made my only error in the two years I presided over the Convention. In those days, the president was his own parliamentarian. Parenthetically, let me say that anyone who says it is not a frightening experience to preside over a Southern Baptist Convention has never presided over it. At that time the Convention used Kerfoot's parliamentary book. (Someone told me that when Dr. George W. Truett was president, he began by saying, "Now, brethren, parliamentary law is just common Christian courtesy, and we will follow that.")

Well, to put it in western rodeo terms, before I got settled in the saddle, I was bucked off. The issue concerned a provision that once the agenda for the Convention is adopted, any other motion is automatically referred to the committee on order of business. In turn, it announces in advance the time for it to be handled. This is done to protect the Convention by enabling anyone for or against that motion to be present. The irony was that I had been involved in making that provision. Dr. White's motion fell into that category.

Forgetting that for the moment, I put the motion to a vote immediately. It was adopted. But a lady rose to call for a point of order. I later learned that she was president of the Woman's Missionary Union of Georgia. She reminded me of the provision for a delayed treatment of such a motion. I acknowledged my error and declared the vote null and void. To a few protests I said, "The chair was in error. When it comes before you again, you can still adopt it if you wish." It was set to be heard the next morning at the first miscellaneous business period.

Later, I wrote this dear lady to thank her. In her reply she said that was the first word she had spoken at a Southern Baptist Convention. But to me, it was a golden word indeed!

That night, I slept very little due to worry about White's motion. Basically, it called for an *affirmation* of Southern Baptists' faith in the Bible and *instructed* the Sunday School Board to withdraw Dr. Elliott's book from publication. Seldom has the Convention *instructed* its agencies, instead simply referring to them matters pertaining to their work. If the messengers rejected the motion on that basis, I could see headlines across the nation to the effect that Southern Baptists had rejected their faith in the Bible. My worry was how to prevent that, so I spent much of the night in bed, worrying and praying.

The answer came the next morning as I was shaving. The motion was really two motions: one to *instruct* the Sunday School Board, the other was to *affirm* our faith in the Bible. I shared this with Frances, and she agreed.

Arriving at the convention hall, I told White my decision to rule that this was two separate motions, and he agreed. The Convention voted to affirm its faith in the Bible. It voted not to instruct the Sunday School Board. Instead, the matter was referred to that Board for its consideration. At its next meeting it did vote to withdraw *The Message of Genesis* from publication. Later, Eerdmans, an independent publisher, agreed to publish it, but that is another story.

The remainder of the San Francisco Convention was largely routine, with the possible exception of the president's address. Prior to this time, this address was more a routine matter, but in 1962, I determined to use it to deal with the pending situation in the Convention. I requested one hour for its delivery, and I read every word of it. My usual style of delivery is more extemporaneous without notes. I noted that fact and explained why I read it: "(1) before I speak, I want to know what I am going to say, (2) as I speak, I want to know what I am saying, and (3) after I have spoken, I want to be able to prove what I have said."

The Convention's response was gratifying. The message received a standing ovation. Also, a motion was adopted to include the entire message in the 1962 *Convention Annual.* The same thing happened with the president's message in 1963. As far as I know, these are the only times this has been done.

We left San Francisco feeling that we had a good Convention. Among other positive things, we had avoided a crisis in the Elliott matter, and we had in place the committee to make a study of "The Baptist Faith and Message" statement of 1925. During my second term as president, I filled the usual numerous speaking engagements which go with the office, but our major emphases were on the above-mentioned matters.

Soon after the 1962 Convention, some of the editors questioned whether or not the committee was qualified to fulfill the responsibility placed upon it with so delicate a matter as our statement of faith. Jack Gritz, editor of the Oklahoma *Baptist Messenger*, had one of his assistants research the matter and ran the result in his paper. It showed that seven of the twenty-four committee members had a Ph.D. from the Southern Baptist Theological Seminary. Thirteen had either a Th.M. or B.D. degree from our seminaries. Two were pastors with college degrees, one was a successful businessman, and one was a lawyer from Washington, D.C. Since no more was heard about it, apparently this laid to rest any concern. To show how seriously the committee faced its task, every meeting of the committee had 100 percent attendance with the exception of the lawyer, who did not attend any of the meetings. I suppose he felt he had nothing to contribute.

At the initial meeting of the committee, Douglas Hudgins of Mississippi was chosen to serve as vice-chairman. In this meeting we also agreed that under the action of the Convention we had three choices as to procedure: (1) recommend a reaffirmation of the 1925 statement, (2) write a new statement altogether, (3) present a revised form of the 1925 statement. We chose the third.

As the committee proceeded with its work we did not study the 1925 statement article by article but word by word. Our procedure is summarized in the introduction or preamble of the 1963 statement.

> It has sought to build upon the structure of the 1925 statement, keeping in mind the "certain needs" of our generation. At times it has reproduced sections of the statement without change. In other instances it has substituted words for clarity or added sentences for emphasis. At certain points it has combined articles, with minor changes in wording, to endeavor to relate certain doctrines to each other. In still others—e.g. "God" and "Salvation"—it has sought to bring together certain truths contained throughout the 1925 statement in order to relate them more clearly and concisely. In no case has it sought to delete from or to add to the basic contents of the 1925 statement.

In our work the committee was always mindful that we were dealing with the faith of all Southern Baptists, not simply one segment of them. For instance, one night at eleven o'clock, we finished with the article on "Baptism." I said, "We are mentally and physically exhausted. Let's get a night's rest and take up the 'Lord's Supper' in the morning." The next morning one member asked if he might read a proposed article on that ordinance. It was closed communion of the strictest sort. Following his reading, a very conservative member of the committee said, "That pleases me very much. It will please the people of my state, for that is what we practice. But we must remember that we are not considering the Baptists of any one state, but all Southern Baptists. And it must be broad enough that all of them will be comfortable with it." The committee agreed.

The committee spent more time on the "Preamble" than on any one article in the statement. Our concern was to protect the individual conscience and to guard against a creedal faith. Since 1963, I have reminded Southern Baptists repeatedly in writing and from the Convention platform that if we disregard the "Preamble" we do not need to get a creed; we already have one. Without the "Preamble" the Convention would not have adopted either the 1925 or 1963 statement. And no Southern Baptist or group of such has the right to try to enforce any article in the statement by disregarding the protections of the "Preamble"!

At the same time no one should say that a person can believe anything he/she wishes and claim to be a Southern Baptist. The "Preamble" closes thus:

> A living faith must experience a growing understanding of truth and must be continually interpreted and related to the needs of each generation. Throughout their history Baptist bodies, both large and small, have issued statements of faith which comprise a consensus of their beliefs. Such statements have never been regarded as complete, infallible statements of faith, nor as official creeds carrying mandatory authority. Thus this generation of Southern Baptists is in historic succession of intent and purpose as it endeavors to state for its time and theological climate those articles of the Christian faith which are most surely held among us.
>
> Baptists emphasize the soul's competency before God, freedom in religion, and the priesthood of the believer. However, this emphasis should not be interpreted to mean that there is an absence of certain definite doctrines that Baptists believe, cherish, and with which they have been and are now closely identified.
>
> It is the purpose of this statement of faith and message to set forth certain teachings which we believe.

Once the first draft of the statement was completed, we sent to each seminary president and to the president of the Sunday School Board enough mimeographed copies to distribute to every professor and Sunday School Board person having to do with theology. Our request was that these people make a careful personal study of the document, then in each of these institutions to have a meeting of its involved personnel to formulate and return to our committee any suggested changes and/or criticisms. None made any suggested changes; all expressed approval of the statement.

There was one exception conveyed to me in a personal letter by Wayne Ward, professor of theology at the Southern Baptist Theological Seminary. In the statement about "God the Son," we said of Him "identifying Himself completely with mankind." He suggested that we add "yet without sin." Of course that was our intent. It is an obvious fact, but it is well to write it out so as to avoid any possible misunderstanding concerning it. Naturally we added those words. I will always be grateful to him for this wise suggestion.

In the 1925 statement, under each article of faith, a few Scripture references supporting it were listed. The 1963 statement contains a more exhaustive list of such. For my own satisfaction as to accuracy I undertook the task of choosing these. I mentioned it to Dick Hall, Jr., a member of the committee, stating that such a tedious task almost had me climbing the walls. He offered to help, so I assigned him a few articles. No reflection on Dick, but for my satisfaction I checked each of these for accuracy. He did an accurate job.

According to instructions from the Convention, by March 1, 1963, we furnished a completed copy of the statement to the general secretary of the Convention. This was to enable him to include it in the *Book of Reports* for the 1963 Convention. He complied with our request to print in parallel columns the 1925 and 1963 statements. This was to enable the messengers to see readily the changes we had made.

Also, we sent a copy to the editor of each of the state Baptist papers. We requested that they run the entire statement in their papers and to editorialize about it. This was to enable Southern Baptists at large to study it. Each editor complied with our request, and each wrote his approval of it. One of them, while approving it, questioned the need for any such statement.

The night before the report of our committee was to be presented to the Convention, Albert McClellan came to our hotel room. He handed me pages he had cut out of leading books on Baptist theology, including the first page of J. M. Pendleton's *Church Manual*. He said, "You may need these tomorrow, but I want them after that."

The day was May 9, 1963. The convention hall was packed. Though air-conditioned, the hall was hot. All week I had had bronchitis. My doctor said he should put me in bed, but knowing what I had before me, he simply gave me the strongest antibiotics available. Following his advice, I went to the Baptist Hospital. I told the nurses to give me a shot of penicillin that would keep me on my feet that week. Later, I heard that they got a laugh out of it. They said, "We stuck the needle so deep he won't be able to sit down for a week."

Fearing that I might have a coughing spell while reading the report, I told Doug Hudgins to be ready to take over. About halfway through the report, the crowd seemed to be weaving back and forth. I knew that if I did not sit down, I would fall down. I sat while Doug finished reading the report.

The committee had agreed that if there was any debate, I should defend the report. The only debate, and very little at that, was on one sentence we had added on "The Church." "The New Testament speaks also of the church as the body of Christ which includes all of the redeemed of all the ages." Fearing that I could not stand, I sat as I defended the statement.

When I figured that the opponents had said all they wished to say, I pulled out the pages given to me by Albert McClellan and explained what they were. Then I said, "If you wish, I will read all of them. But first let me read from the opening page of J. M. Pendleton's *Church Manual*." I am quoting from memory. It read, "The word *ekklesia* is sometimes used in the New Testament to refer to the redeemed in the aggregate." Pendleton is the "patron saint" of those who believe that "church" always refers to the local church. So as when Jesus rebuked the wind and the waves, there was a great calm. When the question was put to a vote, it was adopted overwhelmingly without even changing a punctuation mark. One church history professor said that that one sentence at the close of the article on "The Church" was the first new development in Southern Baptist ecclesiology since 1845.

Later, Ray Summers, then professor of New Testament and Greek at Southwestern Seminary, said, "Herschel, reading that quote from Pendleton was a stroke of genius!" He added that he had a ten-page typewritten statement on the church that he was planning to request the Convention's permission to read. When I read that statement by Pendleton, he folded it and put it in his pocket. I said, "Ray, if there was any genius involved, give Albert McClellan the credit. My only part was the timing as to when to use it."

Meanwhile, when I had to sit down, Frances wanted me to return to the hotel and call a doctor. She feared I had had a heart attack. (The afternoon edition of the *Oklahoma City Times* reported in a front page story that I had had one.) I told Frances, "Hon, I am no hero. But I feel that it is so important to get this statement adopted, I am willing to die on this platform in order to do so."

A medical missionary came to the platform to check my pulse. He said I was all right but simply became overheated. Later, the hotel doctor said I was dehydrated and had not been eating properly. He sent me a large pitcher of orange juice and a rare steak with instructions to consume both. Though the steak was still bloody, I did as told. That night I was feeling fine and presided over the session.

Through the years numerous efforts have been made to change the purpose and/or wording of the statement, but all have failed. For instance, in New Orleans in 1969, a motion was made that all writers for the Sunday School Board be required to sign "The Baptist Faith and Message." Along with others, I opposed it. This was in direct conflict with the "Preamble." The motion failed. In 1970, in Denver, a young man told me he planned to move that "truth, without any mixture of error, for its matter" be deleted and replaced with "infallible." In reply to his question as to what I thought of it, I said, "You have the right to do so, but I will oppose it, for the statement is stronger as it reads." He made the motion. I opposed it, and it failed.

On the other hand, to my knowledge every agency of the Convention voluntarily has adopted it as its statement of faith. Two seminaries are using it as the document which professors must sign. I have not made a survey of this, but insofar as I know, it has been accepted by state conventions, associations, and even many local churches. I have heard of only one local church which has considered and refused to adopt it. It believed the statement, but did not want any outside group telling it what to believe.

It is possible that at some future time the Convention may want to revise the 1963 statement. If so, in my judgment, it should be done through a well-chosen committee as in this case and not by some motion from the floor of the Convention. For the present it seems that the vast majority of the Southern Baptist Convention is comfortable with the statement as it is.

I have been asked many times what I consider my greatest privilege of service in the Southern Baptist Convention has been. My answer is the privilege of being chairman of the committee which drew up the 1963 statement of "The Baptist Faith and Message." A close second would be writing *Studying Adult Life and Work Lessons* for more than twenty-five years.

13

The Great Controversy

Some years ago, Dr. Walter Shurden wrote a book: *Not a Silent People*—the history of controversy in the Southern Baptist Convention. The time span of my ministry has seen four major controversies: fundamentalist-modernist (1920s); Elliott (sixties); *Broadman Commentary* (seventies); present controversy (1979-). I call the present one the "great controversy" because of its length and radical nature.

"Misery loves company." If there is any comfort in this for Southern Baptists it is that other religious bodies have had and are having theirs. But largely they are handled behind closed doors by various boards. The very democratic nature of our Baptist faith and polity invites controversy. Furthermore, Southern Baptists hang their dirty linen on the clothesline for all to see, and if they do not look at it, we call attention to it.

In 1979, the Convention met in Houston, Texas, where two significant things happened. We held a large rally in the Astrodome with Billy Graham as speaker. Its purpose was to launch Bold Mission Thrust, designed to preach the gospel to every person on earth by A.D. 2000. It was also at this Convention that the great controversy began. And while some of the goals of Bold Mission Thrust are on schedule, for the most part, that challenging program has been put on the *back burner*, with the controversy absorbing most of our time and energy.

Someone said that if you build a cathedral to the glory of God, Satan will build a chapel alongside it. This is not to say that those on either side or both are the devil's people. He would rather use good people than bad ones anytime to do his work. After years of involvement in efforts to mediate the problem, I have concluded that there are no "white hats" or "black hats" in the controversy; all wear "gray hats." And each side has something to benefit the other, if only they would share it.

For many years I have been saying that this controversy is the devil's effort to destroy "Bold Mission Thrust." Apparently, it received little attention. In one press conference, Billy Graham said the same thing, and it got wide news coverage. I am just glad that someone said it who could get that much attention.

Church historians probably will go farther back in time to find the roots of this controversy. But having been a pastor as well as being involved in denominational work, in my limited judgment, I see these roots as coming in the late 1940s and early 1950s. Since 1925, "The Baptist Faith and Message" had anchored Southern Baptists to their historical moorings, while many other Christian bodies had drifted from theirs. There had been no controversies of consequence. But during that time, from 1925 to 1960, such giants as Mullins, Truett, Scarborough, Robertson, Sampey, Carver, and Connor had passed from the scene. W. Hersey Davis had become largely incapacitated, later to die in 1950. Kyle M. Yates, Sr. had entered the pastorate.

In 1961, Duke McCall and I were talking about the situation in the Convention. He said, "We are victims of the Depression of the 1930s. At the time when these teachers were nearing the end of their active years, we should have been securing young men to teach alongside them to continue in our Southern Baptist heritage, but we did not have the money. So as these older men began to fall by the wayside, we had to recruit some young pastors and even some still doing graduate work to fill the gap."

In the late 1940s, Southern Seminary trustees, most likely led by the faculty and administration, voted to put less emphasis on Hebrew, Greek, theology, and homiletics, and more on pastoral ministries, psychology, and counseling.

I told one of those trustees that they were going to produce the greatest generation of pastoral counselors the world ever saw, but that most of them would have little or no knowledge or appreciation for Southern Baptist heritage and doctrine. Some would be able to preach in spite of it, but many would not. Much preaching I hear today has the form of a classroom lecture without classroom lecture content. In time, the other seminaries followed suit.

Then in the early 1950s, we let the old Training Union die. I remember during Jerry Lambdin's later years how he opposed any effort to change the format which had been developed over many years. When we let the Training Union die, we lost four months annually of training people in Baptist heritage and doctrine. Along with the Training Union we lost week-long Sunday School and Training Union study courses which included both doctrine and methods. (Today we elect people to offices but seldom tell them their duties.) Keep in mind that I am criticizing my generation, not the present one.

Nevertheless, due to the "sins of the fathers" we now have in both the pulpit and the pew a generation which is sadly lacking in the knowledge of our Baptist heritage and faith. Someone asked me, "Where are the giants today?" Asked to explain, he said, "When Dr. Truett spoke, Southern Baptists listened." I replied, "You cannot compare then and now. If Dr. Truett were speaking to this generation they would not listen to him either."

Several years ago it became evident that the ranks of "old-timers" were growing thin. These included those and their wives who had attended the seminary together or else who had worked together in the Southern Baptist Convention. So David Byrd, then the dean of Boyce School of Theology of Southern Seminary, and James Middleton conceived the idea of having a reunion each summer in Berea, Kentucky. We begin with a dinner in a private dining room on Friday night and close with a luncheon Saturday noon.

Following Friday evening dinner, we sit in a circle about the room. Going around the circle, each person tells what he/she has been doing or any other item of interest. (Bragging about grandchildren is a "no-no," since it would take too much time.)

Since Albert McClellan and I were serving on the Peace Committee, one evening we were asked to give a brief report on the controversy. Present were a seminary professor and his wife. I concluded that I feared present day seminary graduates know systematic theology but not *Southern Baptist* systematic theology. They know what Barth, Brunner, Bultmann, and Tillich wrote, but not what Mullins and Connor wrote. All through my remarks I feared that the professor's wife would break her neck as she nodded in agreement, but I was not certain as to how her husband would react.

But when we adjourned, he came to me. Said he, "Herschel, I think you are correct. I have Mullins and Connor on my recommended reading list, but I teach from a different text-book." (In another seminary, a student had shown me his textbook in that course. I do not recall the author's name; I do remember that it was of German derivation. I am certain that he was not a Southern Baptist. I have no reason to question the soundness of his Christian faith, but I would conclude that it did not have that peculiar Southern Baptist slant to it.)

In reply I told this professor, "Let's suppose that alongside each other are Mullins' *The Christian Religion in Its Doctrinal Expression*, published in 1918, and a book by a non-Baptist author published this year. Which do you suppose the student will read?" He replied, "The new one." More than likely that would be the case.

This is not intended to decry the works of more recent authors. It is to emphasize the importance of preserving the heritage and faith which pertains to Baptists. Neither is it a claim that Southern Baptists have a monopoly on intellect and truth. But as someone said, "If we do not *stand* for something, we will *fall* for everything."

The Southern Baptist Convention owns and provides for six seminaries. Students from other religious persuasions are welcome to attend them, but we do not have these seminaries for them. Their primary purpose is to train leaders for Southern Baptist churches. If these leaders are to lead as Southern Baptists, they must be *indoctrinated* as to those things which Southern Baptists believe and practice. To some, *indoctrination* is a dirty word. But the word basically means *teaching*. It is simply a matter of what one teaches. These six schools are not *universities* but *seminaries*, whose reason for being is to prepare future Southern Baptist leaders for a specific task.

Through the years I have heard much about academic freedom, but I do not hear much about academic responsibility. The only place where absolute freedom exists is a desert island occupied by one person. Wherever we live in community each person must accept limits to freedom so that my freedom does not violate your rights.

In the academic world, whether in a university or a seminary, professors voluntarily accept limitations. "The Baptist Faith and Message" is careful to protect individual freedom, but it also sets forth tenets of faith as safeguards against irresponsible exercise of freedom contrary to the generally accepted faith held by others of that persuasion.

To put it even more plainly, I would fight for your right to teach or preach whatever you wish. But that does not mean that I should provide you a livelihood, building, and a ready-made audience to which to do it. At the same time, I do not have the right to demand that everyone cross every "t" and dot every "i" or use the exact terminology as I do—so long as we both remain true to God's revelation as recorded in His inspired Word. Southern Baptists are a diverse people, but with Christian consideration we can have *unity in diversity* as in love we speak the truth, as we see it. I realize that the foregoing words are not designed to "win friends," but I hope they will "influence [some] people."

Maybe I am like Grandma. One grandchild asked another, "Why does Grandma spend so much time reading the Bible?" The other replied, "I don't know. I guess she is cramming for her *finals*."

Having examined the roots of the controversy, let us endeavor to see how it began and outline its plan of operation. It did not suddenly spring forth, full-grown, in 1979. The vast majority of Southern Baptists have never been extremists in theology, either to the right or the left. They have been a middle-of-the-road people. However, due to our adherence to the doctrine of the priesthood of all believers, some would fall to the left or right of center. When I was president of the

Convention, I estimated that 90 percent were in the middle of the road, with 10 percent equally divided to the right or left of center. A later president, Carl Bates, said he thought I was generous in my estimate; he figured 5 percent to the left or right. And I expect he was correct.

Nevertheless, those to the right felt they were being omitted from places of leadership and/or decision-making positions. However, according to the "historical table" every president (1917-1978) would be placed in the center theologically with a few left-center or right-center. (I picked 1917, J. B. Gambrell, as a starting point, but could have gone on back.) Those chosen to preach the annual sermon during that period would fall in the same category. This does not resolve all the problems faced by the Convention during the last few years, but it does show that there was no conspiracy to exclude any one group.

Eventually, the problem centered in the appointive powers vested in the presidency. But during the period mentioned above I am certain that no conspiracy was evident in the appointing of committees such as the committee on committees and the one on board members. I know it was not true in my case, or to my knowledge, in that of any other president for that matter. For instance, one day I received a call from a longtime friend. He asked me to appoint him on the committee on boards. Said he, "I owe some debts in my state, and I want to repay them." He did not stand a chance of being on that committee! I suppose I lost a friend, for until his death I never heard from him again.

How did the controversy actually begin? For years voices of protest were heard about what was being taught in our seminaries. Unfortunately, these were *blanket* protests. It was the "shotgun" method in which many innocent professors were hurt. In the midst of the controversy, Dr. Landrum Leavell, president of New Orleans Baptist Theological Seminary, said to the Convention that if someone would name a person and present evidence supporting the charge, he would handle it. From experience in other cases, I feel certain that he spoke the sentiments of all the presidents.

But we failed to heed the protests, and this led to a political process. *Someone* or *some ones* found the "Achilles heel" of the

Convention; namely, the appointive powers of the president. Furthermore, the names "Conservatives" and "Moderates" were applied to the resultant contending groups in the Convention. Since neither adequately described the groups, the Baptist news media sought more adequate terms. However, I will use the original terms.

As for the plan, the Conservatives said that if for ten years they could elect persons of their group as the committee on committees and the committee on boards, and if they could lead the Convention to elect their nominees to the various boards which under Convention authority operate the agencies, then in ten years they would control the Convention. Suffice it to say that they did this.

One of the strange things about this controversy is that theologically it has centered in the nature of the Scriptures. The strangeness is that when "The Baptist Faith and Message" of 1963 was adopted, not one word was said about Article 1 on "The Scriptures." The focal point is the portion of one sentence which says that the Bible has "truth, without any mixture of error, for its matter." This refers to the original manuscripts. In St. Louis in 1980, someone said, "But I have never seen the original manuscripts." Another replied, "I have never seen Jesus Christ, but I believe in Him!" I thought that was a good answer.

One day I received a call from Hugh Wamble, then professor of church history at Midwestern Seminary. His students were asking as to the origin of that statement. Had our committee researched it? I said, "No. It was in the New Hampshire Confession of 1833. The 1925 committee relied upon that Confession and retained it. Our committee left it in the 1963 Statement." Dr. Wamble researched it. He found a bound volume of the letters of the English philosopher John Locke.

A young English preacher had asked Locke how to be a success in the ministry. In a letter dated September 1702, Locke said, "Preach the Bible. For 'it has God for its author, salvation for its end, and truth, without any mixture of error, for its matter.'" He died in September 1703. So, "It has God for its author, salvation for its end, and truth, without any mixture of error, for its matter" (exact quote from the BFM) came, not from a preacher or theologian, but from a philosopher.

At the Pittsburgh Convention in 1983, Wayne Dehoney asked how I saw the controversy. I told him that I saw it as a correction course. If a rocket headed for Mars veers off course by only a fraction of a degree, the error, if not corrected will cause that rocket to miss its target by a million miles.

Every so often, usually in one of our seminaries, it is reported that some professor has gotten slightly off course. Then we go through a course correction. In the past they have been of relatively short duration. This time, due to the politics involved, it will be longer, and we will come down a little to the right of center. But we will in due time come back to the center. Responsibility tends to moderate people.

Franklin Paschall, former president of the Southern Baptist Convention, was the first person publicly to propose the need for a Peace Committee. In turn, the state convention presidents followed through on it. Charles Pickering, a lawyer from Laurel, Mississippi, now a federal judge, was named chairman of a committee to propose personnel for such a committee. At the Dallas Convention (1985), Bill Hickem and Franklin Paschall presented a motion calling for such a committee, specifying its purpose and procedure. The motion also named the personnel of the committee. It was adopted.

Members of the Peace Committee had been selected so as to be balanced between the extremes on either side. In the center were people who were not committed to either side. I was one of that group.

This is a good place to state my position in this controversy. I was/am not on either side. Each has some good and some bad in its position. I have friends on both sides. In Indianapolis, many told me that I have the respect of both sides, and I would be lying if I said that does not please me. I feel that my best service can be rendered in efforts of mediation. Once you identify with one group, your ability as a mediator is dead. To borrow a phrase from Albert McClellan, I do not want to be known as a Conservative or a Moderate as those terms are now defined. I simply want to be known as *"an old-time Southern Baptist."*

The first meeting of the Peace Committee was held in Nashville in the summer of 1985. At this first meeting, after a season of prayer, our chairman, Charles Fuller, asked each of us why we were willing to give two years of our time serving on that committee. My reply was that I felt it was the most important committee ever appointed in the history of the Southern Baptist Convention.

Already I had said, "In any division of opinion there are three sides: yours, mine, and the right one. In this case the right one is God's side, and we must find it." Then I added facetiously, "When you return home, write a postcard to all your friends. After we report two years from now, you likely will have no friends." My point was the difficulty in reaching a decision with which everyone would be happy. In fact, I do not think that any member of the Peace Committee was completely happy with the report, for in mediation you give to get.

To avoid any appearance of officialdom we agreed to hold future meetings alternately in airport hotels in Atlanta and Dallas/Fort Worth. The only exceptions were Nashville, at a time we were to make a progress report to the Executive Committee; the prayer retreat at Glorieta; and the meeting in St. Louis prior to the 1987 Convention.

With few exceptions we met monthly for two days. We agreed that tapes of our meetings be sealed for ten years. This was so that committee members would feel free to talk about problems. We also agreed that meetings would not be open to the press. Dan Martin was chosen as our press liaison. He rendered tremendous service in recording every word spoken in our meetings—including stale jokes. Later, we did meet with the press at our second Nashville meeting since the state paper editors were already there for the Executive Committee meeting. Finally, we set April 1, 1987, as the deadline for furnishing to the Convention general secretary a finished report to the Convention. This would enable us to have it printed in the *Book of Reports*. I might add that we agreed unanimously that should anyone suggest we serve a third year, we all would shoot him. Later, that decision would come back to haunt us.

It is not my purpose to recount in detail the various sessions of the Peace Committee. Rather, it is to point out some significant events which throw light on the controversy. In our second committee meeting, our chairman reviewed the instructions of the Convention. We were to work within the framework of "The Baptist Faith and Message" and the Constitution and Bylaws of the Convention. (At our first meeting Charles Fuller had asked me to give an interpretation of "The Baptist Faith and Message.") Specifically, we were requested to do three things: (1) determine the source of the controversy, (2) report our findings, and (3) make recommendations toward resolving it.

Therefore, the first definite move was to appoint subcommittees to visit all Convention agencies. The purpose was not to make charges but to share and discuss correspondence we had received which expressed critical opinions. When the subcommittees had reported, the final conclusion was that the source of the controversy was *theological which produced the politics.*

At the same time, I must add that in my judgment, the theological problems were confined to a few people in two seminaries and were not as serious as some supposed. This was brought out in subcommittee reports. So much so that we immediately gave a clean bill of health to New Orleans, Southwestern, and Golden Gate—and so reported to the Convention at its next session in Atlanta. We were about to include Midwestern when we received a complaint about a book written by one of its professors. In a subsequent report of the subcommittee, we were told that the professor had been misunderstood. We then added Midwestern to the list. We were assured that any existing problems in the other seminaries would be handled by the administrations.

In several subsequent meetings of the committee the discussions turned more to the political aspects of the problem. On one occasion I said to a leading Conservative, "You and I could write out our statements of faith and, except for eschatology, each of us could sign the other's statement." He agreed. "Yet," said I, "you call yourself a Conservative and by your standard I would be called a Moderate, even though we believe the same thing." (One's view on eschatology has never been a test of orthodoxy among Southern Baptists.) I continued, "So I must conclude that it is because I am not on your 'team.' Which tells me that these terms are not theological but political." He agreed. (I choose not to use names where it might embarrass someone. This man and I are good friends.)

Because our concern had turned to politics, a subcommittee on politics was appointed. I was on that committee whose chairman was Charles Pickering. We spent a full day in a Dallas/Fort Worth hotel, interviewing those most closely identified with matters related to politics. I will relate only the two most outstanding ones.

We interviewed Paige Patterson and Judge Paul Pressler. It was being rumored that Paige was one being considered for the presidency of Golden Gate Seminary. Someone asked, "Paige, if you were elected president of one of our seminaries with absolute power to act, would you get rid of all professors who do not believe as you do?" Immediately he replied, "No! Through the process of attrition—death, retirement, or resignation—I would replace them with professors who believe as I do." Such would involve a long process, not an immediate academic blood bath. Since Judge Pressler did not reject what he said, I assume that he was in agreement.

In Dallas in 1985, I was as close to the start of the report about ballot manipulation as I could be without starting it myself. It was on Wednesday night when the former presidents and their wives were presented to the Convention. Due to the large attendance (45,519 messengers plus family members) the platform was so small that only those on the immediate program could be on the platform. The former presidents were seated near the front so as to get on the platform quickly. I sat with a couple, longtime friends, whose integrity and sincerity I do not question even for one moment. He told me that when they came in they saw people giving out ballots to others getting off buses.

Just at that moment, Earl Potts, executive secretary of Alabama Baptists and chairman of the teller committee, came down the aisle. The former president told Earl, who went immediately to tell Lee Porter who was in charge of balloting. Lee went to a microphone to announce it and urge that it not be done since it was against the rules.

When the subcommittee had its first meeting, I related this without using names. The chairman asked if I could get a letter to that effect. Later, I called this friend who promised to write the letter. However, the next morning he called. Since he had no documentary proof, he and his wife felt that it would not be wise to have such a letter in the historical files of the Convention. He said, "I will write you, and without using my name, you may share its contents with the committee." The letter read: "I thought I saw people giving out ballots. I cannot swear that they were ballots. They looked like ballots. I do not know which side they were on."

After sharing the contents, I destroyed the letter.

In our meeting with Lee Porter and Tim Hedquist, manager of Convention arrangements, they differed as to the ratio of people present and ballots cast on that Wednesday evening. Hedquist said he checked with the manager of the convention center, who agreed with Hedquist.

Then they told us the following story. Someone reported to them that two students of Criswell Bible Institute were giving out ballots at a certain entrance. Hedquist literally ran to that entrance, hoping that if it were true he would catch them in the act. Arriving, he found two nicely dressed young men. They had no ballots. They were not Criswell students. They were wearing stickers given out that afternoon at the Southeastern Seminary luncheon.

When I returned home, I related the situation to a lawyer in our church. I asked, "If you went into court with a case based on that kind of evidence what would they do to you?" With a laugh he said, "They would throw the case out of court, and then have me up before the bar association for bringing such a case to court."

I am in neither position nor disposition to judge in any of these or similar matters, but they do suggest that we should exercise caution as to what we hear or speak.

By later summer of 1986, the committee was ready to begin writing our report. A committee had been appointed to write the first draft. However, we were agreed that we needed something to *happen* which would enable us to bring the whole matter together.

We were nearing the close of one of the meetings in Atlanta, so we had a season of prayer. We prayed for God's guidance and that something would happen to enable us to bring together all that we had learned. On our knees we prayed around the group, with Charles Fuller closing the prayer session. We all stood up, except Charles Stanley. When someone knelt down to remind him it was finished, he said, "But we haven't received the answer!" Down on our knees we went and continued praying.

I had to catch a plane to Asheville, North Carolina, in order to speak that night at Ridgecrest during Senior Adult Week. They had assigned me the subject of *prayer*. I must confess that I was peeping at my watch. The time came when I must leave or else miss the flight, but I felt that I would be the world's biggest hypocrite to leave that meeting to make a speech on *prayer*. So I eased out and called Ridgecrest and told them the situation. They understood and got a substitute. Then I rejoined the prayer meeting until it was over.

We did not receive the answer that day. It came a few weeks later at a previously arranged "Prayer Retreat" at Glorieta. The heads of Convention agencies, including WMU, were asked to meet with the committee for fellowship and prayer. These were accomplished the opening night. The next morning the entire group met together. And like a bolt from the blue, Dr. Milton Ferguson, president of Midwestern Seminary and chairman of the seminary presidents group for that year, asked if he might read a statement drawn up by the seminary presidents.

Since the Peace Committee had concluded that the basic source of the controversy was theological, these men said that it was up to the seminaries to take the lead in helping to correct the situation. So they had met in Kansas City, the result of which was what we chose to call "The Glorieta Statement." In essence, it stated the presidents' purpose to lead and/or maintain their institutions to a more conservative position in teaching, lectures, evangelism, and the like. *That was the answer to prayers in both Atlanta and Glorieta!*

That afternoon agency heads except seminary presidents departed. That evening at the committee meeting, Milton reread and interpreted the statement. Some members did not want to release the statement unless Adrian Rogers, then president of the Convention, gave a similar one. He said, "You fellows are trying to pressure me, and I don't work that way."

It was at that point that I said, "Leave Adrian alone! If he wants to make a statement, he will do so. He will not make one under pressure. But even if he did, it would not mean anything. And let's release 'The Glorieta Statement.' This is one of the most prayed for meetings in Southern Baptist history. Even some Methodist churches have written that they are praying for us. If we report that nothing significant happened, we will crush the spirit of our people, even diminish their faith in prayer." The committee voted to release the statement.

The next morning, most of the committee members caught an early flight home. Those of us having a later flight ate breakfast together. Adrian was one of that group. He said, "I want to read something I wrote after going to my room last night and get your reaction." In essence, he commended the seminary presidents for their statement and called on all Southern Baptists to cooperate with them and help them to achieve their goal.

When no one else made a comment, I said, "Adrian, I have one suggestion. Date it, sign it, and give it to the secretary of our committee." When he said he would have to get it typed, I said, "No! No! Just like it is." "But," said he, "I have scratched out words and written others above the line." "Perfect! Perfect!" I said. "I do not compare that with Lincoln's 'Gettysburg Address.' But what price could you put on the original copy if it were like that? That is a historical document. If Joe Dokes had said that, it would not mean a thing. But that is written by the president of the Southern Baptist Convention and should be preserved." He did as I suggested and so it is in our permanent record.

The two statements were published together in the state Baptist papers. I was told that some "Moderate" said that we pressured the presidents into making their statement. In Ephesians 4:15 Paul tells us to speak the truth in love. Such a statement is a double violation of Paul's words. It is not *truth*, and it was not spoken in *love*. This matter was never mentioned in our committee meetings. To my best knowledge none of us expected it. From later developments, apparently none of the faculty members were aware of it. In my judgment, it came as an answer to prayer through the Holy Spirit.

We left Glorieta thinking that at our next meeting we would reach the point where the subcommittee could begin writing the first draft of our report. However, something happened in the meantime which delayed our plans.

The state Baptist papers ran a story about Roy Honeycutt's report to his faculty about the "Glorieta Statement." He was quoted as saying this would not change anything at Southern Seminary. They would continue operating as they were. Without the context of the statement it sounded as if he was backing down on the "Glorieta Statement." Some of our committee were quite upset, so most of that meeting was taken discussing this matter. The subcommittee said it could not do its work until this was resolved. So it was agreed that the chairman and vice-chairman of our committee would confer with Dr. Honeycutt before the next meeting.

At the next meeting they reported that in his report to his faculty he had said that at Southern they were already doing what the "Glorieta Statement" proposed. So for that reason it would not affect them. They would continue to do as they were doing. This satisfied the committee.

I am not implying that the writer of this news report deliberately sought to mislead. It was simply one of those things that happen with the best of intentions. But, at the same time, I want to clarify the matter, especially because later some of the papers were critical of the Peace Committee for being late in getting our report into the hands of the messengers in St. Louis. We missed our original target date of April 1 by almost the time of delay spent in clarifying this matter.

In St. Louis, the Peace Committee held an all-night meeting in order to finish its work, adjourning about 4:00 a.m. After the report was unanimously adopted, Adrian Rogers said, "Mr. Chairman, if the spirit which has developed in this committee could be throughout the Convention, our problems would be behind us." I agree. But unfortunately, fourteen million Southern Baptists cannot spend two years talking and praying together as we had done.

Printed copies were available to the messengers the morning before the Convention voted on it that night. Some complained about this. But as one who attended every meeting of the committee, I can say that we did the best we could do under the circumstances!

The Convention adopted the report overwhelmingly. No computer ballot was necessary. Lee Porter estimated a 97 to 3 margin in favor of the report. I cannot imagine a vote nearer to unanimous on so controversial a matter. In addition to the actual content of the report, that vote said, "We are tired of this controversy and want it stopped!" As I have gone from one side of this country to the other, I hear that everywhere.

After the report was adopted, I heard of one "Moderate" who said, "They gave the 'Conservatives' everything they wanted." In truth he did not know what they wanted. Or the "Moderates" for that matter.

I give one example. In next to the last meeting of the committee before reporting, just before adjournment, one prominent "Conservative" moved that we put in "Findings" the following:

> We, as a Peace Committee, have found that most Southern Baptists see the "truth, without any mixture of error for its matter" as meaning, for example, that
>
> (1) They believe in direct creation of mankind and therefore they believe that Adam and Eve were real persons.
>
> (2) They believe the named authors did indeed write the biblical books attributed to them by those books.
>
> (3) They believe the miracles described in Scripture did indeed occur as supernatural events in history.
>
> (4) They believe that the historical narratives given by biblical authors are indeed accurate and reliable as given by those authors.

I preferred not to use the examples, though I have no problem with them. If you slice the meat too thin, you cut your finger. However, in mediation you give to get. So I voted to put this in "Findings."

But in our all-night meeting, just before we voted on our report, this same person suggested that this be moved from "Findings" to "Recommendations." I said, "No, sir! I voted to put it in 'Findings.' If you move it to 'Recommendations' I want to be recorded as voting against both motions."

Another person said, "If it is true, then we should have the guts [his word] to move it over to 'Recommendations.'" I replied, "It isn't a matter of 'guts' but of brains. Where it is, it is 'Findings.' If we move it to 'Recommendations,' it becomes creedal." The matter was dropped.

As stated previously, early in our work the committee agreed that we did not want to serve a third year. But as we neared the end of the second year, we had to face the fact that we were more familiar with the situation than any other group. So it became logical that we should be the ones to report to the Convention how the agencies were reacting to the Convention's actions in adopting our report. Hence, the recommendation that we continue one more year.

News stories of the report's adoption, (the following day) quoted a seminary professor calling us a "Police Committee." Never in our work did we assume such a role or consider ourselves as such. We never accused anyone; we shared and discussed with concerned agencies or individuals complaints received by mail.

Following the adoption of our report, I did not seek out the seminary presidents, but I happened to run into all of them except Russell Dilday. I asked each of the five what they thought of our report. Each one said, "There is nothing in it with which we cannot live."

In the third year we were authorized to have only one meeting funded by the Convention. With the exception of a pre-Convention meeting in San Antonio, we had only the one meeting in Atlanta. At San Antonio we bore our own expenses and met only to finalize and adopt the concluding report to the Convention.

A faculty member at Southern Seminary told me that when Dr. Honeycutt returned from the St. Louis Convention, he called his faculty together and explained the report adopted by the Convention. Then he added, "We are going to live according to the Convention's action." At our Atlanta meeting of the committee, we requested that each agency head and the chairman of his trustees meet with us on a scheduled basis. Each was asked to report on what his agency was doing to implement the action of the St. Louis Convention. Every report was positive.

When we had finished, a leading "Conservative" said, "Brother Chairman, after what we have heard for the last day and a half, I think we can say that our theological problems are behind us. Our problem now is politics."

Yes, our agencies are living according to the Convention's action, but, sad to say, this is not true of the *warring parties*.

Two of the main recommendations in the Peace Committee report were (1) to appoint balanced committees and board members and (2) to end the politics and the use of inflammatory language. Of the former, the Convention action reads "to select nominees who endorse the Baptist Faith and Message Statement and are drawn in balanced fashion from the broad spectrum of loyal, cooperative Southern Baptists, representative of the diversity of our denomination."

Frankly, I must admit that I do not know enough about the younger generation to make a personal judgment on this. But from information received from some who do know them, it appears that this has not been done. Had this recommendation been followed, I seriously doubt that the Cooperative Baptist Fellowship would have been formed.

Upon their election, I said to three of the presidents during this time, "If you will appoint balanced committees you will have no problems." Each of these stated that as their purpose, but in the end, it was not done. These are honest men. I believe the statement of their purpose. I cannot help but conclude that other influences were brought to bear upon them.

This raises a question which I have not heard mentioned otherwise. All of us will agree that *motions* (not resolutions) adopted by the Southern Baptist Convention are binding upon its *agencies*. What about the Convention's *officers*? Are they not bound by the same so that they are not free to act arbitrarily but in keeping with Convention action? In adopting the Peace Committee's report, the Convention called for balanced appointments. To do otherwise is to act contrary to Convention mandate. This is not intended as criticism of anyone. It is merely to point out something which apparently has been overlooked by all of us.

While on the subject, let me point out another matter. The annual meeting of the Southern Baptist Convention is composed of *messengers*, not *delegates*. A messenger goes to the Convention not instructed as to how to vote. He/she is to go with an open mind, study the issues, listen to discussion—and then vote his/her conscience and judgment. If a person goes instructed how to vote—either by the local church, the pastor, or any other organized group—he/she ceases to be a messenger and becomes a delegate. As such, that person is not eligible to be seated as a messenger. I am not so naive as to think this will ever be enforced. For one thing, who and how could it be determined as to any person's status? But it is a principle of church polity which should be kept in the heart of each attendant at the Convention.

As to the matter of politics and inflammatory language, in spite of the Convention's action, politics has gone on unabated. Indeed, it has been increased *on both sides*. The most evident move has been the organization of the Cooperative Baptist Fellowship. Strangely, some of its leadership served on the Peace Committee which voted unanimously for the report brought to the Convention. All this has our people confused.

I do not go about the Convention territory voluntarily speaking on the issues. But when requested to speak on the controversy at pastors conferences, encampments, and/or Bible conferences for preachers, I try to analyze the situation, dealing with all sides of the issues. At one annual meeting of the state executive secretaries they asked me to take three hours to deal with the issues. Without exception, I am told that I have been helpful in understanding the controversy. Where individuals ask about it with respect to local churches, I point out that it should not affect local churches unless they allow it to do so.

It has now developed into a power struggle at the top. I tell them that I have been up there, and I know how little the "top" has to do with local churches. The base of the Lord's work, missions and evangelism, is the local church. So I say, "Just keep on doing the Lord's work and pay no attention to this struggle at the 'top.'"

What of the future? As for the Cooperative Baptist Fellowship, no one knows. Reports of interviews with some of the leaders reflect their own uncertainty. They have dropped the name "Southern." So, in effect, they have severed that tie. Some have said that they have no intention of leaving the Southern Baptist Convention. Others have suggested the possibility of joining some other existing Baptist body.

But one thing is certain. They have in place everything necessary to becoming a separate Baptist body. By whatever name they may call themselves, they have an executive committee, an executive secretary, a publishing house producing its own literature, a seminary, a mission board with missionaries on the field, a missionary giving program, and separate convention meetings. To move in that direction they only need to vote to do so and have enough churches to support their program.

As for the Southern Baptist Convention itself, I have not been in agreement with many decisions that have been made. But not being privy to all facts involved, I am in no position to make a definitive judgment. I share the concern of some of the more recent Convention presidents about immediately moving one of their people from allowable terms on the Executive Committee to membership on the Foreign Mission Board. This is doing that for which others were criticized in the beginning of the controversy. But it must be admitted that both sides are doing things for which they once criticized the other. If something was wrong for one, it is also wrong for the other.

But I am an incurable optimist. I am convinced that, given time, patience, and Christian love, we have no problems which cannot be solved. The question is, will we wait on the Lord?

The charge has been made in some quarters that the Peace Committee failed. I deny the charge! We were not told to bring peace. Our responsibility was clearly stated: determine the source of the controversy, report our findings, make recommendations designed to bring peace. We did exactly that. No, the Peace Committee did not fail. The contending parties failed in that they have completely ignored the recommendations designed to bring peace.

The report of the Peace Committee cites "reconciliation" as the key to peace. This does not mean that we must *parrot* the same words and phrases. But recognizing our differences and allowing for them, in Christian love, we can have "unity in diversity" as we pursue the mutual purpose of evangelism and missions. *There are more things that unite us than that divide us!*

But let us suppose for a moment that there will be no reconciliation. What then? I can only speak for myself, even though my longtime friend Wayne Dehoney said it for me.

"Simply because they will not let me drive the bus, I am not getting off the bus and walking. Even if I must sit in the back row, I'm staying on the bus."